NATURE IS A HUMAN RIGHT

NATURE IS A HUMAN RIGHT

Why we're fighting for green in a gray world

EDITED BY ELLEN MILES

DISCLAIMERS

Content warning: Traumatic topics – including mental illness, racism, ableism and suicide – are discussed in the text. You can find resources on page 318 if you would like to seek support for any of these topics.

Multi-contributor experiences: The lived experiences, opinions and choice of language expressed in each piece belong to its individual author(s). Some of the text in this book has been edited in an Americanized style.

Protest and trespass: Please note the book contains text about protesting, guerrilla gardening and trespassing. Nothing in this book constitutes legal advice in relation to any form of activism and should not be relied on as such. Your rights to protest differ depending on where you live and you should seek independent legal advice to ensure that your planned actions are lawful. The publisher, editor and authors hereby disclaim any liability arising directly or indirectly from the use, or misuse, of the information contained in this book.

CONTENTS

INJUSTICE How We're Being Deprived of Nature

CHANGE What We Can All Do

Humanity races toward a precipice. Never have we known so much and understood so little about the Earth. The planet swarms with restless information, yet we are disconnected, adrift in increasingly abstract lives. Our roots severed, we're hurtling – like lemmings on hoverchairs – towards social alienation, somatic distress, universal angst and climate chaos. One thing can save us from this freefall: reconnecting with nature.

"Now, over half of us live in an urban environment ... It reminds me of just how easy it is for us to lose our connection with the natural world. Yet it's on this connection that the future of both humanity and the natural world will depend."

Sir David Attenborough,
Planet Earth II (2016)

INTRODUCTION
Ellen Miles

"People today have forgotten they're really just a part of nature."
Akira Kurosawa, *Dreams* (1990)

"We never were separate from nature and never will be,
but the dominant culture on earth has long imagined itself
to be apart from nature and destined one day to transcend it.
We have lived in a mythology of separation."
Charles Eisenstein, *Climate: A New Story* (2018)

What does it mean to be human? To ask this, in itself, points to what makes us unique. While other species feel deeply, use tools, communicate and solve problems, we have unequalled capacities to question, understand and express our complex realities. We painted the Sistine Chapel and split the atom, pondered whether to be or not to be, and believed six impossible things before breakfast. We invented chess, and we invented computers that could beat us at chess. We are a species of storytellers, teachers, designers and dreamers, who can understand the world's past (though we often conveniently forget it) and imagine its possible futures. Our abilities to conjure and create are so vast that, although humans make up just 0.01 per cent of all living things on Earth, we're now the planet's dominant influence, pulling this solar satellite's entire crew with us into the Anthropocene, "the age of humanity".

The Promethean tales and technologies we've built around ourselves are blocking out a truth that we've been running from: we are part of nature. This is as much a part of our humanity as the things that make our species "special". But, for the most part, we've chosen to lose our heads in the clouds, and erase nature from our CV. A standard definition of nature confirms this collective delusion: "the phenomena of the physical world collectively, including plants, animals, the landscape, and other features and products of the earth, *as opposed to humans* or human creations". The phrase "we are nature" may sound like inspirational guff – something you'd find written in cursive over an Instagram stock image or hung on the wall of a backpacker hostel – but it's a truism.

We *are* "products of the earth". The iron in your blood, salt in your sweat and calcium in your bones come from the Earth's crust. The water molecules that make up 60 per cent of your body have flowed down the Nile, rained over the Amazon and drifted across the Atlantic Ocean. You're related to everything that's ever lived on the planet: all life evolved from one single-celled organism; you share DNA with each and every living being, from amoeba to zebra. The visual continuum between human bodies and other elements of nature has its own poetry: our snaking veins run like rivers, neurons crosshatch chaotically like mycelium, and bronchioles branch out like tree limbs. The perfectly imperfect human form – micro to macro, inside and out – is glorious in its nature-ness.

For over 99 per cent of human history, there was nothing other than "nature". Our bodies evolved among a rich tapestry of life, woven from deep relationships between plants, animals, soil, landscape, air, water and weather. Let's say we condensed the 300,000 years that humans have existed into 24 hours, with right now, as you're reading this, being midnight. *Homo sapiens* blinks into existence as the clock starts, and then spends almost the entire day immersed in the wild. It's not until after 11pm that the first Agricultural Revolution – the shift from a roaming hunter-gatherer lifestyle to settlement and farming – comes along. At 11:30pm, the world's first cities rise up from the dust. Giza is pyramid-less until 11:38pm. The Scientific Revolution, and its revelation of a complex, magical world beyond the reach of our naked senses, arrives at 11:57pm. The Industrial Revolution, a minute later. A durable, mass-producible new material called "plastic" is invented with just 33 seconds left of the day. Neil Armstrong takes one small step with 15 seconds to go, and Google launches seven seconds before midnight. From this perspective, it's clear that our severance from the land is a relatively recent phenomenon. Nature is, ahem, our natural habitat.

But our habitats now look very different to our ancestors'. Today, most *Homo sapiens* live in urban environments: mazes of concrete, glass and tarmac in which nature has become an other – compartmentalized, commodified and enjoyed, at best, in doses. Have we adapted to our new, urban surroundings? Unlikely. Genetic variations take thousands of years to emerge, so there's little chance we've evolved to suit the rapid urbanization and industrialization of the last 250. "It took us seven million years to get to where we are now," human evolution expert Professor Kaye Reed explains, nodding back to our first hominin forebears. "*Homo sapiens* that existed 40,000 years ago have essentially the same genome. If we have genes that relate our well-being to nature, they're not going anywhere any time soon."

Influential biologist Edward O. Wilson, dubbed the Darwin of the 21st century, affirms that our need for nature is genetically encoded. Wilson's "biophilia hypothesis" says that humans have an innate need to connect with the kind of lush, life-filled environments that our ancestors would have prospered in. Although it might feel like our glass towers, underground shuttles and digital infrastructure grant us independence from nature, our genes still stubbornly anchor us to it.

Some futurists think we might transcend our Stone Age genetics by other means. Transhumanism is gaining momentum, and there may come a time when we can upload our consciousness to a "cloud"-like digital realm. For now, though, we are incurably carbon-based apes. Our cultural advancements drape like intricate costumes over these simian frames. They empower and entertain us, but they don't change what's underneath.

There are, of course, many wonderful things we can do to alter our bodies; surgeries and prosthetics can be life-changing and -affirming. I've personally chosen to have laser eye surgery, a titanium tooth implant and the contraceptive coil. Accepting our status as animals and our need to connect to living things doesn't restrict life-improving procedures; our ancient genes, whispering of primordial roots, are untouched by such interventions.

Acknowledging our need for nature doesn't mean abandoning civilization's achievements, many of which are improving global quality of life. What it does demand is reframing our understanding of "civilization" to include nature connection, rather than explicitly shunning it. At present, our very concepts of "civilization" and "progress" are understood in terms of moving away from, or taming, nature. As proof of this, Indigenous cultures – whose diverse practices share in common a land-based approach, and respect for nature's balance – have been derided as "uncivilized", or even "barbaric". But it's the rest of us who are causing chaos. Our insistence that we are independent from nature, and that "progress" means widening this gap, is ushering in a host of harms. Some of these rising threats, such as decreased immunity, stress, allergies and diminishing attention spans, manifest within our bodies. Others are visible in our environment: the impacts of widespread ecological unravelling, including extreme weather, rising sea levels and temperatures, the extinction of keystone species, and toxic air, land and water.

We are at a crossroads. Our species has arrived at an embarrassingly teenage phase; lashing out with Oedipal spirit, we seek to both conquer and eliminate our lifesource. To become a mature global civilization (as well as curb the sixth mass extinction) we must accept this simple fact: a need for green is written in our genes. By divorcing ourselves from nature, we are both limiting our potential and losing a part of ourselves. Nature is not an inconvenience or an other; it is not a luxury or a frivolity – nature is a human right.

*

When I came to pick a name for my campaign (which became the title of this book), I thought *Nature is a Human Right* summed the idea up nicely. Resisting the allure of a snappy pun or portmanteau, I hoped that this mouthful would be clear, if not concise. Since then, I've been proved wrong on innumerable occasions, and confronted with various – often valid, occasionally imaginative – alternative interpretations. Before sending you off into the teeming thicket of ideas in this anthology, I should first clarify what we mean when we say "nature is a human right".

Definitions of "nature" are famously mercurial. At one extreme, everything is nature: isn't everything in the universe – sycamore or silicone – from the same cosmic soup? At the other, very little is: parks, ponds and poodles are arguably man-made. I generally use the word "nature" to refer to all life and organic matter on Earth – creatures and features, from rabbits to rocks. In the phrase "nature is a human right", though, "nature" means vegetated environments, sometimes called "green spaces". This includes woodlands, wetlands, meadows and rainforests – and yes, even gardens, parks, fields and allotments. The wilder and more biodiverse the better (as we'll see later on) but planted and pruned spaces count too. So, a more appropriate title for this book might be *Vegetated Environments are a Human Right*.

What does that mean, exactly? Is it our "right" to use and abuse these environments as we please? Of course not. The proclamation "nature is a human right" doesn't mean the Earth is ours to consume or destroy; rights and responsibilities go hand in hand, and our relationship with nature must be symbiotic if it is to be sustainable. Nor does it suggest that humans are *more* important than the rest of nature's players.

It simply means that we *are* important, all of us – important enough to deserve health and happiness (for which we need contact with nature). In fact, the understanding that we are dependents, not masters, of nature is inherent to the idea that we need frequent contact with it.

Making nature contact a human right will actually help promote the rights *of* nature and "deep ecology", the idea that all living beings have intrinsic worth and deserve protection, regardless of their utility to human needs. Why? Because our current lack of respect for the rest of nature – our inability to empathize with other life forms, and the anthropocentric narrative of human supremacy – is a direct symptom of our distance from it. (Clover Hogan and I wax lyrical about this in the final chapter.)

We're now ready to upgrade the title again. May I present *Daily Contact with Vegetated Environments is a Human Right*. I've avoided "access to" in this new and improved name for two reasons. First, to avoid the insinuation that anyone and everyone has a right to access any and every natural environment. People's privacy and native inhabitants' land rights are sacred, and must be protected.

Second, "access" subtly implies an onus on the individual. Is a public park a mile away, or a National Park a train ride away, "accessible"? Where "accessibility" begins and ends is up for debate, and this ambiguity could be leveraged by lazy legislators (snide tongue-twister, that) to avoid making the changes we need. Not everyone has the time, money or physical ability to make such journeys – and it is precisely these people who need nature's tonic most.

Finally, what does "human right" mean? Human rights are inalienable rights, common to all human beings. Their ontology has been debated for centuries: some believe that these rights are objectively woven into the fabric of our being, and exist independently of human judgement; others, like philosopher Jeremy Bentham, think the idea of innate, "god-given" rights is "nonsense upon stilts". I'll let you decide which side of the fence you fall on. Whether these rights exist *a priori*, or whether we've collectively decided that all humans have inherent worth, we can acknowledge that certain things (like the rights to have an opinion and not be enslaved) are essential for a basic standard of freedom, dignity and welfare. These fundamental rights, called human rights, are the foundations of global legislation – making them vital instruments for change.

The seminal text on human rights was the United Nations' *Universal Declaration of Human Rights* (UDHR). Created in 1948, the declaration was a reaction to the "barbarous acts which ... outraged the conscience of mankind" during the Second World War. The text enshrined 30 fundamental rights, including the rights to work, education and a fair trial, and freedom from torture and arbitrary arrest.

The declaration did not, however, consider the natural world's complex role in our welfare – a subject that has, in the past seven decades, risen (with tides and temperatures) to the forefront of global humanitarian concern. In 1948, a time when over two-thirds of the world's population still lived rurally, nature may well have seemed eternal and omnipresent. Since then, however, we have become an urban species, natural spaces have disappeared at an alarming rate, and contact with nature is no longer something we can take for granted. As the voices in the Welfare chapter come together to demonstrate in force, connection to nature is fundamental to our physical, cognitive, emotional, existential, social and spiritual well-being. If work, which doesn't inherently provide any of this, is a legally protected human right, why not nature, which does? Sorry, I mean, why not daily contact with vegetated environments?

Our legislated human rights – intended to prevent injustice and inhumanity – need to adapt to reflect the evolving landscape of oppression. At present, a new form of oppression is growing: nature deprivation. Depriving people of contact with nature is not only unnatural, it is a form of violence. Driving physical, mental and social ills, this violence is often enacted against people in the service of private profiteering. The Injustice chapter unpacks the forces driving nature deprivation, and how it intersects with other forms of oppression and injustice.

To protect present and future generations, we must defend our right to have contact with nature. We can work away in fragments on the ground, scrabbling to save this bit of green space here or create that bit there, or we can fight together to turn the dial globally. Enshrining nature contact in international human rights law is the fastest, farthest-reaching way to do this. By recognizing contact with nature as a human right, we can stop governments and legislators from pursuing expedient policies at the expense of people's welfare. Back to the title. *Daily Contact with Vegetated Environments Should Be a Legally Protected Right for Every Human Being.* I'll file for the trademark now.

*

The goal of making daily contact with vegetated environments a legally protected right for every human being is achievable. Since 1948, dozens of treaties and declarations have supplemented the UDHR and, in 2021, a new right was enshrined: the right to a healthy environment. The six key elements of "the right to a healthy environment" are: clean air; a safe climate; healthy ecosystems and biodiversity; healthy and sustainably produced food; access to clean water and adequate sanitation; and non-toxic environments. This provides hope that ecological and environmental inequalities are now being taken seriously within the human rights arena.

However, in a world in which geoengineering and terraforming are viable climate "solutions", there is a very real threat that we'll lose nature itself in the quest for "a healthy environment". Picture a future in which advanced machines are what's generating the clean air and water, nutritious food, and so on. Given that we're far from comprehensively understanding how nature's cast works together to support life (the calamitous Biosphere 2 project is testament to this), there is a very real danger that we'd miss out on key components of what exactly keeps us happy and healthy (or even alive).

Even the "healthy ecosystems and biodiversity" element could easily preclude nature contact, as prevalent conservation methods involve removing human beings from the equation (ignoring the fact that the planet's healthiest, most biodiverse ecosystems are those protected by resident Indigenous communities). All the more vital, then, to enshrine contact with nature itself – real, leafy, living spaces – as a legally protected right for all.

I asked David R. Boyd, the United Nations' Special

Rapporteur on Human Rights and Environment and spearhead of the "right to a healthy environment", whether he agrees that contact with nature should be a human right. "In an ideal world, of course!" he rhapsodized. "You could argue that this is part of everyone's right to live in a safe, clean, healthy and sustainable environment. This is particularly true as the scientific evidence regarding the health benefits of contact with nature becomes increasingly clear. The content of the right to a healthy environment continues to evolve, and contact with nature could certainly be recognized as a key element."

We can do this. And we have to. Let this book be a clarion call for the conversations we desperately need to have, and the actions we desperately need to take – to build a future of abundant joy, resilience and equality, in which contact with nature is not a rarity, but a birthright.

WELFARE

WELFARE
Ellen Miles

"If we surrendered to earth's intelligence we could rise up rooted, like trees."
Rainer Maria Rilke, *The Book of Hours* (1905)

"In some Native languages the term for plants translates to 'those who take care of us.'"
Robin Wall Kimmerer, *Braiding Sweetgrass* (2013)

Being in nature is good for you. This isn't news to you, of course. We learn in school that plants clean the air, that getting outdoors raises vitamin D levels, sharpens eyesight, and provides room to move. You likely grew up being told to *go and play outside* for precisely these reasons. But stay with me. There is much more to learn about nature's exquisite remedy. So much more, in fact, that scientists are just scratching the surface of it.

Modern medicine has long underestimated nature's influence on our well-being. As recently as 2005, there were only 60 solid studies on the subject. Now, a painful irony is emerging: as the distance between humans and (the rest of) nature grows, so does the evidence that our health and happiness depend on close contact with it. Today, as author Richard Louv points out, a thousand studies "point in one direction: Nature is not only nice to have, but it's a have-to-have" for healthy bodies and minds.

Take mental health. When the world descended into lockdown, it brought a wave of recognition that green, open spaces are a pressure relief valve for frantic minds –

banishing stress, alleviating anxiety, conjuring glints of joy from a vacuum. The emerging evidence not only supports this intuition but goes further, telling us that exposure to green, leafy environments can relieve and prevent debilitating psychiatric disorders, including depression and schizophrenia, suggesting that "accessible natural areas may be *vital* for mental health". Like myself and countless others, Jay Griffiths has been through the mangle of mental illness, and attests to this. In her raw, gripping piece, the author and activist shares how immersion in verdure pierced depression's grey smog (page 54).

Intuition also tells us to head to nature when we need to "clear our head", to experience that undiluted convergence of the senses – the presence, awareness and awakeness – that only the great outdoors can provide. More and more studies substantiate our instinct that greenery fuels brain-power: aiding cognitive development as we grow, slowing its decline as we age, and keeping memory, focus and problem-solving faculties sharp throughout our lives. These brain-boosting effects also conspire to make us more creative, as young writer Daisy Kennedy explores in her colourful inquiry into nature's sway over our right-brained activities (page 92).

As for the rest of the body, we're coming to realize that the "Natural Health Service" works its magic through every somatic system, deterring a host of physical ailments, and making us measurably fitter and more resilient to illness. We now know that office workers get sick less often if they're surrounded by plants, and that hospital patients recover faster if they can see foliage from their beds. While I could continue listing nature's head-to-toe medicinal qualities, I'm no scientist. Thankfully, Professor Qing Li –

possibly the world's most qualified person on this subject – is. His essay reveals many more jaw-dropping revelations about nature's cure-all tonic (page 36).

To experience these benefits more intimately, take Shareefa Energy's guided meditation to a quiet spot in nature (or let it take you there), and learn how to compost with Poppy Okotcha's love letter to this "ancient alchemy" (pages 50 and 86).

*

How do natural surroundings impact our health so drastically? Well, the fact that humans aren't separate from nature can be true spatially as well as taxonomically: there is no real boundary between your body and what's around it. The human body is less a solid, bounded object and more a space through which external matter passes, settles and merges. The epidermis (the outer layer of your skin) is, to paraphrase environmentalist Paul Shepard, more like a pond surface or forest soil than a wall. You don't process fuel (air, food and water) in an isolated chamber, like a car does; you assimilate this matter, using it to power your muscles and brain, and repair and rebuild your cells – influencing how you move, think and heal. Though your body may appear constant, it is, like a river, always being (re)built from new inputs. So, the matter that's around you matters.

Moreover, the non-human bacterial cells in your body outnumber human cells three to one. These organisms form intricate systems that map your body like a power grid, influencing your health as they interact with your immune and digestive systems. In their joint polemic, *Inflamed: Deep Medicine and the Anatomy of Injustice* (2021), medical expert Rupa Marya and social justice academic Raj Patel say, "The study of ecology is becoming indispensable to the study of medicine because humans are not just a single animal, but a multitude; an ecology of beings lives on us, in us, and around us." The more diverse these beings (called microbiota) are, the healthier they become; and they're more diverse the more you are immersed in natural surroundings. Healthy microbiota regulate and reduce inflammation, which Marya and Patel note "accompanies almost every disease in the modern world: heart disease, cancer, inflammatory bowel disease, Alzheimer's, depression, obesity, diabetes, and more."

*

Nature's miracles reach beyond individual health, to our relationships, social connections and community harmony. Green spaces aren't just nice environments to hang out in, they're also places that allow people to see eye to eye, settings where social hierarchies dissolve. A Zurich study found that urban forests and parks are venues where local and immigrant youths can meet on equal footing, increasing social integration among young people from different cultures. The very notion of "common ground" has its roots in these realities.

Green areas also make people calmer and kinder, reducing interpersonal conflict, aggression, and even crime. A study in New Haven, Connecticut (a city with a crime rate twice the United States' national average) discovered that, for every 10 per cent increase in tree canopy cover, there was a 15 per cent decrease in violent crime, and a 14 per cent fall in property crime (theft and arson). Other research indicates that there is less graffiti, vandalism and littering in tree-filled outdoor spaces than in comparable plantless spaces. A study of the infamous Robert Taylor Homes public housing project in Chicago, Illinois found that blocks surrounded by trees and grass reported half the amount of crime and domestic violence, as well as higher social cohesion and happiness, compared to blocks with little-to-no greenery around them. The study's lead scientist, Frances E. Kuo, concluded: "Without vegetation, people are very different beings". In more ways than one, to lose nature is to lose our humanity.

Contact with nature also strengthens the most lasting relationship any of us will know: the one we have with ourselves. Spending time in natural environments improves our self-esteem and body image, helping us develop a lasting sense of respect, reverence and gratitude for ourselves, just as we are.

And it's not just human relationships either: as much as we have a material need to have nature around us, we also have a psychological need for beyond-human connection. Biologist Robin Wall Kimmerer describes humankind as having placed itself in solitary confinement, leading to "'species loneliness'—a deep, unnamed sadness stemming from estrangement from the rest of Creation, from the loss of relationship." Nurturing ecological bonds can heal this collective heartache. In their intimate essays, naturalists So and Pınar Sinopoulos-Lloyd describe the joy and solace that such relationships can provide (pages 66, 68 and 77).

*

The voices in this chapter provide evidence for what many of us intuitively feel: nature is a panacea. Yet it feels wrong to talk of nature's "benefits" when nature – our natural habitat, the environment we need – is something mankind is systematically eradicating. The "boosts" we get from having plant life around us – to health, happiness, brainpower, temperament, community – should be our normal state. Anything less is our loss. It isn't just that time in nature lifts our spirits – lifeless environments are causing chronic mental anguish. Living in greener areas doesn't simply help us live longer – nature deprivation is killing people.

Though full of wonder, this chapter is bittersweet. At every turn, as we marvel at another of nature's gifts, we must also grieve it. As humankind urbanizes and digitizes, these gifts will continue to fade and vanish, unless we protect contact with nature as a right for all.

THE PEACE OF WILD THINGS
Wendell Berry

When despair for the world grows in me
and I wake in the night at the least sound
in fear of what my life and my children's lives may be,
I go and lie down where the wood drake
rests in his beauty on the water, and the great heron feeds.
I come into the peace of wild things
who do not tax their lives with forethought
of grief. I come into the presence of still water.
And I feel above me the day-blind stars
waiting with their light. For a time
I rest in the grace of the world, and am free.

THE SECRET POWER OF THE FOREST: FROM A FEELING TO A SCIENCE
Professor Qing Li, MD, PhD

We all know how good being in nature can make us feel. We have known it for millennia. Since time immemorial, forests have helped us to heal our wounds and to cure our diseases; they have relieved us of our worries, eased our troubled minds, restored and refreshed us. The sounds of life, the scent of soil, the sunlight playing through the leaves, the fresh, clean air—these things give us a sense of comfort, they help us to relax and to think more clearly. We know this deep in our bones. It is an intuition, an instinct, a feeling that is sometimes hard to describe. But what lies behind it? What is this secret power of the forest that makes us so much healthier and happier?

I am a scientist, not a poet, and I have been investigating the science behind that feeling for many years. Some people study forests. Some people study medicine. I study forest medicine, to find out all the ways these environments improve our well-being. Until recently, there was little scientific evidence to support what we have always known about the healing power of the forest. It was not until 2004—when I, with others, founded the Forest Therapy Study Group—that scientific investigation into this matter began in earnest. Since then, I have been researching the beneficial effects of these wild green spaces on human health by studying *shinrin-yoku* (森林浴). *Shinrin* (森林) means "forest" in Japanese, and *yoku* (浴) means "bath." *Shinrin-yoku* is "bathing in the forest atmosphere" or, as it is more often translated, forest-bathing. Forest-bathing is not exercise, nor is it an esoteric meditative practice. It is simply *being*, connecting with the forest through all our senses.

Over the last 17 years, I have discovered that exposure to nature is as vital to our well-being as regular exercise and a healthy diet. That immersion in green spaces can help to boost our immune systems, lower blood pressure and heart rate, aid sleep, improve mood and energy levels, lift depression, sharpen cognitive processes, and increase anti-cancer protein production. Outside my own work, a growing body of evidence shows that greater exposure to nature can also lead to a lower likelihood of cardiovascular disease, obesity, diabetes, asthma hospitalization, mental ill-health, childhood myopia, and, ultimately, death. In an eight-year study of over 100,000 women in the United States, those with the most vegetation around their homes had a 12 per cent lower death rate than those living in the least green areas (even adjusting for risk factors, such as age, ethnicity, smoking, and socioeconomic status). In a study of Tokyo residents aged 75 to 90, those with plentiful green space and street trees in their neighborhoods had a 74 per cent likelihood of survival over a five-year period, versus just 66 per cent for those with very little nearby greenery.

While nature's benefits are too innumerable and unknowable to comprehensively cover in these brief pages, I would like to walk you through some of the most significant scientific discoveries of recent years, which are beginning to show how contact with nature is essential to our health and happiness.

Let's Talk About Stress

"Stress" is a key term when it comes to how contact with nature benefits us, and how being apart from it harms us. Our growing disconnect from nature is stress-inducing, even when we do not realize it. Stress is often called "the health epidemic of the 21st century" and finding ways to manage stress, I believe, will be the most significant health challenge of the future.

We can measure stress by looking at three kinds of hormones: adrenaline (which indicates mental stress), noradrenaline (which indicates physical stress), and cortisol (which can indicate both). In my own scientific research, I have proven that just six hours of forest-bathing in two days can reduce all three.

Blood pressure is another key indicator of stress, and a very important parameter for our health. High blood pressure (hypertension) is a silent killer—it can induce strokes, heart disease, and kidney disease. For context, healthy resting blood pressure is under 130mmHg for systolic blood pressure (SBP), which is the force at which your heart pumps blood, and under 85mmHg for diastolic blood pressure (DBP), which is the resistance to blood flow in your blood vessels. I conducted a study with middle-aged men who had high blood pressure—on average 141/86mmHg (SBP/DBP). After walking in the forest, this average fell to 134/79mmHg, meaning that their DBP had normalized to a healthy level, and SBP had significantly fallen, in very little time at all. The forest provided a decrease in blood pressure comparable to that provided by antihypertensive agents (drugs used to treat hypertension). This is a vital and significant discovery for preventive medicine—we need to take contact with nature seriously when designing healthier futures.

Nature also regulates the nervous system. The nervous system is made up of the sympathetic nervous system (the "fight or flight" part, which gets your heart going), and the parasympathetic nervous system (the "rest and recover" part, which calms everything down). Common sense tells us that spending time in nature helps us relax and feel calm. Through my research, I confirmed that forest-bathing reduces the activity of the sympathetic nervous system and increases the activity of the parasympathetic nervous system, reducing stress and heart rate. This further indicates that helping people to spend time in forested environments could have a preventive effect on heart disease.

Stress can also lead to insomnia and poor quality sleep. Sleeping well is vital for maintaining our health and well-being: it helps our brains to work properly, it balances our hormones, and is essential for the proper functioning of our immune system. Doctors recommend eight hours of good quality sleep a night. In Japan, 30–40 per cent of working-age men say they can't sleep because of stress, and 40 per cent say that they sleep less than six hours a night. Sleep deficiency such as this is linked to numerous health problems, including increased risk of heart disease, kidney disease, high blood pressure, diabetes, and stroke.

In one of my studies, before forest-bathing, participants, on average, slept for less than six and a half hours (383 minutes). During our forest-bathing excursion, this rose to over seven and a half hours (452 minutes). Not only that, the effects lasted after we returned: participants slept for just under seven hours (410 minutes) on the night following the trip. In other words, there was a significant increase in sleep time during—and after—the forest-bathing trip, providing compelling evidence that we sleep better when we spend time in nature, even without a significant increase in physical activity. Participants also reported feeling significantly less sleepy and more refreshed on rising, indicating that forest-bathing not only extended sleep time, but also improved sleep quality.

It is well known that the immune system plays an important part in building our defences against bacteria, viruses, and tumours. It is also well known that stress inhibits immune function. If your immune system is suppressed, you are more likely to be ill; stressed people are frequently ill. The more stress we have, the sicker we get. We have more heart attacks, hypertension, strokes, and cancers; more mental illness, addictions, loneliness, and depression; more sleeping disorders, eating disorders, panic disorders—you name it! One of the ways we test the health of the immune system is by looking at the activity of natural killer (NK) cells, a type of immune cell, so-called because they can attack and kill unwanted cells, for example, those infected with a virus, or tumour cells. They do this with the help of anti-cancer proteins: perforin, granulysin, and granzymes A and B. These proteins drill holes in cell membranes, which causes the target cells to die. People with higher NK activity show a significantly lower incidence of diseases such as cancers.

Across multiple studies (with both men and women) I have found that, after three days and two nights in a forest, participants' NK activity, NK cell numbers, and anti-cancer proteins significantly increase, and that this effect lasts for as long as 30 days afterward. Hence, a monthly forest-bathing excursion is enough to maintain a high level of NK activity. I also found that a single-day forest-bathing trip also boosts immune function, and the effects lasted for a week, meaning that smaller weekly journeys may have the same impact. These studies suggested that forests may have anti-cancer effects.

If you can raise your NK activity just by going for a walk

in a forest, what would be the effect if you lived near trees all the time? How great could the anti-cancer effects be if you lived in a green place? After asking myself these questions, I set out to look at the relationship between forest coverage in Japan and deaths from different kinds of cancers. I found that people who live in areas with fewer trees, not only have significantly higher levels of stress, they also have higher mortality rates from cancers than people who live where there is a good density of trees. We must make all our dwellings green enough for everyone to receive these vital, life-saving benefits.

Senses Are Sensei

Why do freshly cut grass, petrichor (the smell of earth after rain) and sea air smell so good? They're good for us. We developed our finely tuned senses, which pick up on the things we need them to, over millennia. Our senses are ancient and wise; they can teach us about what we need— and they do. You can hear your ancestors whisper through them, guiding you towards certain sights, sounds, and smells. *Shinrin-yoku* is a bridge: by opening our senses, it bridges the gap between us and the natural world.

Cities are wonderful places, full of excitement, innovation, and energy—I love living in Tokyo—but living in these fast-paced, unnatural environments can be an assault on the senses. For one thing, there's city noise. Noise pollution raises blood pressure and heart rate, causes sleep problems, damages hearing, and reduces mental clarity. Nature's sounds, on the other hand, are restorative. The sounds of water, wind, and birdsong have been shown to have a strong link to stress recovery. Like our ears, our eyes weren't designed for cityscapes. Because we evolved in the scenery of the natural world, we're visually fluent in its patterns: processing fluid, organic shapes is easy for our Paleolithic visual cortex. Looking at natural patterns can reduce stress by as much as 60 per cent. This could suggest that the lines and angles we see daily in our offices, subways and apartment blocks are causing us to subconsciously strain our visual processing system, resulting in higher stress levels than we should naturally have.

Our modern-day lives are exhausting—we are pulled in so many different directions at once—and urban environments have been found to provoke anger and irritability. One of the ways we measure the impact of forest-bathing on mood is through the POMS (Profile of Mood States) test. Participants are given a list of 65 emotions and asked to rate the extent to which they are currently experiencing each one, on a scale ranging from "not at all" to "extremely." In my studies, the results show that forest-bathing reduces negative emotions such as anxiety, depression, anger, fatigue, and confusion, and increases positive feelings such as vigor. Even accounting for the mood-enhancing effects of exercise (a walk in downtown Tokyo did not have such benefits!), these effects begin to appear 20 minutes after the forest-bathing begins, even in city parks, suggesting you need to stay at least this long to begin to feel the effects. I also found that a two-hour trip to the forest had a similar effect on POMS scores as even longer excursions. This 120-minute magic time frame (after which, the impacts start to plateau) was affirmed by a 2019 study involving around 20,000 participants. The study also found that two hours was the minimum requirement, but, interestingly, you don't need to do it in one go: several short visits (totalling 120 minutes) had the same effect as one long visit. By bringing forest-like spaces into cities, we can thus help busy people to experience the same essential, mood-enhancing benefits. Perhaps commuters could even walk home through city forests rather than taking a busy metro train.

The mood-boosting effects of nature also help people suffering from more debilitating mental distress. Working with patients in a rehabilitation hospital, I have found that a 20-minute walk in a Japanese garden can reduce depression, anxiety, anger, fatigue, and confusion, and even show a preventive effect on depression. Empirical evidence supports this preventative potentiality. A study in London found that, for every street tree added per kilometre (⅔ mile), there were 1.18 fewer antidepressant prescriptions per 1,000 people. A German study found that individuals with low socioeconomic status were significantly less likely to need antidepressants if they had a high density of street trees in the 100 metres (110 yards) around their home.

What is it about trees that has this effect? How exactly do trees do this? I knew that our five senses played a crucial role in forest-bathing's healing effects—the sights, sounds, smells, tastes, and feel of the forest all have a powerful impact on our state of mind. It is a total effect of five senses. The quiet atmosphere, beautiful scenery, mild climate, pleasant aromas, and fresh, clean air. Of all our senses, smell is the most primal, and I speculated that the sense of smell has the biggest impact. Could it be that trees' subtle aromatherapy provides this mental boost? And could this be linked to our physical health? It took a long time to discover the answer to this. Let me first explain what a phytoncide is.

We know that trees produce the oxygen we need to

breathe. As well as having a higher concentration of oxygen, the air in the forest is also full of phytoncides. Phytoncides are natural oils within a plant. *Phyton* is derived from Ancient Greek (φυτόν) for "plant" (specifically, a leaf and its stem, from which you can propagate a new plant), and the *-cide* suffix means "to kill" (as in homicide, pesticide, and ecocide). In this case, the *-cide* is a good thing (if you're a tree at least): phytoncides are part of a tree's defence system; they release these chemicals as protection against bacteria, insects, and fungi. Phytoncides are also part of the communication pathway between trees: the way trees talk to each other. The concentration of phytoncides in the air depends on the temperature and other changes that take place throughout the year. The warmer it is, the more airborne phytoncides there are (concentration is highest at around 30°C (86°F). Evergreens like pine trees, cedars, spruces, and conifers are the largest producer of phytoncides. The main components of phytoncides are terpenes: the aromatic compounds you smell. The major terpenes are: Alpha-pinene (nature's most common terpene), which has a fresh, piney scent; Beta-pinene, which smells herby, like basil or dill; camphene, which has a turpentine-like, resinous smell; and D-limonene, which smells (you guessed it) lemony!

We have known for generations that people liked these smells, that we were naturally drawn to them, but we didn't know why. So, I decided to test them. Incubating human NK cells with phytoncides, I found that both the NK activity and the presence of anti-cancer proteins in the cells had increased. This was the world's first investigation into the effect of phytoncides on NK cell function—I was amazed by the results, though not surprised. The next thing to do was to test the effect of phytoncides on immune function.

One of the most familiar smells in Japan (and my personal favourite phytoncide smell) is the scent of the *hinoki* cypress, *Chamaecyparis obtusa*. It is a very nostalgic scent for me, reminding me of many happy times.

I took 12 healthy middle-aged men to stay at a hotel in Tokyo and gave them a choice of different wood essential oils, but they all preferred *hinoki*—like me! I diffused *hinoki* stem oil into the participants' rooms as they slept. The results of the *hinoki* phytoncides on participants were:

1 Significantly increased numbers of NK cells and NK activity
2 Enhanced anti-cancer proteins
3 Significantly decreased levels of stress hormones
4 Increased hours of sleep
5 Decreased tension, anxiety, anger, hostility, fatigue and confusion

So, the smells that we are drawn to in nature are good for us—we have evolved to love these scents because they can help us to be healthy.

Another important forest smell is geosmin, the terpene (produced by soil microbes) that gives soil its characteristic "petrichor" smell. Researchers at Brown University discovered the origins of this odor in 2007. Ten years later, a South Korean team examined the effects of smelling geosmin, and found that it is linked with calm, relaxed brain states, particularly in women. We've also since learned that human noses are 200,000 times more sensitive to the smell of geosmin than sharks are to blood.

Why do we like this smell so much? And why does it have this relaxing effect on us? Scientists are now discovering that it may have something to do with *Mycobacterium vaccae*, a bacterium found in soil, which accompanies geosmin. Soils rich in organic matter will smell earthy, whereas depleted soils don't have much smell at all. If you can smell geosmin, the soil will be healthy and full of microscopic life and, very likely, *M. vaccae*.

Mycobacterium vaccae has incredible, mind-altering properties, similar to antidepressants: it stimulates the brain's production of serotonin, the "happy hormone" that stabilizes our mood and promotes feelings of happiness and contentment, and decreases anxiety, fear, and stress responses.

If you have ever had the urge to deeply inhale the earthy smell of soil, or to dig your hands into it—this is why. Our bodies intuitively know that it's good for us. Every time you dig around in your garden, or pluck a vegetable from the ground, you'll be ingesting *M. vaccae* and receiving its bountiful boost.

So, our bodies are innately smart when it comes to seeking out nature's remedy. But nature can help sharpen our mind too. Not only do trees make us healthier and happier; they help us think more clearly. Spending just one hour in nature can improve your memory and attention span by 20 per cent, and a four-day trip can boost problem-solving ability by 50 per cent. Growing up in greener environments has a beneficial association with children's cognitive development. A Belgian study found that a 3 per cent increase in green space boosted the IQ of children living in an urban environment by 2.6 points.

It can also help children to overcome challenging behavioural problems: green outdoor settings appear to reduce children's ADHD symptoms across a wide range of age, gender, and income groups, community types, geographic regions, and diagnoses. Not only does living in a greener environment improve cognitive development as we grow, it slows cognitive decline as we age. Researchers performed a 10-year follow-up of 6,500 people aged 45 to 68 in the UK, and found that the decline in cognitive scores over this period was 4.6 per cent smaller in participants living in greener neighborhoods.

A Need for Nature

With its astounding benefits, forest-bathing is becoming a focus of public attention in Japan. It is now recognized as both a therapeutic activity and a method of preventing disease and promoting health. Slowly, acknowledgement of nature as medicine is catching on worldwide. Doctors from New Zealand to Scotland have begun to prescribe "green prescriptions," such as listening to birdsong or taking a walk in a natural environment. The "Nature Prescriptions" calendar, created by RSPB Scotland in partnership with NHS Shetland, suggests daily activities such as "Step outside—be still for three minutes and listen," and to "Really look at a lichen." Creating and improving public pockets of greenery—especially in neighborhoods whose residents already face high health risks—would be a simple, powerful, practical public health intervention that would help to prevent and mitigate health inequalities.

Forests occupy 68 per cent of the land in Japan, meaning forest-bathing is accessible to those who can afford the time and expense of the trip. But, with our busy lifestyles, and unequal societies, we shouldn't expect people to make a journey to receive nature's tonic. Instead, we must bring the best of the forest environment into people's habitats. Doing so not only provides all the well-being benefits I've explained, but also presents additional benefits in urban contexts: urban trees remove tons of pollution, store tons of carbon and help mitigate extreme temperatures. Their root systems absorb water and help with excess rainfall. They provide respite and relief from noise and dirt. Trees are a vital and integral part of our urban lives, as important a part of a city's infrastructure as roads and broadband—and much more beautiful than either.

Clearly, there are vital benefits to being immersed in an ecologically rich, verdant environment, and I expect many more will be discovered. To quell the stress epidemic of our times, and avoid countless other easily preventable harms, we must protect people's right to have contact with nature— and bring the power of the forest to everyone.

WALK THROUGH THE JUNGLE
Shareefa Energy

Taking you on a journey
A sacred place within
Let your mind wander
To a place of comfort

I want you to close your eyes
Close the doors on all demanding
Relax your shoulders
Feel the weight you're carrying leave your body

Let the stresses of life fly by
Don't give them power inside you to reside
Every struggle you face today is temporary
Remember to breathe

Surrender to nature's abundance
Take a walk with me
Away from the concrete
This place you call home, your city

Take my hand
Take hold of my palm firmly
Step out of the concrete
Journey to the jungle with me

The rainforest, she is solace
Her beauty blooms
She brings calm to my spirit
She makes my struggles feel miniscule
Her bright shades of green

Her demand for my attention
She brings me back to grounding
She forces me to be present

Don't be afraid to step out of the concrete
Make time for yourself
Don't be afraid when your mind's overwhelmed
When you want to numb your stresses
When you want the pain to go
When you feel misunderstood
When nobody seems to be listening
When you feel like you're all alone
When your world feels like it's going to cave in
Don't be afraid

Find a safe space inside yourself
Step out into the world
Fill your lungs with clean air
Climb, stretch, play like you did as a child
Find what you enjoy
Make time for yourself

Don't be afraid to spend time with yourself
Journey in life by yourself
When we be more gentle with ourselves
When we show our self more compassion
The world reflects this love back

Show love to yourself
Speak encouraging words to yourself
Prioritize yourself
Look after your health

What we eat impacts our mind and body
Eat nutritious food that uplifts
Eat fruit in generous portions
Fruit that makes you feel alive full of good vibes
Papaya, fresh coconut water and berries

Step out of the concrete
Take a walk in a park
In a forest
Go for a hike
Climbing mountains, new horizons bring us perspective in life

When you feel overwhelmed and stressed
When the pain hurts too much inside your chest
Take a moment and breathe
Take a walk away from the concrete
Into the jungle with me

Our body heals
Our heart heals
Our mind heals
What weighed heavy on you yesterday
You don't have to carry into tomorrow

When the sun shines
When it's spring or summertime
Close your eyes
Feel the sun kissing your skin
Feel her healing you
Feel her giving you energy
Feel her hands lifting your burdens
Feel her working her magic

Pay attention to the whistles of the birds
The jovial honeybees
A part of us heals when our eyes meet
Let Nature bless your eyes, your soul
Keep a plant in your room
Drink plenty of spring water
Staying hydrated makes us clear headed

Discipline your mind
Pick up a martial art
Give your mind constructive focus
Let your body express itself
Never suppress yourself
Find healthy outlets
Find a space where you feel safe
The Bruce Lees of this world
Spent valuable time humbled in forests

Don't be afraid to be different
Don't be afraid to try something new
Don't be afraid of change
There's always blessings when we embrace the new

Take a walk through the jungle with me
Leave your troubles and your stresses in the concrete
Believe life is going to get better
Your burdens less heavier –
Take a walk through the jungle with me

THE NECESSARY MEDICINE
Jay Griffiths

Depression. Its colour is grey. Of all the psyche's pains, it is the dullest, the most stagnant ache. It is stale with unhappiness, misery at its most lifeless. Often, it is compounded by the low-level, nerve-eroding hum of constant anxiety.

Studies illustrate that people in urban areas who live near parks and green spaces suffer less depression. Taking socioeconomic status into account, research shows that those who "move to greener areas have significant and long-lasting improvements in mental health."

Green is good for you. Ecotherapy, supported by MIND among others, is a form of treatment shown to be effective for mental health issues. There are studies which link proximity to green space with physical fitness but, although exercise is good for depressives, there is more going on when it comes to mental health and nature. Our minds are not Lego sets built for a Bauhaus world. We are not machines; we are animals. Incontrovertibly so, and a cause for celebration. The prevalence of mental health distress tells us one thing as a society: we must be kinder to our human nature and these, our animal bodies. And the necessary medicine is green.

What is it that happens to the human mind in the natural world which no study can ever quite grasp and pin down? The studies, taken collectively, demonstrate the fact that the green stuff is good for the psyche, but they seldom say exactly *why* this is the case. And in that margin, many of us who know both depression and a love for the green world may feel our way, tendril by tendril, like ivy asking questions of the gaps between the railings and the branch.

In depression, the psyche turns inwards, feeding on itself, for the ill mind demands attention as much as the ill body does. In green spaces, though, the mind is gently, repeatedly invited to turn its gaze outward, to notice, see and hear. When the great psychiatrist and Holocaust survivor Viktor E. Frankl articulated *Man's Search for Meaning*, one of the areas of meaning he describes as life-saving is that of simply being attentive to, and appreciative of, the natural world. No product. No price. No profit. Nature takes us outside ourselves, making us convivial with the carnival green of the vivid and turning world.

Nature is good medicine for the sick psyche. Nature doesn't judge and cannot lie, and those are healing qualities. Judgementalism and inauthenticity or dishonesty are two responses from the outside world which depressives rightly abhor. Many depressives feel torn between needing company and needing solitude: nature provides both, at the same time.

What else happens, then, in this meeting of mind and green? *Life* happens, wriggly, thriving and green. In all its turning cycles – a season, a snail, a whirlpool of leaves in the wind – the sheer liveliness of the green world is good for the mind, for our psyches are life-lit, and on the lookout for all the vital signs, written in green.

I have felt the benefits of nature all my life. But I have felt the urgent and essential need for it when I have been at my lowest points of depression. These are the times when nature is the necessary medicine, and more even than that: it is a human right, our birthright.

Some years ago, living in a small flat in North London, a long way from the forests, I had become very ill with depression. Quite how bad it would have got, I cannot tell you, if I hadn't spoken one word in answer to one question.

The word was "Yes."

I remember saying that word as if my life depended on it and perhaps – I'll never know – it did.

I didn't even manage to say it loudly. I said it with my eyes shut, as someone might plead for help, or as a child would make a wish, or as a singer might close their eyes at the most significant note of the song.

It was a heartfelt yes, but whispered, because whispering was all I could manage. It is the whisper which often starts the story. Hush. The noise of traffic fades. Station announcements fall silent. Trains grow quiet. Quiet. Quiet as the pause when you wait for the right word. *Zurrumurru* – whisper, in the Basque language. Hush. Step out of the station, step sideways into the woods. Step across the boundary and the trespass of story will begin. Just say yes.

My story began when I had been suffering depression for months. Many people know that lifeless place, where every way you look seems closed off to you: *No* is written on all sides, on every path.

I was lost in that bleak, hollow emptiness, haunted by thoughts of suicide, all my vitality gone. Then, one day, into this abyss of lifelessness someone threw me a rope, a lifeline. An anthropologist who knew my situation telephoned me and invited me to go with him to the Peruvian Amazon to visit shamans who worked with the formidable mind-medicines of the forests.

I had to say yes to the journey and yes to the story, because sometimes the tree of life may be a literal thing.

From Lima, we took a small plane, then a car, then a *peque peque:* one of the little motorized dugout canoes which zip up and down the rivers of the Amazon. From the river, we walked to the shamans' centre, through the forest, which stings you, bites you, then strokes you with leaves soft as a kitten's ears. One tree's bark smelt of nutmeg, and the air was alive with smells, from honey-scented flowers to the zinging smell of sap and the sour smell of a mossy fetid pool. I could almost smell the sunlight. Palm fronds rattled in the hot, moist air, and the whole forest surged with life.

As evening came, we settled into the shamans' hut; and a long night of the mind began. The medicine they gave me was like drinking hemlock and stars, as bitter as the one, as brilliant as the other. Cicadas and a whirring night bird feathered the night with noises and all the forest seemed mating and purring, rustling, cocooning and watching. I was surrounded by the warmth and breath of the forest, green and vital, and it was as if I were drinking in something of its essence, its spirit, its soul – and I needed that so badly because I had lost my own.

Before I visited these shamans, I would never have used the term soul-loss, but that was what I felt, my psyche unhappily lost and lonely. Shamans consider that their job is to travel in the landscape of the mind, to search for someone's spirit and to bring it back strong.

*

There are some terms of psychological well-being which can sound like descriptions of trees: to be "grounded" and "well-rooted", able both to "stand firm" and also to "branch out". Forests have long been linked to the psyche, and it seems a human universal to see trees as good ways of seeking truths. Across the world, people have trusted trees for their solidity and steadfastness, both literally and metaphorically. Intriguingly, the words "tree", "trust" and "truth" are all related words, as if the human race has always trusted trees to embody truth.

One Amazonian elder says the Amazon is "a wide expanse, similar to a perceptive human head." We speak of the "tree of knowledge" and trees have long been associated with wisdom; the Buddha meditated under a tree and in India, Sadhus have always retreated to the forests for wisdom. Native Americans honoured the idea of a Sacred Tree. I've been with Indigenous people in the Amazon when they have watched their forests cut down, their lands obliterated. They wept. "Destroying the forests is the same as destroying us," they said. "We are the land." The deforestation of the Amazon is also a deforestation of the human mind.

Shamans are the forest's doctors and therapists; their medicines are a free pharmacy. The Amazon has its artists, musicians and philosophers, who intricately link the forests with the pathways of the mind. Forests are rich in all the psyche's expressions of art, music, language and culture, and the destruction of the Amazon is like napalming the Berlin Philharmonic; burning gas flares through the Louvre; slashing every copy of Shakespeare; bulldozing the Sydney Opera House; and torching the scores of Mozart.

Meanwhile, as I lay in the shamans' hut, the forest night was quite literally en-chanted. One of the shamans chanted incantations, the songs or *icaros* which are the Songlines of the Amazon. Ethereal, quiet almost to inaudibility, the songs are sometimes whistled, sometimes voiced, and sometimes they sound like panpipes from miles away, music half-heard from a source unknown, where melody is more like scent, a sweet resin in the air from an unseen tree. I felt as if I was not only drinking the forest but hearing its essence. The shaman fell quiet for a while, and then began another song, from his own locale, the specific trees and groves of forest. He was singing one of his own Songlines. Although it is the Songlines of Indigenous Australia which are the most famous, I would argue that the whole world is wreathed in Songlines, people's love of land made into music.

The song lay in hot silence for a while, unsung, then from the shadows came a tiny leaf sprout of song. All the songs seemed sung in the key of green. The song seemed alive like a plant, and in a whistle I heard a wisp of slender stem, and then the music grew, elastic and gently energetic as a sapling sprung with green meaning; the Songline twined like a vine, melody winding into leaf. This music was green and vivid and was so strongly suggestive of plants that I felt myself plantlike, rooted in brown leaf mould and thirsty for the sun. The music jumped up to the light, clambered like a vine, streaked for the heat of noon and wetness. Then, at its height, the music descended a few tones as a leaf would drop, swinging down from the canopy to the forest floor.

It's common knowledge that the Amazon is the source of huge numbers of medicines for curing diseases of the body, but it is also a cure for the mind. Not, I would emphasize, in the form of chemical extraction, turned into pills, but the true and whole curing, resulting from the totality of medicine, shaman, song and forest. What they amounted to was, in a word, life. It is this which can be found in the forests of Britain or Australia, the forests of the Americas and beyond: wherever there are forests there is life. And the shamanic role? It is findable, wherever there are musicians, artists, poet-seers and writers willing to go to the trees for wisdom; willing to listen to earthsong.

That the forests are the lungs of the world, we know. That the world needs the forests in order to breathe, we know. But forests are also sources of psychological health, as I found when my spirit was so lost. The terms for "spirit" and "breath" are linked in many languages: *anima* (Latin) means both "breath" and "soul"; *psyche* (Greek) means "breath" and "soul". My acute feeling of soul-loss, of being dangerously de-animated, was cured by the animation, the spirit, of the forests.

The forests are a place of transformation, of shapeshifting. In the woods, the spirit can stretch and change, can move like a willow, elastic in spring. The whole tone of a day can be shifted by taking a walk through the trees in the park, even in a city centre. Woodlands can absorb bad moods and calm headaches. They change us. In the woods, you may be lost in your thoughts, willingly lost, creatively lost, which allows you to enter the mind's forests, where the wind within can blow you somewhere sought and as yet unfound. A child may go to the woods to dream themselves into a different character, to effect their changeling masquerades away from the eyes of adults. In the wild dreamwood of childhood, children can play disguise-games which begin "Let's pretend ..." and if children can't pretend, then they are condemned to reality.

Scented with story as it is with wild garlic, the woods may be a moment of beginning, the pause on the threshold before the journey, and then the woodlands may tell an unending story. I felt the most powerful sense of cure in the Amazon forest, but *all* woodlands are medicine for the mind. Children know it, when they are upset and take their troubles to a tree. A child, leaning against a tree, may listen to a blackbird, watch a rabbit, a fox or – if they are very lucky – a badger. In the forest is a child. But inside the child will always be the forest. Breathe the forest deeply enough in childhood, and the birds will still be singing 70 years on.

*

After my stay with the shamans in the Amazon, I felt happy as a grasshopper. The depression I had felt did not return for years. What was so effective? A combination of the shamanic treatment and music, but also the sheer shining vitality of the forests which, as all wild places, was in itself a tonic for the human spirit.

Our minds need what is wild, that unmistakable, unforgettable, elemental thing: wildness, the universal Songline, sung in green-gold, which we recognize the moment we hear it. We come from this wild song and we are most fully alive when we resonate to its wildest pitch with intense and necessary love.

All humans are essentially wild creatures and hate confinement. We need what is wild, and we thrill to it, our wildness bubbling over with an anarchic *joie de vivre*. We glint when the wild light shines. The more suffocatingly enclosed we are (tamed by television, controlled by mortgages and bureaucracy), the louder our wild genes scream in aggression, anger and depression.

Walk. The drum begins. Follow it. Follow the drums of thunder. Follow the sun. Follow the stars at night as they lean their long slant down the far side of the sky. Follow the lightning and the open road. Follow your compulsion.

Follow your calling. Put your boots on.

We were made to walk through our lives wildly awake: our minds mobile, quick, changeable. To be a nomad in one's mind is our gift: to move and learn, to be a student always. The mind, let loose, is a walking, asking, searching thing, questioning, questioning, whose root, of course, is to seek, to go on a quest.

It is as if a tragedy has been written into the world. People prey to depression feel that tragedy individually, but I think there is something far wider happening: the tragedy of divorce from the essential wildness of life, and separation from its fundamentally comedic nature. Tragedy works through crushing the spirit, in overwork, commuting, rush-hour exhaustion; worries, debts, bills, stress and the bad news which we all know. But tragedy is not the whole of the picture.

For still, in spite of it all, there are still the trees. Still, the wild reverie of the woodlands is within ourselves and the forests are enchanted; sung. Among all the tragedies of destruction, still, comedy erupts on the wild side, growth an absolute demand, new shoots thrusting up, yearning for sky. For, at some level, we have never really forgotten the comedy of life.

The spirit of comedy is the spirit of life, both leguminous, a vegetable exuberance. It is playful, this spirit. Wildness and comedy share a love of rudeness, tickling the pink with the horn of plenty. The comedy of life is rebellious, in the riotously festive nature of nature. Everything and everyone is a player in this harlequinade. Comedy unfurls through life, with its generous, regenerative grace, *fill it till it spills and lick it up again*. The earth is hot with, bursting with, fermenting with, dizzy with, hooting with – life, life which will always walk the wild way, the curly way, in fecund riot and feral grace.

The forests are, for me, the opposite of depression. Where depression is dull, the forests shimmer with vitality. Whereas depression is a congealed stasis, the forests wriggle, dance and jump. Where depression is a horribly lonely illness, the heart of forest-wisdom is the irrefutable interconnectedness of all life. Having felt condemned to depression, I experienced the shapeshifting transformation of the forests. Having felt the cold, silent approach of something potentially fatal in depression, I found in the Amazon something which spoke of the warmest opposite, a riot of language in irrepressible gusto, life growling, flowering, leafing, hooting and budding, flickering in a forest fiesta of verdant and noisy verbs, the forest chattering with language, a whole universe laughing with life.

And what it says is – *yes*.

EMPATHY AS RESISTANCE
Sophia "So" Sinopoulos-Lloyd

If you want to learn how to belong

on /this/ land

watch the creatures

who live here

for whom nature is not just a backdrop

for a spiritual experience.

See how the bobcat and lion

walk along the edges of things

even at night

they walk in moonshadow!

See how the birds

warn the whole forest of danger

and claim their territory

with a song.

Watch them if you can

because here's the irony:

When beings become expert at belonging

They can appear invisible to us.

When beings become expert at belonging

They can appear invisible to us.

64

This includes

human beings.

There are good reasons for stealth

for example,

Survival.

But do me a favor

& don't simply add this

to your list of naturalist facts.

It is easy to watch a documentary

where the narrator informs you

of scientific reasons for things.

What is hard

is learning

the psycho-spiritual reasons

for stealth

and silence.

When we learn that

we are finally able

to sit with our relatives

And Listen.

ANIMISM(S) AND OUR NEED FOR BEYOND-HUMAN KINSHIP
Sophia and Pınar Ateş Sinopoulos-Lloyd

It has been well established that social bonds are essential for our development, well-being, and survival. Relationships with companion animals have received welcome scholarly attention as well, reminding us that our pets are often some of the most intimate and supportive relationships we have. However, we neglect the suggestion that relationships with trees, plants, fungi, wild mammals, songbirds, and other nonhuman residents of our environments are necessary for our well-being—in spite of the fact that Indigenous peoples the world over practice lifeways derived from webs of beyond-human kinship.

From the Latin *anima*, meaning "soul," the word "animism" generally describes a way of being that is open— and oriented—to interpersonal relationship with other-than-human beings, and which sees these beings as "animated," or "imbued with soul." As religious studies scholar Graham Harvey puts it, animism centers an acknowledgment that the world is "full of persons, only some of which are human." Chickasaw scholar and poet Linda Hogan emphasizes that for her—and many First Nations people—what this academic word refers to is "simply called tradition." Honoring the multitude of relations and kinships with "earth beings" (as Peruvian anthropologist Marisol de la Cadena describes extra-human agencies like rivers and mountains) does not proceed from an intellectual endeavor but is continually enacted through place-tending (and -defending) practices that the modern European perspective often divides up into disparate labels:

"conservation," "religion," "spirituality," "activism," "land use," and so on.

Interpersonal relationships with local wild species and abiotic elements of the natural world were (and sometimes still are) a part of normal human social, emotional, and spiritual activity for most of our species' history. Based on this observation, there are those who claim, as American writer Joshua Michael Schrei does, that "animism is normative consciousness." In other words: identifying personhood, agency, and the activity of soul in our environments is native, or normal, to human ways of thinking and being. The small sliver of history we now find ourselves in, where the soul is often dismissed from our framing of the nonhuman world, is indeed the deviation from the norm set by the larger human story.

RESTOR(Y)ING PLACE: TRACKING AND THE NECESSITY OF ECOLOGICAL INTIMACY
Sophia "So" Sinopoulos-Lloyd

When a bird-watcher, or birder, spots a beloved and familiar bird, something amazing happens: the part of their brain responsible for human facial recognition is activated. "Birding," ornithologist Richard Prum reflects, "trains your brain to transform a stream of natural history perceptions into encounters with identifiable individuals." In other words, with enough immersive study and love, we see birds as unique persons.

I would wager that similar dynamics occur in many seekers of wild flora and fauna, whether their favored activity is mushroom hunting, scouting for snakes and lizards, or identifying tracks and remnants left by animals. In the course of learning wildlife tracking, my attachment systems seem to have slowly expanded beyond the human. I have found deep attachment to, and even identity with, the animals and landscapes around me. My queerness—assumed by many to be a postmodern identity—may be as influenced by coyote and deer as by feminist theory.

Familiarity and intimacy with wild beings and the living landscape can be a deep source of joy, awe, and spiritual well-being. Too often we are deprived of this source of pleasure and refuge. Barriers to accessing and interpreting ecologically rich places are deeply interwoven with wealth, race, and privilege. But the more cryptic barriers are those erected in our minds and spirits by ideologies that have emerged, or at least conspired more fully, in the last few hundred years: the myth of human supremacy; the arrogance of empiricism, which tells us that the universe contains nothing more than what human science can divine, that we can (and should) vanquish the world of all mystery; and the idea that "nature" lacks inherent value or personhood, and is something to be dissected and ultimately harnessed for human use. These systems guide what and whom we pay attention to and designate ecological attention as the provenance of an elite few (funded scientists, for example), dispossessing ordinary people from the deeply human (and animal) gifts of paying attention to—and tracking—our environments.

The loss of access to cross-species relationality does not just create personal spiritual voids, it harms culture. Excluding wild beings and landscapes from our social-emotional worlds contributes to a dangerous pattern whereby stories—and one important source of stories: relationships—are progressively severed from place, and our bodies and senses are not trusted as mediums for generating, identifying, and stewarding truths and knowledge. Today, many people (especially here, in North America) are affected by the complex trauma of stories being disembedded from places and from particular terrains. Many settler religions are centered around far-flung locales that we may never see. People Indigenous to this continent have often been forcibly relocated from their spiritual centers and their stories of place outlawed. When efforts are made to regenerate these connections, the effects are remarkable: a project connecting young Heiltsuk people to their ancestral lands and lifeways through place-based skills helped end a tragic surge of suicides within the community.

We find ourselves in a time of so-called "post-truth,"

where the ancient community-building technology of story is both misused and mistrusted. It seems beyond time to heal our relationship with story—and this process must be intertwined with healing our dissociation from place and "nature." Tracking—a story about our surroundings that we write with our senses—offers timeless clues to what this could look like.

On the most basic level, tracking is the recognition and interpretation of marks, tracks, traces, and signs—often called "spoor"—left by other animals on the landscape. The art and science of tracking involves interpreting many kinds of evidence of behavior and passage—footprints, scrapes, antler rubs, scat, scent mounds, beds, and other signs. It also involves associating and aging collections of tracks and signs to imagine fairly accurate anecdotes— where a deer slept last night, where a coyote took a drink of water, or where a bear feasted on grubs. While perfect foot (or paw) prints may be hard to find in many landscapes, subtler forms of tracks and signs abound nearly everywhere humans live and beyond, if we look close enough. Such signs ride a ghostly line between absence and presence as they point to the multi-species biographies of the living or the recently dead.

Tracking, for me, has become a practice of devotion to the world, a pastoral ritual of listening during times marked with ecological fracture and loss, and a portal to the possibility of science as a local and community practice. I delight in the miniscule or subtle signs—the clipped grass at the edge of vole tunnels, the faint marks made by squirrels marking tree bark with their teeth, or the few strands of fur twisted around a barb in a wire fence. Such signs continue to help me redefine what I see (and was taught to see) as information. When we grow up thinking information lies only in two-dimensional (or even dimensionless) black and white, as text, numbers, or computer code—human-made artifacts—we are less aware of information in the world around us and on just about any surface on which life occurs.

When I was first introduced to tracking, I was quickly amazed at how seeing the land as not just a static "text," but actually alive with stories all of the time, transformed my relationship to nature. Tracking felt like a way to access an old-fashioned practice of natural history in which we rely on our senses to arrive at local truths, very often broaching a realm of specificity and "microhistory" that a field guide or internet search could never illuminate; the particular way the moose laid in the snow, or the emergent relationship between the neighborhood fox and the weasel. Since then, tracking has been a powerful way for me to become more aware of the nonhuman others whose lives (and trails) are constantly weaving around me. It has become a means to the broad end of relationship building and bearing witness, and folded within that is a means to better grasp my own impact on the world around me.

A big part of why I return to tracking almost daily is for what some might call, on an individual level, mental health or, on a collective level, cultural health. In the moment, it helps slow down my thinking, reminds me to focus more on questions than answers, and time after time it forces me to *look closer* and question my assumptions, no matter how familiar or simple something might look. Often, it takes me weeks or even months to figure out why or how a track or sign was made, or by whom. Here, I learn, knowledge is the outcome of relationship—it's not something we're ever entitled to. And in our information-saturated world, there's something comforting about that; it lets us off the illusory hook of having so many answers seemingly at our fingertips.

As someone who struggles with attention in an overstimulating world, tracking has been something I am miraculously able to focus on for hours, perhaps because in the animate, organic world, it's clear that no two traces (or bodies) are ever exactly the same. While print and digital culture has perfected the copy, nonhuman culture is populated not by copies but iterations. The furred and scaled feet that make tracks are not inanimate stamps but living variations on a theme, woven together by the warp and weft of genes, soul, and land.

Over time, tracking has helped me work toward what seems like a more secure attachment to place(s) than I've known before. Wherever I am, whether it is a city park, a highway overpass, or a rural forest, I now pay attention to who is there who is not human and how they make their home there. It is almost a way of shaking hands with the places that I find myself in, or getting to know seemingly familiar places in a strange and welcome new light—the picturesque covered bridges in small-town Vermont concealing in their shadows a family of roosting bats, or the ancient ruins in rural Greece where jackals and wild boar leave their tracks at night after the tourists leave. As a transgender person, I (like many of the plants and animals I have come to know) have not always felt like I could rely on the human world to welcome me in a given place, whereas nonhuman animals and ecologies are much more neutral—appraising humans based on whether we pose a threat rather than by our social norms.

Following fresh trails has shown me places in landscapes that I would have never navigated to by myself. Trailing, the practice of following trackways, creates an embodied empathy with other beings, through a mimicry of their movements across (and with) the land. You are—almost literally—walking a mile in someone else's shoes. Sensing the landscape in this way provides an experience of place that extends beyond the human, to a shared perspective. Critically, it also has helped me sense when and where I may not be welcome in a place—and has forced me to look more closely at the ripples of impact my presence can create on the landscape, across nonhuman and human worlds alike.

Humanist geographer Yi-Fu Tuan helped evolve our collective understanding of what makes space into place. We gain a sense of place, Tuan taught, through intimate and emotional encounters with(in) space. Place is the awareness of being amidst an ecosystem, which is made up of relationships. To witness the tracks, trails, and traces of our wild relatives is to witness the threads with which place is woven. Through tracking, we realize that all spaces on the land are already places to someone else, human or not. On the flipside of this, we realize that colonial and imperial processes have been responsible for the turning of place into space, through seizing land, border-making, monocultures, and other industrial food systems and through narrative control.

As well as witnessing and generating local stories and science, tracking is also about local spirituality. Ways of being that honor multi-species, cross-species, and "transbiological" relationships have historically been labeled "animism." It has been impossible for me to become a naturalist without being, in some way, an animist! Instead of providing yet more maps and references of the world, animistic ways of being ask us to map what is unfolding now, in real time, in this place, in relationship. Tracking is to me an animistic practice—a way of seeing that anticipates animacy everywhere by looking for its effects on matter. This includes the scuff of paw on dirt but also extends to the low-hanging branch sweeping a crescent on the ground below as the wind blows, the seaweed and driftwood etching a waterline across the beach. Rare is the surface or substrate that is free from traces of the animate.

I hesitate to use the term "worldview" to describe animisms, just as I hesitate to leave "animism" in the singular, lest we think that it is some sort of universal formula. Instead, it is helpful to consider animisms as ways of being—orientations—of bodies in place. As scholars Naveh and Bird-David explain, animisms are intensely local and are often about immediate encounters between people within place. Further, they are about the business of maintaining relationships that occur in particular places with their particular ecosystems, patterns, and webs of kinship.

The essence of animisms often live in a rather mundane (but also sacred) place of listening and responding to beings and forces within our shared habitats from a place of humility and reverence for the differing abilities, capacities, and inherent mysteries held by each and every species and by other "earth beings." Thus, I don't invite deeper relationship with "animisms" as a self-help fix but as opting-in to a necessary spiritual paradigm shift and rite-of-passage for a good portion of the human species—who may even find themselves reading this volume.

Through better articulation of these relationships, we may begin to talk of being mentored in belonging and survival, not just by the socially acceptable and "charismatic" animals, but by the very animals we often demonize, like coyotes, jackals, or rats. We may begin to talk of being raised by a certain landscape in addition to being raised by a human caregiver or primary attachment figure. However, such relationships hold the promise of emotional experiences other than just comfort and security—notably, the experience of awe; the emotion felt in the presence of sublime mystery and otherness. I often say that mystery is a primary need, along with shelter, water, food, and companionship. Because contemporary societies can provide water, food, and shelter without requiring deep relationship-building with nonhumans and natural materials, we can get tricked into thinking that the wild world is nonessential—a space for recreation. However, our needs for spiritual mystery and diverse emotional attachment can only be met by such places.

Mainstream society has undervalued the stories about the land that people gather inside themselves just through the course of living. But witnessing matters, as many Indigenous peoples of the circumpolar regions of Earth have demonstrated as they track sensitive ecosystems shifting dramatically over generations of time, providing perspective that Western science can't. Conservationists call what they do "ecological monitoring," with its echoes of surveillance—and maybe there's an honesty to that. But what, too, of witnessing, of beholding, of paying attention to beloved friends and neighbors? The "natural history" of an area (or an entire country or continent) is only limited by what we choose to pay attention to. However, crucially, what we pay attention to shifts when our cosmologies, worldviews, and habits shift. If we consider animals to have personhood, consciousness, even sentience, how do we look at their tracks and trails (and our own) on the landscape differently? Mary Oliver wrote that "attention is the beginning of devotion." In an age where so many stories are prepackaged for easy consumption on page and screen, the intimate act of paying attention has become ensnared and the muscle for discerning and decrypting stories atrophied. Perhaps then it's time, we choose carefully what, or to whom, we are devoted to.

WHEN SEEING THE WORLD AS ALIVE IS CALLED MADNESS
Pınar Ateş Sinopoulos-Lloyd

After immigrating to Turtle Island (North America) at age eight, I became cognizant of my difference from others, and I felt alone. I was experiencing culture shock on multiple levels, I had been rotating through different primary caregivers, and I did not know English. The human world was coming to seem chaotic, concerning, and difficult to understand—I felt it needed to be monitored and studied. I didn't speak much for a few years and spent a lot of time watching people and listening. I also watched the nonhuman world, which felt much less threatening and more familiar. In kinship with cats in particular, I sensed a shared experience of studying humans with curiosity and a little wariness.

Silent observation was a survival strategy, especially as an autistic kid. It was also humorous. There was an absurdity I found in human interactions and cultural and social norms that helped diffuse the culture shock and social discomfort, and I grew to love people-watching. I learned how to mimic the baselines of the world around me, which helped me conceal things about myself that were seen as "weird" or unusual. I also read people's body language to discern whether I would be safe, since I had been abused by some of my caregivers. Most youth who grow up in one culture don't really know what culture is when they are that young, but for me, as a "third culture" kid, the cultural shifts I experienced were a crash course in human culture—like how we gain a fuller understanding of what grammar and syntax are when we learn a second language.

Even when I started to learn English, I was not very talkative. Talking less and observing more helped me tune in to the ways that nonhuman animals are often not heard or regarded. My silence became a portal to solidarity with other nonverbal beings. I became friends with pigeons and squirrels—animals that are often demonized by contemporary Western culture—at suburban or city parks. The whole concept of varmints, vermin, or pests in colonial wildlife management is abhorrent to me; it shows how beings with their own unique dignity and ecological niche are seen as disposable, when they are actually just resourceful and adaptive. Their ability to adapt to immense and truly apocalyptic change is viewed as a threat by many humans. There are many parallels between conquering cultures' treatment of these types of wildlife and their treatment of Indigenous people—when a species or organism survives a cataclysmic event that helped establish the dominant human culture, its very existence can be seen to undermine that culture. This is why I often say that, as a trans neurodivergent Indigenous person, my existence itself is a form of resistance.

When I lived in the Bay Area (traditional Tamien land) as an adolescent, I was enchanted by the huge diversity of deciduous trees and their impressive palette of fall colors, and I collected their leaves. With the deep kinships I was developing with nonhumans, I felt like I didn't need human friends that much. Some people may interpret this as me feeling like an "alien," and I realize some people frame their experiences of marginality that way. But I don't see this experience of creaturely witnessing as unearthly; it's actually a very terrestrial, animal act. Many years later, I learned that for many nations, Indigenous to the Americas, being silent is respected and seen as a sign of peace and wisdom. This was a revelation, since US culture frames silence as a sign that something is wrong or needs to be fixed in the individual (as opposed to in the culture).

I didn't have much guidance or mentorship to help me navigate and make sense of my relationships with the more-than-human world, access socially accepted avenues for nature connection, or contextualize these relationships into any sort of cultural heritage or framework. I also started to experience parallel realities with entities that I later understood to be ancestors or what Europeans might call *genius loci*, spirits of places. I feel a lot of the pain of the earth, but more specifically, the pain that lives in places. This pain can manifest in different ways, through neglect of beings (human and nonhuman) and their histories, or by demonizing certain beings, or seeing them only for their economic or aesthetic value, or through pollution and deforestation. I tried to figure it out on my own and kept getting pathologized for my ways of being in the world. This included my gender identity and sexuality. I found mentors in the more-than-human world, but when I shared these experiences with adults, they grew concerned and thought I was experiencing hallucinations. Interestingly, hallucination is just a clinical term that can pathologize visions, which in some cultural contexts are normal and necessary.

When I was 14 years old, I survived suicide. In despair, I had swallowed a bottle of pills in a bathroom at my high school and fell unconscious in class. I was taken to the emergency room of Stanford University Hospital, where my heart stopped for a few minutes before I was revived. When I was clinically dead, I had an experience of my ancestors calling me back to the world of the living. This gave me clarity: so much of the pain I was feeling was related to intergenerational trauma and memory. I was followed around and harassed by police that year before my suicide, and it contributed to a feeling of being constantly surveilled and mistrusted by adults, which was enraging since these were the very people I needed guidance and trust from. We must learn to trust our youth even if we don't always understand them. Youth can keenly feel the grief and contradictions present in the world, and they are ecological indicators for the health of cultures.

This was at least a decade or more before we saw mainstream discourse about "ecological grief" or the connection between climate change/ecocide and public mental health. When I was 22, I was at a loss for who to turn to to make sense of these experiences and voluntarily visited a psychiatrist. I described my feelings of deep ecological grief and shock, the impacts of species loneliness, and expressed maybe needing antidepressants to function. However, the psychiatrist diagnosed me with schizophrenia—something I only found out when reading my medical records later—and prescribed me with antipsychotics. It felt like the psychiatric and medical world wanted to privatize and isolate these monumental feelings I was having, placing the onus on me to change, instead of society. Explicitly naming Indigenous grief in this project of settler colonialism ended in one of the deepest forms of colonialism there is—breaking down the bedrock of Indigenous reality and infusing the idea of "craziness" that acts as a mechanism for self-colonizing.

One of the first times I experienced what I'm referring to as parallel realities was when I was 19 and heavily involved in frontline environmental activism. I was living in Phoenix, Arizona, a sprawling desert city, and I couldn't shake this experience of grief that felt like it was radiating from the place. It was a feeling of not being able to breathe, or being crushed. Out of impulse, I went to the nearby South Mountain and started following a hiking trail from the parking lot. I soon walked off the trail and came to a rocky ledge. Looking down at the city, I felt like I could breathe deeply for the first time in a while. Parts of my brain were online that couldn't be when I was down there. After this, I started to look into the history of Phoenix—the experiences of the Indigenous peoples there, how Native aesthetics had been commodified by capitalist culture, and how South Mountain is a sacred site. I realized that I was feeling the active wound in that place, which is not a metaphor, it's a real wound that is still open and infected.

I have learned that intimacy with the more-than-human world is not just necessary for my well-being; it has been necessary for my survival. Finding ecological co-regulation remains inaccessible to many of us TQIBIPOC (trans, queer, intersex, Black, Indigenous, and People of Color). Co-regulation is a term used for mutual nervous system regulation between two or more beings. Ecological co-regulation is when we engage in a mutual nervous system regulation with the more-than-human world. On the flip side, living rurally often means we are often unable to access cultural co-regulation—finding refuge among those with whom we share the same culture(s). TQIBIPOC have to choose between connection to nature or connection to other humans who reflect our own cultural, social, and demographic intersections.

One of my most important primary attachment figures is a creek in the Southwest, a being I often describe as helping raise me like a parent. When I met the creek, I was in the midst of struggling with bulimia. I had heard about this creek, several hours outside of the city where I lived at the time. I drove out with my camping gear, and I felt such a sense of familiarity when the landscape greeted me. The treasure of a riparian ecosystem within a desert, with its spiky yucca and sensuous cottonwood trees, enchanted me. I went to meet the water, which was eerily warm, fed by a warm spring. It was when I fully submerged myself in the creek that I had a very visceral feeling of recognition, like a memory. I knew the fish, the cattails, the horsetail, and the sycamore trees, but I didn't exactly know how I knew them, like a déjà vu.

I had experienced rivers and creeks as sovereign beings, as persons, before that, but this had the added layer of an intensely emotional interpersonal encounter—like falling in love. The creek felt like a refuge or a nest where my body and soul could finally relax and just be, and embody who I was without question. This made me painfully realize that finding refuge is political, and nervous system privilege—that some bodies can benefit from feeling safe while others cannot—exists.

In one conversation with this creek, I recalled that I, too, was once a creek and had decided to enter the human world, to help other humans understand that rivers are people and should be treated with dignity. After a time, I had begun to feel that I wanted to return to creek form, announcing that I was tired of the human world. The creek scolded me, like a selfish child, telling me that I had to go out beyond the bounds of this refuge and continue my work as a human in the world. I felt like a fledgling being pushed out of their nest. Through the creek reparenting me, I gained enough emotional resources and secure attachment to survive without their constant guidance and to accept that I was, for now, human.

In many ways, the creek and I healed together. I found out that they used to be dammed. The year that I met them, they had just been undammed and began to be protected as a wild and scenic river—a rare designation. Simultaneously, I began to heal from my eating disorder, as I gained more resources and frameworks—in part thanks to the creek's mentorship—to process intergenerational trauma.

Many Black and Indigenous animists get pathologized. Black and Indigenous realities, cosmologies, and survival strategies, which are so centered on relationships, collectivity, mutual aid, and DIYing our own community care systems, are so often pathologized and punished. I love the term animism, and I relate to it deeply, but I don't love that some people seem to be able to explore it freely while others don't or can't. In order for us to fully experience the magic of seeing the world as alive and full of personhood and soul, we must be able to fully see the personhood and dignity in our fellow humans, across differences of ability, class, race, and gender, and through the beautiful prism of difference, because that is what our bodies of experience are—they are gems that refract light in diverse and enchanting ways. It is not until this that we will truly be animists.

My breath escapes
Into the opposite
Side of green as I
Peel away the gloves
That hide away
My speckled banana skin
Just translucent enough
To see the steeped colour
Of burgundy earth
Pulsing steady through
A collective of snakes
Forming tributaries that
Drip molasses towards
The skipping stone
Smooth pads of my fingertips
And settle into the silt
Underneath the cracked
Eggshells of my nail beds
Only to be disrupted
Into an urgent reversal
Towards the liminal air
Carrying the smell of home
Finding itself back to me

THE ANCIENT ALCHEMY OF COMPOSTING
Poppy Okotcha

Composting is the natural process that recycles organic matter into beautiful, dark, decomposed "black gold", stable carbon that can be locked away in the soil. It's moisture retentive and full of fertile goodness – a gift to the soil life and so the plants. To me, there's no better way to connect with the natural world and its rhythms than through the alchemy of composting. It's mucky, mysterious and transforms potentially pollutant waste into an incredibly valuable resource ... I almost get more excited watching waste turn to compost than seeing a seed germinate!

If you grow a garden – in the ground or in pots – composting is a beautiful way to form a truly reciprocal relationship with your plants. If not, you can still compost your scraps, and give your compost away to loved ones, local community gardens, or underloved public plants in your area. There are many ways to compost, but my favourite is worm composting, or vermicomposting, which harnesses red worms' incredible ability to munch through pretty much any organic material. Simply feed them kitchen or garden scraps, and they poop out magical worm castings – rocket fuel for plants, teeming with microorganisms and micronutrients. It's easy to do at home, even if you don't have much space at all, and it's very clean and shouldn't smell – making it the perfect method for small, urban spaces (as I learned when living on a canal boat in London). Plus, you get a bunch of wriggly friends!

Making Your Worm Farm

You can buy swanky ready-made worm farms (some of them

are very stylish!), but here's how to make your own, using an old sink, bathtub or bucket. Before you get started, choose a spot for it to live that's relatively sheltered, warm and out of direct sunlight (think under the kitchen sink, the corner of a balcony, in a shed or by the back door). Bear in mind that composting worms (also known as brandling worms, red wigglers, manure, red or tiger worms) are different to the common earthworms you'll find in the soil. You can buy them online (they come in the post!) or find out if someone you know has a worm farm with some going spare.

SINK OR BATH METHOD (BEST FOR OUTSIDE)

1   Cover the plughole with **gauze** and place a small **stone or brick** loosely on top to keep the gauze in place while letting the liquid drain out.
2   Place the container at an angle, so that the drainage hole is at the lowest point. This will ensure gravity draws the liquid down and out of your container so your worms don't get flooded. **Logs or bricks** are useful supports.
3   Place a **jug** under the drainage hole, to gather the "worm tea" liquid runoff.
4   Spread a layer of **bedding** (well-rotted manure, straw, hay, or shredded paper or card) at the bottom, and cover with a layer of **organic matter** for your worms to feed on.
5   Pop your **worms** in their new home, and give it all a good soaking with water.
6   **Cover** your container. A wooden board, tarpaulin or dustbin lid can work well.

BUCKET METHOD (BEST FOR INSIDE)

1   Find **two buckets** of the same size, which can stack into each other, and ideally have a lid.

2   **Drill or hammer** a few drainage holes into the bottom of
    Bucket 1. They should be no bigger than about 2mm
    (⅟₁₆in) in diameter, to reduce the chances of worm escapes!

3   **Pop Bucket 1** inside **Bucket 2**. Bucket 1 will hold your
    worm farm, while Bucket 2 will catch the "worm tea"
    liquid runoff.

4   Spread a layer of **bedding** (well-rotted manure, straw,
    hay, or shredded paper or card) at the bottom of
    Bucket 1 along with an initial layer of **organic matter**
    for the worms to feed on.

5   Add your **worms**, and give everything a good soaking
    with water.

6   Pop a **lid** on Bucket 1 (you can make one if the bucket
    doesn't come with one).

Looking After Your Worm Farm

- **Feeding:** Feed your worms with the right kinds of
  organic matter every few days. This gives them time to
  work through their food, and shows you how hungry
  they are. Wait until they've made a good dent in their
  previous feed before you give them more.
  - **DO feed your worms:** Raw fruit and vegetable
    kitchen scraps; green waste from your garden or pot
    plants (e.g. soft prunings, lawn trimmings and
    weeds); crushed egg shells; coffee grounds (in small
    amounts) and loose tea (remove the teabag, as many
    have plastic in them); some shredded paper and card.
  - **AVOID feeding your worms:** Citrus fruits; alliums,
    which includes onions, garlic, shallots and leeks; large
    pieces of tough woody material (e.g. branches); cooked
    food; meat, dairy or fats (so try to rinse off any oily
    dressing before you feed leftover salad leaves to them).

- **Moisture:** The worms' living environment should be moist, but without any puddles of water.
  - If it is too wet: Add shredded paper or card, and ease up on your feedings – organic matter is full of moisture!
  - If it is too dry: Give them a good watering and include more moist vegetables (e.g. cucumber peel, celery bums, leaves).

Using Your Compost

Every few days, you can gather the "worm tea", a brilliant plant food, full of nutrients, minerals and microorganisms. You can spray your worm tea on your plant leaves as a foliar feed (plants absorb nutrients through their leaves too!) or water directly onto the root zone. You can either use it straight or dilute it, at 1:3 parts worm tea:water.

Every three months, you can harvest your compost. Simply dig into your worm farm using either your hands or a makeshift scoop (a bowl will do!), fishing out any worms and putting them back in their home.

*

So much of how I lead my life is rooted in what I've learned from composting. The process teaches us so beautifully about the interconnection of all things – we support the land, and the land supports us. It is a cycle of exchange: the soil feeds the plants, which feed us; our scraps rot down as compost and feed the soil; again the soil will feed the plants, and on and on. Visualizing this eternal cycle is awe-inspiring. Seeing how we fit into that cycle is at once deeply comforting and mind blowing. This cycle has also taught me how the death of the old will give rise to, and sustain, the new. Seen this way, engaging with the natural world (and the world as a whole) is so much less scary – "failures" become compost, to try again.

FROM *31 WORDS* * *PROSE POEMS*

Evie Shockley

highly visual rural winter image seeks lyric poem (14-30 lines) for mutual enrichment and long-term relationship. image offers potential lines about fog-covered fields where snow seems to rise toward its origins.

IS NATURE CAFFEINE FOR CREATIVITY?
Daisy Kennedy

The relationship between nature and creativity has fascinated me since primary school. Tongue sticking out, crayon in a tight fist, viciously rubbing paper against a tree – I remember feeling like time was endless, like nature was my infinite playground.

This fascination extends far beyond me. Since the dawn of human history, creativity and nature have been linked. Of course they were; when *Homo sapiens* were painting on cave walls 45,000 years ago, there was little else to work with, content- and medium-wise (biro and paper were out of the question, let alone NFTs). Since then, nature has continued to provide inspiration and refuge to poets, painters and pianists alike. So much so that Post-Impressionist Pierre Bonnard asserted, "Art will never be able to exist without nature."

History is on his side. Wherever we look, we find nature-inspired art. Ancient Roman cities were decorated with frescoes and mosaics of natural scenes: songbirds perching in bushes, colourful blossoms, fruit-laden trees. In 17th-century Japan, haiku brought drama to fleeting natural phenomena, while paintings and prints by the likes of Hokusai depicted trees, mountains and waves. In 19th-century Britain, the Romanticists wove descriptions of landscape with emotional undertones; William Wordsworth was a self-professed "worshipper of nature".

Bonnard's claim also has scientific backing: it seems that nature makes us (more) creative. The University of Kansas and the University of Utah conducted an experiment in which they gave participants three seemingly random words – for example, "cream", "skate" and "water" – and asked them to find a fourth term that links them. In this case, it could be "ice". After a few days immersed in nature – backpacking in Alaska, Colorado, Maine or Washington state – the "naive hikers" were 50 per cent better at coming up with the umbrella links. In another study, a German research team found that just a glimpse of green makes us more creative: participants were 20 per cent better at coming up with different uses for a common object when they'd seen the leafy colour beforehand.

What is this magic that nature works on our right-brained activity? To really investigate how nature and creativity are intertwined, we need to examine what rouses the creative mind.

Safe Space

Creativity demands a kind of bravery. Perhaps we can only truly have this bravery when we feel sufficiently safe and secure. According to Prospect-Refuge Theory, evolution has adapted us to feel safe and calm in environments in which our ancestors could discover opportunities (prospect) and find shelter (refuge). These spaces typically involved trees, which provide both a vantage point and hiding place, while affirming the land's fertility. In simple terms, we all want a nice view, access to clean water, and to avoid animals that can kill us. As Professor Qing Li has written, "We are reassured by green on a very primitive level. Where there is green, there is water. And where there is water, we can find food. When the world around us contains plenty of green, we can relax."

The safety we intuit in lush, green spaces kickstarts the

parasympathetic nervous system, freeing us from "fight or flight" mode and translating to a calmer mind – the perfect petri dish to breed creative thoughts and ideas. When I spoke to illustrator Molly Fairhurst about how nature influences her practice, she confirmed that, for her: "Green is relaxing, and green feels safe."

Nature is also important for mental health and, while that is an entirely different essay (Jay Griffiths's, to be precise), mental health and creativity are closely linked. Often, the mind needs to be nourished and restored before new creative thoughts and ideas can be explored, incubated or realized. Molly explains that she likes to head outside everyday "for creative reasons, but largely sanity", adding that, if she doesn't, she ends up "going stir, questioning everything." Poet Hollie McNish echoes that her creative process will "factor in spending time outside – for my sanity."

Not only does time in nature aid our mental health, cradling creativity, in turn creativity can become part of what heals our minds. Nature writer Richard Mabey, in his book *Nature Cure*, attributes a turning point in his recovery from depression to a moment in which creative outlet and nature connection fused – sitting under a beech tree, pen in hand. "What healed me, I think, was that flash of loving inspiration ... nature entering me, firing up the wild bits of my imagination. If there was a single moment I was 'cured' it was ... those first stumbling acts [of writing]".

Art and ART

Attention Restoration Theory (ART) is the theory that nature can renew our focus and mental energy. The theory emerged from psychologists Rachel and Stephen Kaplan at the dawn of the 1990s – the onset of the ubiquitous digitalization of our daily lives. In a nutshell, ART says that, because we evolved to look at nature's forms, they demand an effortless kind of attention, leaving the mind restored from the stresses of screens glowing with algorithmic addictivity.

Now, some artists like to hyper-focus: shoving their headphones on, getting their heads down and working. Journalist and author Will Storr likes to close the curtains and write in the darkness; Roald Dahl famously wrote his novels in his garden shed, all blacked out apart from candlelight. However, surprisingly enough, the human brain isn't designed to stare, unremittingly, at a computer screen or piece of paper for hours on end.

Stop.

Think of your happiest memory right now. Go on. I'll give you five seconds. 1. 2. 3. 4. 5.

Did you look away? Did you stare off into the distance as the mechanics in your brain began to turn? When we search for ideas, problem solve or retrieve memories, the brain struggles to focus on a task and simultaneously retrieve information, never mind produce earth-shattering, revolutionary creative ideas. Author and science journalist Daniel Goleman explains how mind wandering such as this allows the brain to make connections that can't be created when the mind is concentrating. Molly is no stranger to this phenomenon. She goes so far as to say, "I would describe looking out of windows as one of my hobbies."

Artist Nathan Wyburn also told me he felt "off with the fairies" when a creative idea is incubating in his mind, and described the outdoors as his "thinking time ... time to breathe". Nature is a paradox: ever-changing, moving and dynamic, yet somehow staying the same. We know what to expect, so it's the perfect thing to gaze at while the mind does its job. Nathan's comments and ART remind me of Jane Austen's observation (spoken through Frances "Fanny" Price) that, "To sit in the shade on a fine day and look upon verdure is the most perfect refreshment."

What's behind this timeless feeling? ART suggests that nature only demands a kind of "soft focus", or "soft fascination". Fiercely juxtaposing a bright computer screen, which demands a "hard fascination", the effortless focus that natural scenes require acts as a balm for burnout, refreshing and restoring our mental energy.

This "soft fascination" occurs because our eyes and brain are evolved to perceive natural shapes, colours and motion. A commonly occurring example is fractals, patterns that repeat in decreasing magnification. Fractals can be found in tree branches, mycelium, river systems, lung bronchi, leaf veins, human veins, cortical neurons and more.

In the 1990s, physicist and artist Richard Taylor examined a series of Jackson Pollock's poured paintings from the 1950s – created a quarter of a century before the scientific discovery of fractals – and discovered that the works mimicked the fractal patterns found in nature. Curious about whether this fractal quality was the reason people were so drawn to Pollock's work, Taylor ran a series of experiments to measure people's physiological responses to looking at fractals. He discovered that our responses to these natural patterns suggest that we are naturally attuned to looking at them: people recovered from stress 60 per cent better when looking at the fractal patterns. Other mysterious, unnameable qualities in artworks, which resonate with us in ineffable ways, may have their basis in our innate need for nature.

Nature's Soundtrack

I don't know about you, but every time I walk out of the house I put my earphones straight in. I do *try* to take them out to hear the sound of leaves crunching under my feet, the rustle of the trees, the poetic splash of water as a frog jumps in. However, I can never listen to nature's sounds for long – my short attention span and addiction to podcasts means I plug my ears and congratulate myself for being at one with nature for a whole 30 seconds.

Silence is a luxury. Or should I say, nature's unaltered soundscape is a luxury. If you live in a city, experiencing total immersion in a natural environment is difficult to come by. Many creatives live a very fast-paced life with little to no time to travel and spend time in the vast outdoors, making it almost impossible to be without human-made sound.

Doctors Eva Selhub and Alan C. Logan describe noise as a "plague", detailing how environmental noises increase stress and compromise cognitive and academic performance. They also explain that "machine-derived noise can quickly undo many of the positive attributes of nature" so, even if you are soaking up nature's sensory offerings, the sound of a nearby motorway can majorly boost annoyance and can leave you just as stressed as before. That juicy mind wandering and activated creative brain can get distracted and led astray very easily, especially with attention spans decreasing due to junk food technologies.

It's important to indulge your ears in sonic forest-bathing every now and again. So, the next time you go for a walk, take out your earphones and listen to nature's own podcast. Who knows, you might feel the urge to start that screenplay you've always wanted to write.

Wild Beauty

Nature's beauty is not only inspiring, it's also good for us. Beauty chimes with our souls in a way that brings a sense of fulfillment, comfort and joy. And, as Richard Taylor's research shows, we are built to find nature's forms beautiful. Writer and activist Alice Walker famously said of our fondness for nature's forms: "In nature, nothing is perfect and everything is perfect. Trees can be contorted, bent in weird ways, and they're still beautiful."

Data scientist Doctor Chanuki Illushka Seresinhe is an expert on how nature's beauty benefits us. Through several studies, involving tens of thousands of participants, she's discovered that beautiful places improve people's health and happiness. Especially interesting, she says, was her finding that, if a scene is full of a variety of natural features (like trees or valley contours), it was considered more beautiful; if it was just flat grass, people rated it lower. "Just green wasn't good enough," she explains. "Not all green space is created equal. People will say, 'OK, you have to put some green space in that neighbourhood', but nobody considers how important it is to make that green space *beautiful*. Without this, people aren't going to use it, or benefit from it, in the same way. Nature is important, but you can't just slap some lawn down and go 'that's fine'. There's something about wilder nature that people need, and are innately drawn to."

Molly confirms this innate desire for wildness: "I was raised in North Yorkshire and, while the rolling Dales were beautiful, the rugged moorland always caught my eye more. My work is rooted in uneven and unpredictable textures, in mess, in roughness. I want to be as wild as those heathers and rocks." Painter Tai Shan Schierenberg's childhood also sowed the seeds for a relationship with the wild. Growing up on a farm, he says, has left him with "a strange relationship with nature: I understand that almost none of the landscape we enjoy is natural ... and that nature is pretty brutal."

Nature's beauty also elicits a sense of awe. Psychologists Stacker Keltner and Jonathan Haidt define "awe" as a feeling we get when confronted with something vast, that transcends our frame of reference, that we struggle to understand. Awe, and being awe-struck, can bring a host of benefits – including boosting creativity. Feeling awe makes time feel abundant, offering a creative haven for the mind to incubate ideas and wander freely. From ancient paintings of the vast night sky, to clickbait articles promising "10 Images of the Deep Sea that Will Shock You", the overwhelming sense of awe is both a stimulus and springboard for creativity.

Creative City Living

In *The Rise of the Creative Class*, urbanism theorist Richard L. Florida asserts: "Cities are the key economic and social organizing units of the Creative Age. They speed the metabolism of daily life, accelerating the combinations and recombinations of people that spur innovation". We often think of the bustling city as the modern creative's natural habitat – colourful, culture-filled spots, offering greater collaboration and audiences.

This suggests a disconnect between the science behind the brain on nature and the geography of artistic locations. Our brains use trees and the earth as fuel for happiness, health and creativity, however, it's evident that cities are where the creative industries thrive. It has become the norm to sacrifice nature for a career – it would be absurd for an actor to live in the Scottish Highlands (unless they had lots of time and money to spare on the commute) – and a vibrant source of diverse inspirations.

The artists I spoke to have an apprehension about living in the countryside, feeling more directly inspired by people and the messiness of human behaviour. Hollie encapsulates this idea nicely: "I think I'm more creative in cities (though I've never lived in one). I find people as inspiring as nature and I find cities – with everything going on and all the conversations you hear, the colour and art and parks and all of that – inspiring. I hate adverts and billboards in cities, but the things I hate inspire me just as much to write as things I love. Which is maybe why I'm less inspired in very remote rural areas, because they're quiet."

There seems to be a push-pull effect: the artists I spoke to are simultaneously drawn to cities, but seek to escape them. Tai Shan also offers his seesaw experience with being an artist in the city: "My creative juices and energy levels are much improved after a visit to the countryside, standing in the fields under the open skies. However, on occasions when I have spent longer there, the positive effects wear off and all that space – both geographically and socially – causes me to lose my moorings somewhat ... the idea of moving to the countryside and living and working there fills me with dread!"

Many other artists also escape to nature. Filmmaker Derek Jarman, after being diagnosed with HIV, retreated to Dungeness, on England's south-east coast, to immerse himself in creativity and experimentation through gardening and writing, as captured in his "diary of the garden and meditation", *Modern Nature* (1991).

It seems that creative people are drawn to cities' lifestyle and buzz – not their lack of nature. So what if we had cities that were full of nature? Imagine a world where green spaces were more accessible and everyone, no matter where, could have access to full nature immersion everyday. Blimey, imagine the artwork and innovative ideas that would be produced!

Tangential Inspiration

For many modern creatives, the majority of their work isn't a direct response to the natural world. But is it, to an extent, still influenced by it? Like when a child starts scribbling the sun in the corner of their paper before starting on the house – nature is arguably always present in the background, acting as an anchor or foundation for other ideas.

On the flip side, art that at first seems to be about nature can be a vessel for totally different themes. Hollie McNish confesses: "Until last week I thought I created a lot of work directly about nature, but then my boyfriend told me that actually what I do is write about sex, through talking about animals and nature – and apparently that's not the same!"

This is a prime example of how the natural world acts as a universally understood reference point – it is so familiar to us, that metaphors can layer on twists and surprises. Is writing about sex through the language of the natural world even really different to writing about nature itself? Using nature as a way to describe something else has been a device used since the haiku, and will never be outdated or unoriginal.

Tai Shan also uses nature as a Trojan horse for other ideas. He tells me that, "in recent years, what I want to say about landscape has changed and become more autobiographical and narrative-driven." To create art about nature is often to create an allegory – rarely commenting on its form plainly, nature in art often sequesters deeper meaning. There is comfort in the fact that everyone on Earth knows what a tree is (at least for now), and we can form human connection through this common ground.

Art Returns the Favour

As artists, we have a responsibility to put a mirror to society. This means showing the very real and shocking ways in which human-driven climate change is wreaking havoc on the natural world. Artist and activist Gustav Metzger's 2015 project, Remember Nature, invited art students to take part in an exhibition highlighting issues surrounding extinction and environmental degradation. The 2021 book *140 Artists' Ideas for Planet Earth*, inspired by Metzger's work, invited artists (including Ayesha Tan-Jones and Olafur Eliasson) to contribute images, poems, experiments, recipes, gardening guides and ideas for insurgency to guide readers to "a new worldview; where you and the planet are one". Metzger said the artist's task is to "protect nature as far as we can and by doing so art will enter new territories that are inherently creative, that are primarily for the good of the universe".

When the world is in trouble, people turn to art. Art is a universal language, so it makes sense that activists create imagery to convey compelling messages – Banksy's political undertones have made his work renowned the world over. As I walk through the city of Bristol, Extinction Rebellion's logo and messages are projected onto buildings, chalk climate warnings are scrawled on the pavement, and a painting of Greta Thunberg covers a billboard right next to my local supermarket.

Artists and activists are using the resources nature has gifted them to give something back. Now, we all need to use our creativity to repay nature for all it has given us. As

Satish Kumar says, "Artists have always recognized the sacred quality of nature. Now it is imperative that scientists, industrialists and politicians do the same."

*

About the Artists

Molly Fairhurst is a Bristol-based illustrator and animator, originally from North Yorkshire. Her soft, organic forms combine reality with absurdity. Molly's work has been published in *The New York Times*, *It's Nice That* and *Intern Magazine*.

Hollie McNish is a poet and author based between Cambridge and Glasgow. She writes incredibly raw, honest, brilliantly funny work. She has published three books, co-written a play, and constantly tours, performing her poetry to sold-out theatres.

Nathan Wyburn is a Welsh artist known for creating celebrity portraits and pop culture imagery using non-traditional mediums, in particular food (including baked beans, sweets and slices of toast) and other everyday materials (such as soil, toothpaste and motor oil).

Tai Shan Schierenberg is a portrait and landscape painter based in London. He is the head of painting at The Art Academy and judges Sky's Landscape and Portrait Artist of the Year awards. He has painted Professor Stephen Hawking and Queen Elizabeth II, among others.

INJUSTICE

INJUSTICE
Ellen Miles

"[I]s the privilege of space, and light, and air, and beauty not to be considered for the small shopkeeper, for the hard-working clerk, who will probably never own a square yard of ... land ...?"
Octavia Hill, *Our Common Land* (1877)

"Urban nature is like living with mass conditions. It sometimes feels like a myth & you are its scribe."
Eileen Myles

The world is getting greyer by the second. In 1900, fewer than one in every six human beings lived in urban areas. By 2050, it'll be more than four in six. As urbanization sprawls, tentacles of cement, gravel and tarmac are engulfing nature. Concrete is the second most used substance on Earth, after water – it already outweighs every tree, bush and shrub on the planet.

Beyond being ecologically destructive, this global greyification is violating human rights. Both the quality and length of human lives are diminished by the absence of nature. As a city dweller (even as a middle class, white Londoner – an absurdly privileged demographic), I've been subject to such effects: I'm 39 per cent more likely to suffer from depression (*tick*), 21 per cent more likely to have anxiety (*tick*), and my life expectancy is two years shorter (*I guess we'll see*), than if I'd been born and raised rurally. My heart and lung health, memory and immune system have also likely been compromised by my unnaturally natureless surroundings.

Governments should be legally accountable for

protecting citizens from such harms, but neoliberal urbanization has left hundreds of millions deprived of nature. In the United States, 100 million people don't have a park within a half-mile (0.8km) radius from home. In England, one in five live in the nation's most nature-devoid neighbourhoods. As urban populations boom in their billions, these numbers will rise exponentially over the coming decades, unless we take drastic action.

*

Nature deprivation doesn't have an equal opportunities policy. It's an injustice that maps onto social inequalities, reflecting structural biases towards income, mental and physical ability, education, employment status, "race" and ethnicity. Wealthier, whiter urban neighbourhoods are significantly greener and leafier than those whose residents are low-paid or people of colour. In the United States, people of colour are three times more likely than their white counterparts to live in especially nature-deprived neighbourhoods. England's most affluent urban neighbourhoods have five times more public green space than its most deprived wards – and that's before private gardens are taken into consideration.

What's more, a Portuguese review found that parks in deprived neighbourhoods "presented significantly more safety concerns, signs of damage, lack of equipment to engage in active leisure activities, and had significantly less amenities" than those in well-to-do areas. These bare, unkept spaces, adorned with "No ball games" signs, remind locals that nature is a luxury they can't afford.

The correlation between wealth and flourishing nature

extends, beyond postcodes, to entire regions. Across England, 2.7 million people have no green space within a half-mile (0.8km) from home. London – the country's financial heart, and home to 17 per cent of its total population – contains only 0.44 per cent of the 2.7 million. Moving north, towards underfunded, historically exploited counties, this proportion leaps up. For instance, in the North West – a region formerly known for coal mining, and today manufacturing – you'll find 7.4 per cent of the 2.7 million, despite the fact that the region's populace is 1.5 million people short of the capital's.

These figures paint a vivid picture of how nature-access maps onto wealth, "class" and power – but statistics only tell us so much. What does it *feel* like to live in these places? In this chapter, Michelle Barrett, a writer from the North West of England, brings us down to the pavement, walking us through time and place in her neighbourhood (page 112). Across the pond, Hila "the Killa" Perry lyrically shares her story of growing up as a New York City kid (page 124).

*

How did we get here? A tangle of social, political and economic currents have carried us to this point, and continue to erode people's exposure to nature. Some of these, like urbanization, are global. Others are more pinpointed. The Crossfire essays focus on localized forces: Elizabeth Soumya denounces India's caste system (page 127), Celine Isimbi reflects on the legacy of South African Apartheid (page 132), and Linda Ludbarza discusses the impact of Soviet architecture in Eastern Europe (page 136). Elsewhere, Nick Hayes explains how England's long, violent history of land enclosure has left the public with meagre rights in the country's great outdoors (page 154).

In the United States, the discrepancy in nature-access "reflects structural racism dating all the way back to redlining" says Linda Hwang, a director of The Trust for Public Land. One case, in Philadelphia, Pennsylvania, reveals a tenfold discrepancy: Chestnut Hill, described by *The New York Times* as "one of the most prestigious areas in the city", is over 60 per cent covered in trees; to the southeast, in the formerly redlined area of Nicetown-Tioga, trees cover just 6 per cent of the ground.

This discrepancy is a matter of life and death. The average temperature in Nicetown-Tioga is a whopping 10°F (5.6°C) hotter than Chestnut Hill, even though the neighbourhoods are just 5 miles (8km) apart. Claiming 1,300 lives a year, heat kills more people in the United States than any other kind of extreme weather. If Americans were to lose their existing urban trees, this figure would almost double. The problem is even worse elsewhere: a 2015 heatwave in the city of Karachi, Pakistan, killed 1,500.

Increased outdoor air pollution is another lethal outcome of a foliage deficit – it's responsible for over 4 million deaths worldwide every year. In the UK, air pollution is 25 times more lethal than car crashes. And your income and ethnicity dictate how much of it you are subject to.

Behind each of these statistics lie human stories of life and loss. Of the millions of deaths attributable to air pollution, perhaps none is better known than that of Ella Adoo-Kissi-Debrah. Ella was just nine years old when she died in 2013, from a fatal asthma attack aggravated by the fuel-filled air around her. In December 2020, following years of tireless campaigning by her mother, Rosamund,

Ella became the first British person to have air pollution cited as an official cause of death.

The tragedy of Ella's case is a reminder that our physiological states are shaped by a network of external sociopolitical influences. Simply by being Black, Ella was more likely to be exposed to illegal levels of air pollution. Simply by living in a borough where two in five residents are people of colour, Ella had II times less greenery around her than people in overwhelmingly white neighbourhoods.

Health is not only biological, it is political, economic and ecological. As sociologist Dr Adam Elliott-Cooper has said, "... Ella's case tells us one of the ways in which racism and state power and capitalism come together in ways which can [not only] oppress people, exploit people, but also lead to premature death ... We can see this in areas like the East End of London, but we also see it in the Niger Delta in Nigeria ... We see it all over the world ..."

If health is wealth, the current distribution of urban green space is making the rich richer and the poor poorer. Nature deprivation is a "threat multiplier": it exacerbates existing inequalities. In the UK, for instance, Black people are five times more likely to die in childbirth than white people. This is due to a web of factors, including underfunded local services, social and economic disenfranchisement, staff bias, and the fact that medical research is canonically biased towards white bodies. Nature deprivation is also a factor: in addition to their body-wide benefits, greener surroundings support healthy fetal growth, suggesting that Black people's higher likelihood of nature deprivation may well be compounding this injustice.

The barriers that disabled people often face in accessing and engaging with natural spaces can likewise exacerbate health problems, both mental and physical. For some, opening a door and going outside isn't easy, let alone visiting a park or mountain range. Syren Nagakyrie, founder of Disabled Hikers, shares their own experiences of exclusion in the outdoors, and the importance of making natural environments accessible to every body (page 170).

The typical, eyeroll-inducing retort to all this is "just move then". Not only is moving to greener pastures financially unviable for most people living in nature-deprived areas but, as Louisa Adjoa Parker's essay explains (page 141), rural, less metropolitan areas are often unsafe for people of colour and other marginalized groups. In the words of urban revitalization champion Majora Carter: "You shouldn't have to leave your neighbourhood to live in a better one". Instead, governments and local authorities must take responsibility to provide all their constituents with ample greenery. In a fair and humane society, it should be impossible – and illegal – for anyone to be nature deprived.

THE ENCLOSED PLACE
Michelle Barrett

The evening air balmy, our feet firm on potholed tarmac, small bodies gathering and knocking together in excitement. To our right, the Anglican Cathedral looms shouldering the sky, all brown and brick. Down south, towards the River Mersey, the clanging comings and goings of the docks echo across the murky water. From the grey, pebble-dashed block of flats, a young Scouse woman squawks, "Cohme an luhk aht dis!" We rush out, eyes towards the sky, squinting west in wonder at the suspended streak of white. The year is 1997 and the Hale–Bopp comet is careering through the cosmos above our council estate. For once, nature, in all its expansive vividness, had come to us.

Shortly after the arrival of my younger brother, in 1990 our newly expanded family moved from our council flat to a council house in Toxteth, Liverpool. Our house belonged to one of two intertwining streets which made up our estate, a small parish community served by St Patrick's Catholic church and primary school. Encircled by main roads, the positioning of the estate – marooned between motors – lent a sense of enclosure. A quality the area seemed fated to: Toxteth (or "Stochestede", as it appears in the Domesday Book of 1086) means "the enclosed place".

Up until the 18th century, L8 (Toxteth's area code) was largely rural agricultural land, and prior to this, for 400 years, it was a royal hunting forest, rich in wild land and life. It's difficult to imagine the area unspoiled – a land of raw, natural beauty where groves of silver birches and oaks matured. Where tumbling brooks pooled in lakes and otter populations thrived.

In the 1700s, Merseyside merchants claimed their wealth trading enslaved people and cotton. The shipping industry continued to boom, and warehouses multiplied along the length of the river. Excavation across the city began. The landscape became entrenched with docks, canals, tunnels and rail lines – necessary infrastructure to store and transport growing cargos. Meanwhile, Toxteth's streams were filled in and the land parcelled up, leased off bit by bit to developers. Slum housing skyrocketed to accommodate the swelling working class and immigrant population. The decimation of the land was rapid; the otters didn't stand a chance. Within a hundred years, Liverpool's population had ballooned from 5,700 to 77,000 – the majority of whom were living in squalor. Following the Industrial Revolution, construction jobs offered a significant uplift for droves of unemployed workers. The 20th century saw the erection of many Liverpool landmarks, including the Royal Liver Building and the Anglican Cathedral. Liverpool today is famous for its cityscape, a ridge of protruding buildings: bulky blocks, spires and cement towers.

Numerous studies have shown that working class people and people of colour have less access to nature than white and wealthy people, so it came as no surprise that Toxteth was recently categorized as an E-rated "red zone" for green space: a dangerously grey epicentre of nature deprivation. "Deprivation" is a term synonymous with the area. A quick internet search of L8 will have you moping over depressing socioeconomic statistics. Figures my family and neighbours contributed to: unemployed, unskilled, uneducated, unhealthy. A lot of "uns" to undo when you're uninspired.

When I arrived in Toxteth, the landscape and community had far from healed from Margaret Thatcher's austerity.

Most of the local factories had closed down. Buildings were left to rot. The Dockers' Dispute escalated as workers protested against their diminishing rights (the strikes spanned three long, bleak years in the late 1990s). Unemployment soared and up to 50 per cent of young people were out of work. Who could blame the boys on my street for selling drugs? Police cars would circle our estate, shark-like, their sirens and lights off, clandestinely cruising for easy targets. The lads would scatter instinctively, escaping the inevitable stop and search. They had good reason to run. I once witnessed a police officer slap a Black male friend hard in the face during a pat down. They'd unearthed nothing during the frisk, he was bountyless. A bemused eyeroll was enough to warrant a smack. Anger and frustration, fear and revolt rippled the air. Life, for most, had not improved and one could still feel the same sense of inequality and racism that had led to the infamous 1981 Toxteth Riots.

My parents were young, skint and probably worried most of the time. My mum worked night shifts in a residential care home ("professional arse wiper" as she blithely referred to it) and my dad was a kitchen porter, although the kitchen he served in changed every few months. He wouldn't tolerate demeaning bosses, so would throw the towel in and the middle finger up as he walked out of the door, mid-shift.

We were lucky enough to have a front and back garden, alive with fluttering cherry blossom trees and shin-high dandelions. They didn't last. My mum had the trees chopped down and the wildflowers and grass replaced with Subbuteo green plastic turf and grey flagstones. She didn't envision a garden as a space to create, express, heal or nourish. Gardening was another job, another expense. Exhaustion outweighed curiosity. Television adverts flogging chemical-laden foams and sprays had worked their magic. Zoomed-in images of soil-stained whites, infested with micro-mutants, had convinced her that nature was dirty and so our small shot at paradise was sanitized away. Inside the house, things were much the same. Fresh fruit and veg was scarce – our kitchen cupboards were filled with brightly packaged, processed, cheap and easy foods – and house plants were out of the question, just another thing to worry about. The whole neighbourhood seemed totally alienated from nature. Some of the older folks in the area kept pretty, if somewhat sterile gardens: neat lawns, the odd rose bush. Other people left their gardens to it: skyward grass, discarded mattresses slumped heavily against fences. Bushes ballooned, absorbing the light, sealing elusive neighbours in or perhaps locking the world out. The enclosed place. What middle-class onlookers might today herald a heroic act of "rewilding" felt, to us, like dereliction. Over the years, my mum allowed encroaching brambles and weeds to multiply across our patch too, until they eventually colonized the back of the garden. She erected a fence, near enough halving our garden space, to block out the invasion of unwanted, alien life. Privacy was established, safety retained and tidiness resumed.

I often think about that wild parcel of land in our back garden. Undisturbed by human hands, untouched for nearly 25 years now. Originally a boundary, grown as a means for human peace and protection, now a biodiverse habitat in our area. A playground for plant and pigeon, squirrel and robin. A fluke forest garden in the bowels of a council estate. Technically it's inaccessible, fenced off, but to know it's there – to stand on the periphery and visualize the world within, a secret life contained – is to cross a mental threshold. It's a sign of what could be, of what's possible.

I've been long-attuned to crossing mental thresholds in order to reach wild, natural places. My childhood bedroom window faced south-west and – beyond the roads and hunkering industrial buildings – I could see the Clwydian mountain range in North Wales. The mountains, on clear days, wore their seasons – snow cloaked throughout winter and beckoning and green come spring. We never got a car, meaning there were no day trips to National Parks or rolling countryside. No one we knew escaped the estate, never mind reached the far-off mountains. Perched in my bedroom window, overlooking those peaks every day, a great sense of longing started to root, and I began to search for language to make sense of my growing pains. I started to make deals, promising myself that one day I'd make it to those hills. I knew that they had something to offer me, though they were giving me so much already, simply by being in view.

The strange thing about growing up in an urban, developed area, is that you don't necessarily understand yourself to be nature deprived. I spent a lot of my early adulthood trying to put a name to the ambiguous, guttural sense of loss and longing which niggled my insides.

I felt stuck. I loved being outdoors but I had no resources to explore nature as a passion or as a tool to live well; and so I was locked out of a world I ached to be a part of and locked into a world of prescribed pathways. Out of touch with my desires and needs I went to university and emerged three years later bored senseless and heavily in debt. I got a job, accumulated and paid bills. "Is this it?" I thought. I became nihilistic, feeling I was predestined to a life of fruitless subservience. All of my grandparents had passed away from cancer, strokes and heart attacks. Chronic illness crept up on my mum – fibromyalgia, then diabetes – her mobility and mental health scuppered. My family never had access to nature; the door hadn't been opened and they'd been too poor and busy to knock.

How can you want what you've never had? What even was nature and what could it do for me and I for it? I wasn't sure, but something was missing from my life, I knew that much. The "something" I couldn't quite grasp.

Back then, our immediate community green space was the fly-tipped field at the end of the road. It was the closest thing to nature that most kids I grew up with had. A desolate, rusty railed square of unloved wasteland. Scorch marks pocked the littered grass and wisely scribed graffiti informed us: DON'T TRUST SNAKES. This was our Garden of Eden.

The lack of green spaces meant that, as children, we had to find other ways to entertain ourselves. Instead of trees, we climbed bus stops and phone boxes. Rather than lighting campfires, the boys set cars ablaze. I remember walking into my mum and dad's bedroom one day and noticing a small pockmark in the window. I placed my hand on the glass, my finger snug in the smooth groove: an impact dent; a bullet hole. Nothing too sinister. Probably a bored kid with an air rifle, blindly taking aim.

The local cemetery, a five-minute walk from home, was the second-closest patch of green we had – a hop, skip and jump over a busy A road. Rows of moss- and lichen-covered gravestones murmured the names of children from long-forgotten orphanages. Wild garlic carpeted slopes of mass graves, where unnamed poor people were laid to rest throughout the 1800s. Rabbits darted between decaying tree trunks. The place was morbidly alive. I recall pointing a rabbit out to my dad. Its sighting swift as it moved between shrub and crypt – a spectre. My dad thought I was seeing things. It might seem strange that he wouldn't believe me but, up until that point, he'd never seen wild rabbits in Toxteth. Thankfully, we spotted a couple more hopping about and the question of my having hallucinated was quashed. The cemetery was a thoroughfare, connecting Toxteth to the city centre. On our way into town for food shopping, my mum, a brilliant raconteur, would guide us past the graves and caves, reciting ghost stories. The cemetery sits on the site of a former stone quarry. Caves and tunnels etched into the rock throughout the grounds housed a small community of homeless people. All of the caves are bricked up or railed off now, the odd crushed can of cider remains, a relic of times gone by and peoples moved on.

I have my dad to thank for my sprees to the trees. He was our green-space guide. Whenever he was off work, my dad would take my brother and I, as well as an entourage of kids from our estate, to the parks on weekends, where we'd watch men fish for bulging carp and visit the peacocks in the old aviary – privileges that come with growing up in a two-parent household. The reality is that parks exist as occasional, day-out destinations for resource-poor locals. If your guardian had the energy to walk you to the park at weekends, you were lucky. For many, the pretty ponds and stalking herons are a world away.

Parks alone can't alleviate green poverty; their presence does not warrant access. First off, you have to be able to get there. This means having the physical and mental vitality to take on the journey, and to enjoy and explore the place upon arrival. Second, you need a few resources to hand – having enough time usually helps. You also need to feel safe. Princes Park and Sefton Park – L8's sprawling pastures, celebrated city-wide for their size and organized beauty – are out of sight and beyond reach for many of Toxteth's 44,000 plus residents. As a young girl, my mum had been knocked down by a car, a trauma which she carried with her into motherhood. My brother and I weren't allowed to cross main roads unsupervised and, like most kids our age, the 30-minute walk to the park was off limits. TV screens projected *Crimewatch* over *Countryfile*, and some parents viewed our public green spaces as dangerous places. Back in the 1990s, the main route leading to the park was dotted with men and women engaged in illicit enterprises. Jobs were scarce, there were mouths to feed, so drug deals and sex work bloomed up and down the tree-lined avenue.

Schools can play a vital role in filling green gaps. My brother and I walked to primary school unaccompanied from a young age. Ours was at the bottom of the estate, there were no thunderous roads to cross, no cars to dodge – the journey took minutes. We'd start the day in the playground, playing tick or football or Red Rover before the morning bell went. I loved primary school. Even amidst the concrete, we managed to tease out some "nature play" from our environment: making "potions" out of dandelions and daisies, plucked from pavement cracks. Traversing the periphery wall of the local field, gripping onto the railings, we pretended we were mountain climbers. We grew cress from egg cartons on sunny windowsills – babes sowing seeds, observing the cycles of life. We knew that spiders had eight legs, while insects had six; that bees were the bastions of life on Earth (though we learnt all of this through chalkboards and text books, under suspended ceilings and halogen lights).

I remember a few outdoor art classes, rubbing crayon over a piece of paper placed across a wall or grit floor – the end result being a collage of various concrete surface textures. Had we a small patch of vegetation, for there was certainly room, we might have observed bugs – tallied up hairy limbs, or learnt the names of certain plants. Instead we were set loose across gravelly plains. A patch of grass might have prevented stone embedded, bloody knees after ambitious games of skipping.

We averaged around seven hours of outdoor play in school per week, which could have amounted to a transformative chunk of green immersion and nature play for kids, who otherwise were utilizing bus stops, pavements and doorways as playgrounds. Worryingly, three-quarters of UK children spend less time outdoors than prison inmates. By the time I was in sixth form, a couple of the white working-class boys – friends I'd shared milk with in primary school – were in prison for charges relating to motor theft and drugs. By the time I hit my early thirties, three of my Black classmates were dead. A shocking reminder that for some, drugs and guns are easier to access than green spaces.

Frances E. Kuo from the University of Illinois tells us that "people need trees". Her research found that "trees draw people out from behind walls of brick and glass, and in coming together, neighbors forge relationships, nurture children, and build a sense of community." There's mounting and compelling evidence that shines light on the fact that trees and green spaces can have a significant impact on the reduction of crime and violence. In Philadelphia an inexpensive project to "green" scrap land led to a 29 per cent fall in gun violence, as well as drops in vandalism and burglaries, in those neighbourhoods. Residents began to venture outdoors more often, fearless and enthused by their greener, safer streets.

I did have school to thank for my first real trip into nature. My class were sent to Colomendy – an outdoor learning facility inside an Area of Outstanding Natural Beauty in North Wales – for two days of outdoor exploration and dormitory living. Our first activity took us through the loamy woodlands of Loggerheads Country Park, where we ascended through towering pines and dropped down to Devil's Gorge. We stood at the entrance of the gorge, peering into the void. The stacked rocks resembled monstrous jaws, damp breath hanging at the entrance. Ferns uncurled from the top lip of rock, like a moustache. Following our guide, we entered the gaping mouth. The guide had promised free reign of the tuck shop for anyone who survived the expedition with dry feet – a sarcastic tease, designed to raise our hopes. She knew we had no chance of staying dry. Before we knew it we were chest deep in chilly water, wading through the cave, all of us screaming and happy. I peered back towards the opening, the light stark through the chink in the rocks. We had entered a portal, where sweets didn't matter and wet feet were the ultimate prize.

We spent the rest of the trip abseiling, wild swimming, and listening out for Peg Leg (Colomendy's resident ghost). On the last day, we set out to summit Moel Famau. We marched past saluting conifers before scrambling springy marshland all the way to the top. Sweaty and accomplished, we stood wide-eyed at the view. Our teacher guided our stares with a finger, pointing out Snowdon, the Irish Sea and, finally, Liverpool. I looked out to my city beyond the spread of hills and trees, and imagined my house, somewhere among the chaos of buildings. I pictured myself at my bedroom window, staring back, as I stood atop the highest hill in the Clwydian Range. I had made it.

During the walk back to the dorm on our last night, our guide asked if any of us could imagine living at Colomendy. A pensive discussion ensued as we weighed television and Tammy Girl against waterfalls and wellies. The Colomendy tuck shop versus our sweet shop at home. At last, most concluded that there was too much in the city to part with. I kept my thoughts to myself: as soon as the question was poised, I'd known my answer to be with nature. The question stuck though. Now I see it as a false dilemma: city or nature? Why not both?

Over the years, people have rallied, campaigned and acted to reinstate and protect local green spaces. My experiences of growing up in nature-deprived areas are not unique, and the battle to access and preserve green space is ongoing. Toxteth nowadays is celebrated for its ethnic and cultural diversity and its working-class roots. People come searching for community and cheap housing close to the city centre. My mum has received numerous invites to council consultations where developers present plans to build multi-storey flats at the bottom of the estate. The flats would completely block her view of the Clwydian mountains, limiting what little wild nature remains in her life. Highways England have proposed a dual carriageway which would tear through the length of Rimrose Valley, a park near to my current home and the only green space for thousands of residents. The road would split a community in half, whilst desecrating the diverse habitat, replacing green playscape with an ecosystem of car and tar.

Safe to say, I never did abandon my hometown for Colomendy. In fact, I moved to another nature-deprived area. For me, nature's tonic is most potent when it infiltrates the mundanity of daily life. Watering my plants in the morning, sowing lamb's lettuce seeds at my kitchen sink after a busy day of work, watching the crows from my window – these small immersive acts bring so much joy. I don't drive, rail travel is expensive, so I treasure what's on my doorstep, for there is so much to notice, celebrate and protect. Being non-disabled and child-free affords me privileges. I make daily pilgrimages, walking 25 minutes to Waterloo Beach, its fiery sunset is among the best on Earth (so I hear), or to Rimrose Valley Country Park, where bluebells colour the canalside. The more time I spend in my local green spaces, the more I connect with place and people around me. I belong.

As I stand on the shore watching the sun, radiant, dip low, I receive a message from my mum. She's at home, a few miles down the river, admiring the orange light streaming in through slats of semi-drawn blinds. Her way of engaging with nature. She's sent me a picture. Together, we watch the sun go down, squinting into the far-off light.

CITY KID
Hila the Killa

City kid
Witty kid
Hila Killa shit
Spittin' what I've written for a minute
Yeah I live in it—the concrete
Bakin' in the summer like some raw meat
They said I didn't need nature,
I think they conned me

It dawned on me, city air is hard to breathe
I'm asthmatic. What happened? Facing smoke and debris
Cement and concrete replace soils and leaves
But I don't wanna leave, I'm here to heal and believe

Only trees on my block was the weed in my socks
Someone sold me oregano ...
Sittin on spring, Poland Spring on the rocks
I've never seen a rooster, but I've seen plenty of ...

Turkey, at the deli, when I'd rather have veggie
More cops than compost, so the city mad smelly
Where does food come from? Are we trying to be healthy?
There must be berry bushes. All I see is the jelly

It's 1993, I see syringes but I'm scared of bees
It's spring time all these flowers make me sneeze
Allergies rampant cuz they planted male trees
Females bare fruit, why wouldn't we want these?

First time I was in a forest I was fourteen
Looking up at canopies never before seen
I was feeling quite swell, I was more serene
Trees keep the mind well, we need the city to be green

We need the city to the city to be green.
City Kid. I want green on my grid.

Water running from the tap, no cap, no lead
Off the top, I should know about my watershed
How to collect rain, how to care for garden beds
How to keep the peace, how to really make amends

I never swam in the river, pollution be flowing
Wanna reduce crime? Let the greens grow in
Manhattan had a pond, now no one is rowing
Lenape land, in my hand, as a kid not knowing

Let the buffalo roam, let the birds make a nest
Make the city go green, then let everyone rest
We got diversity of people, New York is the best
Plants, animals, and fungi, is how we invest

It's a test, what happens in the next few years
I'm blessed, not stressed, time to crank up the gears
Turn gray into green, thank the life that appears
The Earth is here we're nature consciousness engineers

CROSSFIRE: GLOBAL INTERSECTIONS
Ellen Miles

Nature deprivation stands at a busy junction of injustices. Structural racism, socioeconomic exploitation and ecological plunder are, as we have seen, familiar accomplices, thickly matted into this metastasizing issue. It is also often a factor bound up in some of the most harrowing human rights violations.

For the countless people currently confined to sweatshops, migrant detention centres and internment camps, the lack of greenery in their austere surroundings is contributing to even harsher living conditions and more intense distress. Though, it goes without saying, the lack of nature is not the most acute abuse they suffer, it is nonetheless a symptom of, and a tool for, their continued oppression. This is also true of nature deprivation as a function of state tyranny, colonization and social segregation, as the stories told here reveal.

These three snapshots peer at the issue of nature deprivation through disparate lenses: India's caste system, South African Apartheid, and Soviet occupation in Latvia. The writers' unique perspectives offer universal lessons about the issue's underlying currents, and the kinds of society that allow this injustice to occur.

NATURE'S OUTCASTES
Elizabeth Soumya

Jamun, *Syzygium cumini*, is a tree native to India. It bears glossy, dark fruit that stains one's hands with dabs of beautiful purple, and tastes sour-sweet. A soothing respite from the furious summer sun. Two young boys in a village, aged 10 and 11, decided to forage from a jamun tree after school. They picked up overripe fallen fruits, then tugged and pulled the tree's droopy limbs for more. A few hours later, they were found tied to the trunk of the tree, unconscious, having been beaten for hours. Their crime – to have had the nerve to pluck fruits from someone else's tree while being Dalits (communities stigmatized as "outcastes"). The incident, reported in June 2021, is hardly an aberration. Instead, it is a tiresome recurrence.

India's caste system stratifies its society into different castes based on graded inequality. Those lowest in the rung were deemed "untouchables", and have faced dehumanizing penalties for more than 3,000 years. They were assigned menial, degrading work and exploited in a fashion akin to slavery. But they themselves were considered "polluted"; their touch, spit and very shadow were said to defile. So, they were shunned by "upper caste" people to live in caste ghettos in the peripheries of the village.

Their unequal status was reinforced by stripping them of basic claims to nature. Upper caste people forbade them from owning the land they tilled. A meagre, cruelly insufficient portion of what they grew with their own hands was rationed to them. Their feet could not touch the paths that upper caste people walked on. No matter how parched their throats, they were not allowed to draw water from common ponds.

Natural resources imagined as "commons" were denied to them. Writer Ravikumar questions this notion of commons: "A 'common well' means one from which an untouchable cannot draw water, a 'common funeral ground' means a place where the body of the untouchable cannot be cremated, a 'common market' is where an untouchable cannot even sit." When caste limits were trespassed, Dalit people were ostracized, beaten, sexually assaulted or even killed. These penalties, despite laws against them, are imposed openly by dominant caste people in many Indian villages to this day.

In contrast, India's cities – though exploding at the seams and choking with traffic – offer some opportunities and relief. The anonymity and multitude of unknown bodies, the busyness of the city's capitalistic aspirations, seem to dilute caste, making it less obvious. But the big city recalibrates caste. Urban marginalized communities in congested slums experience a new ghettoization, on the framework of old caste order. Anthropologist Joel Lee, writes, "caste hierarchy has always been in place: etched into residential patterns, encoded in rural and urban infrastructure, implanted in the environment – the āb-o hawā, as Urdu fittingly puts it, the water and air that we breathe and drink."

Though there is freedom to dream in the city, the disadvantages of caste are inherited in poverty, caste-based occupations and a lack of networks, maintaining Dalit communities' isolation. India's biggest cities (Bangalore, Chennai, Delhi, Kolkata and Mumbai) are highly segregated based on caste. This means the city's resources are divided as well. Where one lives determines one's access to basic resources, like water, sewage systems and waste disposal, but also to nature – including parks, walking paths, sunlight and open skies.

In Bangalore, a city of over 10 million people, I live a stone's throw away from a settlement of Dalit and lower caste people. Most men work as drivers, electricians and plumbers, while the women make a living as domestic helpers, cooks and street vendors, selling vegetables and flowers in the evening. There are no garden patches or trees for shade in these lanes. Children manage to fit their games into narrow alleys.

Known as the "garden city" for its greenery, Bangalore is loved for its tree-lined roads, and has different tree species flowering each month. The city's older, richer parts, like Basavanagudi and Malleswaram (which developed as clusters of upper caste people) and its centre (which was a British military cantonment) are protected by privileged tree cover of old raintrees and Indian elms. But, here, it's hard to tell which of the city's trees are exploding with fragrant blooms.

When trees are felled for widening roads and building flyovers, for the marginalized, it isn't just a loss of "greenery". People working as hawkers, street vendors and cobblers lose their places of livelihood and the shade that sheltered them from the blazing sun.

Though Dalit communities experience environmental neglect, the city recruits them for its essential environmental services. Almost all of India's sanitation workers are from Dalit communities, historically associated with "unclean" jobs. All garbage is collected by them, the city is swept and cleaned by Dalit women. It is exclusively Dalit men who clean India's sewers descending into death chambers of manholes – 340 men died, asphyxiated by noxious gases in sewers, between 2015 and 2020.

These very communities are settled into caste ghettos with poor access to basic services. As in villages, where defecation grounds are close to untouchable ghettos, garbage piles up in slums without facilities of waste disposal. The city then frames them as dirty, polluted and an environmental eyesore.

People from oppressed castes were historically exploited as agricultural labourers. Even today, 71 per cent of Dalits in agriculture are landless labourers (in some Indian states this number is much higher). Despite this history, they are not perceived as having a connection with nature. They may have the know-how of growing food, but their lack of space and land, and the price of inputs, mean that owning a garden is out of reach.

Even in Bangalore, with one of India's most thriving gardening communities, there are almost no community gardens or initiatives that make gardening accessible in slums. The idea of allotments has yet to catch on, but there is evidence that city land negotiations recreate agrarian caste dynamics. Permaculture and regenerative farming spaces are dominated by upper caste people who can afford land and knowledge.

In spite of many hurdles, Dalits have an intimate experience of nature. Memories of taking a dip in a river, hearing a birdsong, saving seeds or foraging for wild greens became pauses of solace. In her book, *Sangati*, writer Bama describes Dalit women socializing and enjoying a swim in a well, in fields meant only for untouchables, when upper caste women, bound by rules of modesty, could not step out of their homes: "When we went there to bathe, we dived into the water, jumping from the room above where the pump-set was and making a great splash. Then we swam about."

Nature is not remembered from a distance, as pristine and pure, but through a relationship with it. It not only provides feelings of "wellness" but is a resource for living.

In South Asia, colonialism and capitalism have operated on a much older, complex foundation of inequity. Caste draws visible and invisible limits. Its shadow still falls on access to all environmental resources. To imagine a future of nature for all, we must also imagine a future without caste.

AFTER APARTHEID, GREEN SPACES ARE STILL WHITE SPACES
Celine Isimbi

"When we plant trees, we plant the seeds of peace and hope."
Wangari Maathai

My ancestral lineage is from East Africa (Rwanda and the Democratic Republic of the Congo), but I was born in Zambia in the year 2000, and my family finally settled in South Africa as UNHCR protected refugees in 2001. South Africa is thousands of miles away from my ancestral homes but, along with 2 million others, the 1994 Rwandan genocide forced my parents to flee the country as refugees.

Growing up in a supposed "post-Apartheid" South Africa, a country richly diverse in culture, language, and the natural environment, I had thought nature, the outdoors, and green space, were for everyone, equally. I first came to realize this wasn't the case at age 14, when I started at a new school in a middle-to-upper class neighborhood at the foot of Newlands Forest, the eastern slope of Table Mountain. Two buses and a train away from home, the long commutes to and from school—watching the tree density and scenery change—provided a life-size graph of greenery, charting that certain groups got to truly enjoy and experience nature, while others (my community included) did not. More recently, I have come to realize why this is.

South Africa's Apartheid government, founded in white supremacist and settler colonialism, had, for decades, systematically ensured that Indigenous South Africans and racialized people did not have access to basic freedoms, rights, and resources. Apartheid was a political system of institutionalized racial segregation that relegated Indigenous peoples and racialized people in South Africa to second-class citizens.

Apartheid segregated people across economic, social, environmental, and political dimensions. The racial classifications that the Apartheid government defined people by included "Black," "Indian/Asian," "Colored," and "White." Black people were at the very lowest end of this hierarchy; whiteness was at the very top.

With this division of society, space and place were then racialized and divided: "The archetypal 'Apartheid city' was designed around the spatial segregation of these race groups, with people forcibly removed to 'group areas' and regulations around social interaction in public space." Power, in this way, was organized through space. As sociologist Henri Lefebvre suggested, space "serves as a tool of thought and of action ... a means of control, and hence of domination, of power."

Apartheid was dismantled in 1994, with the first democratic elections after years of revolutionary struggle against the Apartheid regime. South African anti-Apartheid leaders were voted into government, and Nelson Mandela became the first democratic president. However, when space and place have been so deeply politicized, and designed and structured specifically to maintain a racial divide, this inequity still persists, even almost three decades post-Apartheid. For Black Africans, the situation has actually worsened. A 2020 report into the impact of Apartheid on South Africa's urban green space concluded: "The inequity in neighbourhood greenness levels has been maintained (for Indian and Coloured areas) and *further entrenched* (for Black African areas) since the end of Apartheid in 1994 across the country."

If this injustice is the case for Indigenous South Africans, what hope do Black immigrants, refugees, the undocumented, asylum holders, and those fleeing from their ancestral homelands have for living in green neighborhoods? From my experience: virtually none. Growing up, I lived in various neighborhoods, as my family attempted to settle in and make a home out of South Africa. Our social and economic class determined where we got to live, right down to our postal code, disconnecting me from green and blue natural spaces when I was growing up. Though I could tantalizingly glimpse far-off foliage and smell the saltiness of the cold ocean in the air, there was always a road or railway that physically separated us from the beaches and forests.

As much as my Rwandan family, coming from a country with a vast and rich natural environment, enjoyed hikes, park visits, and simply lounging on the beach, these activities felt unsafe as a girl—especially as a Black, refugee girl. For South African women, girls, trans and nonbinary folx, a sense of unease is consistently in the back of our minds; we grow up knowing the dangers of the outdoors, with its threats of gender-based violence. Being Black, dark-skinned and foreign added layers of safety concerns; if I attempted to go to the only park in my very gray neighborhood, I asked myself if I would be the next missing person or the next victim of a hate crime.

If you were to look at South Africa on a map, you may wonder how it is possible for a country so abundant in nature to have so many residents who cannot access it. Unfortunately, not only has the legacy of Apartheid and the institutionalization of the race and class divide through urban planning and policy allowed for this, so has the fact that South Africa operates within more ubiquitous, global systems of oppression—white supremacy, capitalism, ableism, cisnormativity, heteronormativity, and patriarchy—making the outdoors unsafe for people, like myself, who have multiple marginalized identities.

Through all of this, I have learned the importance of community-centered and place-based solutions and resistance. This looks like urban community gardens, which help heal the physical, psychological, and emotional rifts between marginalized groups and the land.

Abalimi Bezekhaya is a South African organization working with people living in Cape Town's vast informal settlements, known as townships, which are home to over 1 million people. They help these communities to initiate, replicate, and sustain food growing and local greening, by providing training, affordable resources, infrastructure, and market access.

Some Black South Africans are flipping industrial infrastructure to communities' advantage. The Siyazama Community Allotment Garden Association (SCAGA), in which women grow organic vegetables to help feed their communities, was only possible because the power lines above the site mean that no one can build on the land.

Today's solutions also look like guerrilla gardening in gray zones (as done by the Ujamaa group in the Khayelitsha community) and community groups such as Hiking with iDaki, who organize weekly hikes, park visits, and beach visits, to reclaim these experiences. If we can reclaim the outdoors and heal connections to the land, we can work toward a future in which nature truly is for everyone.

LATVIA'S SOVIET HOUSING: A GREY LEGACY IN A GREEN NATION
Linda Ludbarza

"The human heart's love for nature cannot ultimately be concreted over."
Jay Griffiths, *A Country Called Childhood* (2014)

"Old love does not rust."
Latvian proverb

When imagining Eastern Europe, people often conjure the same image: an endless maze of run-down Soviet housing blocks, where everything is grey, including the people. This perception is exacerbated by Western pop culture, which uses this trope for either comic effect or as a lingering rhetoric of Cold War era propaganda. In the movie *EuroTrip* (2004), a group of American teenagers unwittingly find themselves in Bratislava, Slovakia. The camera cuts to an unending, post-apocalyptic row of apartments – grey, graffitied and bleak. "Dear God, we're in *Eastern Europe*", one of the protagonists wails as an imperial dirge crescendos, soundtracking vignettes of poverty: a woman throwing dirty water from a window, a man washing himself in the street. The punchline comes from a resident, "It's good you came in summer, in winter it can get very depressing."

Fortunately, this kind of depiction is starting to be called out as an unfair generalization and example of poor taste. In reality, Eastern Europe's rich history is reflected in its diverse architecture. In the cities of Latvia – my nation – you'll find Gothic, Baroque and Art Nouveau styles nestled among traditional wooden homes and gleaming modern architecture. Besides, over half of Latvia remains covered in forest, and most of our historically pagan nation's traditions and folklore centre around the turning of the seasons and the power of nature. These traditions, deeply rooted in the Latvian culture, have survived many attempts to eradicate them. But there is some truth to the tropes; the USSR did indeed leave a legacy of grey in our green nation.

Latvia was occupied by the Soviet forces in 1940, Nazi Germany in 1941, and again by the Soviets in 1944. This last occupation resulted in a 47-year rule, during which an unidentifiable number of people across the Union migrated to cities. Today, the vast majority of Latvians (68 per cent) live in urban areas, with a third of the population living in the capital, Riga. To accommodate the post-World War II urban influx and solve the housing shortage, from 1950, Moscow city Community Party leader Nikita Khrushchev declared the building of mass housing, designed by state architects. The low-cost, low-rise residential buildings were designed for one purpose – to house as many people as possible, as quickly as possible – and were not designed to last more than 25 years (during which time Khrushchev believed "true communism" would be achieved). The result was tens of thousands of hastily constructed, prefab living complexes christened *Khrushchyovkas*, combining Khrushchev's name with the Russian word *trushchoba*, meaning "slum".

Scattered stacks of "temporary" housing blocks (four or five floors high, divided into sections in which apartments branched off a central staircase) sprung up across Eastern Europe, culminating in a labyrinth of identical structures.

Soviet rule was ostensibly principled on the communist belief that everyone should have and own the same – a utopian dream of equality. The mass housing was built abiding by this principle as a means of enforcing standardized living; housing was to be a social good, rather than a commodity. International onlookers were impressed by the speed and scale of construction. "What the Russians have done," an official from the United States said, "is to develop the only technology in the world to produce acceptable, low-cost housing on a large scale." But for residents living in these apartments, each just 30–60 sq. m (300–650 sq. ft), the reality was bleak. The blocks were often built near busy roads, highways or train tracks, exposing residents to noise and air pollution. Made out of standardized concrete panels to ensure quick assembly, the buildings lacked sufficient isolation from the elements and pollutants.

These decisions went directly against the way of life that people had long been used to. Historically, most families lived in a house with a garden, and possibly some land. They had a space to enjoy nature and grow their own food. Most of these properties were confiscated by the state during the occupation, displacing or eliminating the families that lived there. The larger houses were divided into smaller flats and redistributed. In a country that values and relies on nature, these forced living conditions are a daily reminder of the disruption created by hostile forces.

Thirty years after the fall of the Soviet Union and the Iron Curtain, the houses, as well as the social injustice they brought, remain. In 1995, almost 60 million residents of the former Soviet Union still lived in these buildings. Speaking to a friend who grew up in a Soviet-built apartment, it's clear that 50 years of state ownership and neglect have shifted people's perception of public space – they value their own, private spaces and mistrust public ones. He explained how the small spaces left between flats, though designed to encourage a community space, are now used as walkways or car parks. How the very few green spaces around were not taken care of, as they were not part of anyone's private property. "If someone felt inclined to attempt to use them, they'd find themselves among trash, animal droppings and parked cars", he shrugged. The romantic notion of proletarian neighbours that come together and share outside space was never fulfilled. Instead, the reality is a bare landscape with no opportunity for people to enjoy the outdoors.

I myself have escaped living in these Soviet structures – a result of my mother's fervent desire to never return to one. When speaking of the living conditions she experienced while growing up in the 1960s, she recalls how trapped she felt in a sea of equally trapped neighbours, lamenting that green, beautiful scenery and privacy were a mere dream. She eventually became an interior designer – and has worked with people who reside in these blocks to improve their living conditions. But poor planning and material deterioration limit what spatial improvements are possible.

The expansion of cities and the necessity of affordable housing is still a global concern. Sadly, in Eastern Europe, these issues were tackled by a regime that did not care for people's welfare, despite its promise of a communist utopia. The consequences of these decisions will haunt many generations to come. To rebuild is costly, to tear down displaces hundreds of thousands of people.

Today's city planners have inherited a daunting task. Some attempts to beautify these structures have been made, if only from the exterior. In Tartu, Estonia, an EU-funded project, SmartEnCity, is tackling the sustainability of these types of houses: turning block flats into smart homes by improving their insulation, ventilation and providing sustainable energy sources, aiming to turn them from class F or H to class A energy efficiency.

Further improvements in infrastructure need to be made to rehabilitate the green areas surrounding the block flats, building a healthier relationship between the resident and communal space. To do so, we can draw from ancient Latvian folklore and traditions, which, like us, survived the Soviet concrete. Most are still being practised today, proving the importance of nature not only to our mental and physical well-being, but also to the identity of our small nation.

HOW CAN WE END RURAL RACISM? IT'S TIME TO REIMAGINE THE COUNTRYSIDE
Louisa Adjoa Parker

Why are there so few people of colour in the countryside? Whether we're looking at residents or visitors, *"race"* plays a huge part in the unequal access to the "great outdoors": the deeply embedded racism present in the countryside across the United States, United Kingdom and much of the West prevents many African diaspora, South, East, and South-East Asian diaspora people from feeling safe and welcome in rural environments or enjoying outdoor activities in the ways their white counterparts can. Throughout Europe and North America, there has been a historic disconnect between Black and ethnically diverse people and nature although – thanks to a rising wave of campaigns and initiatives – this is now beginning to shift.

Let's start with a bird's-eye view. The vast majority of the UK's ethnically diverse population is concentrated in urban areas: people from Pakistani (99.1 per cent), Bangladeshi (98.7 per cent) and Black African (98.2 per cent) backgrounds are overwhelmingly likely to live in urban locations; whereas census data in 2011 recorded a total Black and minority ethnic population in South West England, where I live, of 242,506 out of a total population of 5,288,935 – or 4.6 per cent.

When it comes to visiting National Parks, both "race" and income play a part. For instance, 93 per cent of visitors to British National Parks get there in their own car, with only a small number using public transport, yet 40 per cent of Black people have no access to a car or van. In the US, just 1 per cent of National Park visitors are Black, while white people make up 95 per cent of visitors. There is evidently a problem here, and governments aren't doing enough to tackle these glaring inequalities – indeed, a widely criticized report by the British government in 2021 actually denied the existence of institutional racism in the UK. This suggests a clear lack of understanding of racism, the nuances involved, and the different forms it can take, at governmental level.

I was born in Yorkshire in the early 1970s, a time of overt and unashamed racism in Britain, as a child of English and Ghanaian heritage. Since then, I have spent most of my life living in the largely rural British counties of Devon, Dorset and Somerset. I have never lived in an area that wasn't predominantly white. My best memories from a troubled adolescence are of time spent in the South Devon countryside, with its terracotta-coloured earth, sand and cliffs, its fields and woods and rivers and beaches. I first visited Devon aged six, to visit my English grandparents who retired there. For a mixed-race young person, whose face looked "wrong" against an olde-English, chocolate-box backdrop, this connection with self and land was important. When I was younger, I struggled with my identity – I experienced constant racism, had no idea how to look after my hair, and was usually the only brown-skinned person in any social setting. Not seeing yourself – or anyone who looks like you – reflected in the landscape around you takes its toll, and I believe the trauma of racism contributed to a lifetime of poor mental health. It wasn't all bad, and I learnt to be resilient – I made lots of friends and enjoyed fully inhabiting the landscape and the sense of freedom which life in the countryside brought. But it was hard going.

Life wasn't much better when I moved to Dorset as a single mum. I experienced constant microaggressions – including comments about my hair or skin, being told racist jokes in the pub, people assuming anyone standing near me with brown skin was a relative – and it was only when I embarked on a journey of discovery, through education, writing and researching Black British history, that I finally began to feel I belonged. When I came across the work of photographer Ingrid Pollard, *Pastoral Interlude* (1988), one of the first recognized artworks which highlighted the experience of Black people in rural areas, I was moved and empowered. I had never seen an image of a Black person – other than myself or my family – in a rural setting. These moments of recognition – that actually, you *do* belong – are like nuggets of gold: life-changing, all-powerful.

The reasons behind the comparatively low numbers of ethnically diverse populations in rural areas are knotted and complex, spanning the historical, logistical and economic. When our parents or grandparents migrated to the UK they went to cities, where there was the possibility of work and community. Job opportunities are rarer in rural areas, and if you add "race" into the equation, your chances are even slimmer. Black and brown communities, although already in existence, grew rapidly during the 1950s period of immigration from Africa and other former British colonies. Humans have always migrated; we go to where we have the best chance of survival. As well as this, I can't help feeling that peoples whose ancestry was so linked to slavery and colonization might not have wanted to spend time in fields or working the land.

There is a problematic perception of the countryside in ethnically diverse communities. In the US, there is a long and violent history which includes the hunting of escaped enslaved Africans, woods and trees and lynching. Although white supremacy is woven into the fabric of the United States, the more rural parts, such as the Deep South, are especially known for their violent racism. In the UK, although we don't share the same history of violence, a growing body of evidence shows that those with African or Asian heritage experience racism in rural spaces, ranging from inappropriate terminology and microaggressions to verbal and physical assaults.

Microaggressions, or covert racism, might seem harmless to those who haven't experienced them: the room falling silent when you walk into a country pub and heads turning so quickly you fear for the owners' necks; having constant, irritating questions asked of you; having to justify your existence and explain your heritage; being the "only one"; being asked where you're *really* from and being told you're exotic; having to witness white people wearing blackface and an afro wig because of "tradition" or "fun". Recently I was chairing a panel on "race" and representation in the Exeter Northcott Theatre archives. A member of the audience asked why I had chosen to stay and work in the South West, as a creative of colour. "It's my home", I replied, bristling somewhat. To my knowledge, my white friends and family haven't been asked why *they* stayed.

No matter the degree of racism, the body of qualitative and quantitative data – including a "race map" illustrating that Black, Asian and minority ethnic people are much more likely to be the victim of racist assault in rural areas than in cities – backs up this widely held perception by those who experience racism: the countryside doesn't feel safe if you have black or brown skin. Neil Chakraborti, a criminology professor and the editor of *Rural Racism*, has concluded that "experiences of racism in rural towns and villages are actually much more common, and much more disturbing, than is generally thought."

I've been researching the ethnically diverse British rural experience for nearly two decades, telling my own and others' stories. Although we are all individuals, there are common themes – many of us have witnessed and/or experienced racism; many African diaspora people have experienced microaggressions (including the far-too-common experience of having white strangers touch our hair); many express feelings of isolation, with no others who share our ethnic or cultural heritage around and feel there is a lack of access to our needs relating to culture and heritage. In a place that's often viewed as the last connection with Empire, a mythical "golden" age when everyone was supposedly white (spoiler alert: they weren't), living while Black or brown can be challenging. We are both highly visible, in that we stand out, yet invisible when it comes to having our needs met.

Children and young people are not immune from rural racism. In 2019, I interviewed Fin from Cornwall (aged eight at the time) for my *Where are you really from?* project. He told me, "I like being mixed race. It's when people are racist to me, I don't like it. It makes me feel I don't fit in. People stare at me and touch my hair without asking too ... People say the N-word, that I should go back to Africa where I belong. The first time it happened, I was in Year 1. A kid called me a stupid African and hit me. I talked to the teachers, but they said, 'Just deal with it, it's fine.'"

At the time of writing, BBC South have just aired the story of a 12-year-old's social media post which highlighted her experience of being mixed race in Dorset. Marli McNab, who describes herself as half Black Caribbean and half British, describes being racially abused and told to "go back to the cotton-picking farm" she came from. "Even though some of these things don't sound bad, she wrote, "they do hurt badly. They make me feel worthless and not welcome."

There has been much in the media recently highlighting the problem. In 2020, a video (which went viral) captured Amy Cooper, a white woman, calling the police on Christian Cooper, a birdwatcher (or birder), when he asked her to put her dog on a lead – a rule in that part of the park, to protect the birds. We watch as she tells Christian: "I am going to call the police and tell them an African American man is threatening my life."

An example of rural racism in action in the UK is the story of poet Benjamin Zephaniah's visit to a friend's farm in the Essex countryside. He told *The Guardian*: "I ... went for a long jog. Never left his land. When I got back to his house, the place was surrounded by police, a helicopter circling above. 'We have had reports of a suspicious jogger,' the police said."

Another reason for the disconnect between people of colour and the countryside, I believe, is due to the myth that Black equals "urban", which has been perpetuated by our media and literature. Black and brown people tend to be underrepresented in a range of sectors, but when we are visible, we are usually portrayed as urban creatures, wearing the latest trainers. This perception is so ingrained that, for decades, the word "urban" has been used as a synonym for "Black", with racist connotations.

This myth feeds into the rhetoric that we "belong" in urban areas. This has certainly been my experience. As a child, white people assumed I was from Africa. As an adult, I have been told, you must be from a city, not from here. We need to recognize that African and Asian diaspora people, like anyone else, have multiple identities and live in a multitude of places. We, too, enjoy nature, and are not all afraid of getting muddy (although we might be afraid of racism) and some of us have created Black or Asian rural identities, in spite of the tension that has been involved in this.

We need to consider the history around ethnically diverse peoples' connection to the countryside. Part of the problem stems, I believe, from the way our global history has been told. New conversations around decolonization are beginning to unpick this narrative and reimagine our histories. Yes, numbers are comparatively lower, but the idea that rural Britain is, and always has been, *exclusively* white is a myth. There are many of us living in the British countryside, and this population has increased in recent years.

There is a long history of connections between rural Britain and Africa, Asia, the Americas and the Caribbean, and arguably the infrastructure of the British countryside was built on the proceeds from transatlantic slavery, and country estates and manor houses are intimately connected with these histories. African and Asian diaspora people have been coming here from the former colonies for centuries: as enslaved servants, soldiers, teachers, entertainers, and more recently as students, migrant workers and healthcare workers. The stories are there, if we look for them, although because they haven't fitted the view of the countryside as belonging to white people, the histories have been whitewashed. We need to remember, however, not all our stories are of victimhood, but also of resilience, contribution and joy.

It might feel to people living in the "green and pleasant" parts of the UK, that we're far removed from the white supremacy that rears its ugly head elsewhere. Yet history tells us otherwise. In fact, many of the men who were instrumental in setting up the global system of white supremacy came from places like South West England –

they travelled the globe, colonizing, conquering, stealing, enslaving and murdering peoples they saw as less than human along the way.

Professor Corinne Fowler, who led the Colonial Countryside Project and wrote the book *Green Unpleasant Land*, told me, "The countryside is almost sacred to many Britons. The shock response to the project suggests quite how close to the bone this topic is. Inclusive, evidence-based histories of the countryside in relationship to imperialism are seen as a threat to the countryside's supposed whiteness. My work seeks to open up the colonial histories of country houses, pastoral writing, rural industries like wool and copper production, village, moorland and coastlines. By following local history, Britons can begin to discover the distinctive ways that their region's history was shaped by Empire. Rural lives were connected in myriad ways by the lives of people who were colonized and enslaved. There's much more to research and we should all be heading to look at parish records and records offices to learn more."

So, what is being done to dismantle barriers relating to "race" and support people of colour to reconnect with nature? British initiatives include Black2Nature, Black Girls Hike UK, BLM in the Stix, Black Girls Camping Trip, Flock Together and Mosaic Outdoors. In the US, initiatives include Outdoor Afro, We Go Outside Too, Diversify Outdoors, In Solidarity Project, Melanin Basecamp and Wild Diversity.

Young people of colour are spearheading this wave of change. Selma Maloumi is one of them. Driven by her love for nature and the community, Selma started organizing hikes for women from ethnic minority communities. She tells me that her aim was to "create safe spaces in nature, to explore the beautiful lands of the country we were born and/or raised in and to develop a stronger connection to the outdoors." The trigger for organizing the hikes came after realizing that many of her friends had never visited the beautiful English coastlines or explored hiking trails. Hiking, she reflects, "allows for city folk to see life beyond the confines of the grey urban landscapes we are so accustomed to". For Selma, the hikes have also become "a quiet form of activism. As people from ethnic minorities, we are constantly required to navigate difficult feelings of belonging, constantly being questioned about our identity despite being born and raised in the UK." She also takes a private stand, prioritizing her own right to connect to nature. "I still regularly seek out local parks for my daily nature fix," she says, "to exercise, to write, to reflect, to gain clarity, to watch the clouds, and feel nature envelop me in her warm embrace."

There is a great deal of grassroots activism taking place, with more and more people joining the movement but there is also a need for change at a structural level. Over the past year, I've worked with a range of organizations who are trying to be more inclusive, owning up to their lack of knowledge about "race", and aiming to do better. This includes CPRE, the countryside charity, who told me: "We know the countryside can enrich all our lives, so we've been looking at what social and cultural hurdles are in place that mean people of colour are less likely to feel connected to or more likely to feel unwelcome in rural landscapes. This has been as much about looking at ourselves as it has been about looking externally; our work has focussed on working with the policy 'nothing about us without us' – and co-creating work that challenges racism in rural areas and builds a more inclusive understanding of the countryside. We know building trust between the organization and Black people and people of colour is central to building trust in the countryside."

But the work brings fresh challenges, such as backlash and denial. I read an anonymous quote, "The denial of racism is the new form of racism", and this certainly rings true. For instance, in 2020 the BBC's *Countryfile* aired a piece on rural racism, inspired by the DEFRA review of England's National Parks, which found that the countryside is seen by both ethnically diverse people and white people alike as "a 'white' environment". The piece led to an outcry on Twitter. "The countryside is free!" proclaimed keyboard warriors. "Of *course* they can come here." The countryside *is* – mostly – free, and in an ideal world everyone could access it. Yet saying it's open to all ignores the very real barrier of rural racism – the existence of which was demonstrated beautifully by the backlash on social media. Other responses I've come across include accusations of "race-baiting" or a "woke agenda", anger, racial gaslighting and accusations of lying. After I spoke to Sky News for a piece on a research project they are partnering on, The Forgotten People, a Twitter user said I was "spreading lies, attention-seeking, and painting Somerset as racist".

Of course, any change will bring with it resistance. And a sad but necessary part of the work is understanding that new conversations around "race" and decolonization can trigger a strong negative response. Moves to decolonize South West England, for instance the tearing down of the statue of Edward Colston in Bristol, sparked a fierce response from the self-declared "anti-woke" who wish to "protect" our heritage. We need to find solutions to challenge and manage this backlash. It helps, I feel, to be clear about why we are doing this work, the benefits it brings, and to whom. We will all benefit from having green spaces and a countryside that are welcoming to all. When it comes to decolonization, telling the stories of the colonized as well as those of the colonizer can only be a good thing; that we will gain from the richness that diverse perspectives bring to any conversation. By having a wider, more inclusive, shared global history, it will help us heal the hurts from the past, so we can do better in the future.

Mohammed Dhalech, founder of Mosaic Outdoors, notes that "One of the biggest barriers to access is the lack of information, awareness and understanding." Community-led initiatives certainly have an important role to play in bringing about change, but so too do education and awareness-raising in schools, universities, colleges and other institutions. Local authorities can play a part, as can governments, as can individuals who wish to act as allies. Now more than ever before, it's easy to educate ourselves on anti-racism, the history of Empire and colonialism. It's all there at our fingertips if we choose to find it.

This is a historic moment. There is a growing movement to eradicate racism, in all its guises, in all the spaces it exists. We need to keep the momentum going, so things continue to shift; keep the conversation moving, widen it out and consider other intersections – gender identity, sexuality and disability – as well as class or deprivation. We need to consider children and young people, and the importance of connecting with nature for them. We need to consider mental health and well-being – how can we protect people from the damaging impact of racism in green spaces? And how can we ensure anti-racist activists with lived experience are not retraumatized or exploited? There is much to consider, but I remain hopeful that access to the natural environment and green spaces can become a right for all, rather than a privilege for some.

Yes, I am from here, *really*,
but also from there. My feet
connect me to this piece of earth
which rolls away in green waves,

this piece of earth inhabited
by people who do not look like me.
This is how I wear my skin:
it tells the story of another place;

an imagined country
with dusty roads, hot nights,
which I have yet to see.
We all lean into the dark

towards our ancestors, who lean
towards us, with bent spines,
trying to tell us where we are from,
where we are going.

THE ROAD TO COMMON GROUND: TRESPASSING WITH NICK HAYES
Ellen Miles interviews Nick Hayes

"There have existed men who had the power to hold or to give exclusive possession of portions of the earth's surface, but when and where did there exist the human being who had the right?"
Henry George, *Progress and Poverty* (1879)

"As long as you respect
that this is Mother Nature's home:
feel free to wander;
you have the Right to Roam"
Right to Roam campaign poster (2021)
Stuck over "No Trespassing" signs across England

Though we don't acknowledge it, there's no mistaking that our innocent stroll has just become a trespass. As we clamber over the barbed wire, our conversation flows unbroken, mimicking the wind and wild garlic's disregard for the lightly weaponized boundary. Even so, I feel the impish flutter of doing something *a bit naughty*. But what makes *this* side of the fence so different to *that*?

I've come to Winsley, Wiltshire, to speak to professional trespasser Nick Hayes. It's a bright spring morning; George Floyd's murderer has just been found guilty on all counts; football fans are bringing down the proposed European Super League – the fabric of reality feels lucid, charged with possibility. We're veering onto private farmland for reasons both practical and political: the secluded riverside perch provides not only a stunning setting but an apt one, given what we're here to discuss.

In England, the public are forbidden from accessing 92 per cent of the country's land and 97 per cent of its waterways. Placing just a toe into these spaces is considered trespassing, a civil offence that can quite easily be upgraded to a criminal charge. Unsurprisingly, this private acreage isn't distributed evenly: half of England is owned by just 1 per cent of its population; a third of Britain belongs to the "aristocracy". Take the Duke of Buccleuch, for instance. His family estate, Boughton House, is over 30 times the size of Hyde Park. Not only that, he owns a further 270,000 acres (110,000 ha) of the British Isles. That's equivalent to around 19 Manhattan Islands, or 10 Paris cities. Bear in mind, a third of people in the UK don't own a home at all, and one in every 200 people in England are homeless.

People have fought against England's oppressive land system for centuries. In the spring of 1649, a group of 40 radicals began planting vegetables on St George's Hill, near the town of Weybridge. The Diggers, as they're now known, sought to make "the Earth a Common Treasury for All, both Rich and Poor, That every one that is born in the Land, may be fed by the Earth". Their camp didn't even last the summer. The local landowner, with military support, drove them out, accusing the group of illegal assembly, riot and trespass.

I decided to find out what had become of St George's Hill. The first link Google hands me, a property website, displays a list of £15 million mansions, bordering a golf club. The second, an article, tells me that St George's Hill is now "one of, if not THE most exclusive private residential address outside of London". The article's introduction proudly states, "Naturally, access is restricted." Naturally.

Not only are we forbidden from accessing most of the country, the slivers of England that we are allowed to set foot on hardly constitute freedom. Often remote, they're inaccessible to anyone who doesn't own a car or can't afford the train journey. Not only that but, in a Monty Python-esque farce, several areas marked out for public use can't technically be reached at all – they have no public paths leading to them. As for the strips we can set foot on, we're permitted to do little more than that ...

So Nick, what rights *do* we have, land-wise?

You have the right to walk in a thin line on a ribbon through nature. The restriction of all the activities you're allowed to do – swimming, raving and wild camping included – means that, unless you bloody love walking and looking at things, there's nothing for you to do in the country. That's the state of the nation: we treat the countryside like it's a museum, not a place you can feel at home in. The whole inclination of the law says "this is not for you", and that's permeated our orthodoxy, what we consider to be the norm.

We may consider this normal today, but what did things look like a thousand years ago?

The Anglo-Saxons had a far more egalitarian concept of rights in land. It wasn't a non-hierarchical utopia – thanes and earls owned the land, and took tithes – but people had long-established rights to use vast tracts of that land, called "commons", to grow crops, graze animals, hunt, cut wood, forage (whatever their local resource accommodated) in return for simply giving their time and taking responsibility to collectively manage it. They believed that you never own the land, you borrow it off your grandchildren; they practiced rotational farming – there was a built-in notion of sustainability before the concept even existed, a way of keeping nature's balance.

It was William the Conqueror who imported the idea of private property and the law of "forest" (from the Latin *forīs*, meaning "outside of", as it was outside of common law), which repurposed commons as private hunting grounds for the aristocracy. That was revolutionary. A hundred years after the Battle of Hastings, a quarter of England had been forested. In the 13th century, Parliament introduced "enclosure", the systematic privatization of land that robbed countless people of their food and homes. The Tudors invented new systems of land measurement, turning what was once a right for all into a quantifiable commodity, bought and sold by a handful of people.

They were displacing people, starving people ... Was that legal?

At times, it was literally illegal. The Midland Revolt (a peasant uprising in 1607) is a great example – the protestors said they were defending England against thieves, because 350 farms had been unlawfully destroyed and almost 150,000 people made homeless. For trying to fight back against that, these starving men, women and children were cruelly, gruesomely killed.

In Tudor times, various acts made enclosure "legal" to specific areas of land because the unreformed government said so. Who was that government? The landowners! The economist Guy Standing talks about how justice itself is a commons, but justice has been privatized in a load of nuances, like the costs of court proceedings or how, when the penalty for a crime is a fine, that penalty only exists for the poor. "Justice" is bent in favour of those that have the coin – and everyone knows it.

How has enclosure and the apportioning of land affected other rights?

Enclosure not only allowed private ownership and profit to dominate the countryside, it also forced a load of self-subsistent workers off the land and into wage servitude. The commons were England's welfare system, without the stigma. All of a sudden, you weren't able to provide for your family by going out and doing it yourself – you had to rely on whatever your boss handed out. The fight then moved from "let us retain rights to the land" to "safeguard our rights within this new wage arena". People weren't campaigning anymore for the woodland to remain unenclosed, they were campaigning to not have to work 12-hour Saturdays.

This also foreshadowed colonialism; it's like we practised seizing land and exploiting labour on our own soil before we exported it to other nations. And it was this exploitation of our own soil, our own population, that paid for this malevolence in Africa, the Caribbean and India.

Today, the act of demolishing a wall would be considered violent, but they were built by violence. And they're still violent: walls destroy links between people, they're monuments to imbalance in society. Today's climate and ecological crises, food insecurity, housing crisis, rising social inequality and urban environmental inequality are all linked to the current definition of private property rights, the total dominion given to owners, and the restrictions on public access to land.

Are things getting better? Or worse?

People think of enclosure as a historic phenomenon, but I'm constantly sent examples of localized enclosure: landowners blocking access to woodland so that they can chainsaw it down and create warehouse space; developers blocking up the right of way on a riverbank to put luxury flats there instead. Covid-19 has meant that a load of permissive paths have been closed by landowners, just because they can. We also now have "stopping up orders" that allow landowners to own highways.

In the last 100 years, we've lost half of England's remaining public footpaths. Now, any path not registered on a new "definitive map" by 2026 will be automatically extinguished. The onus lies on regular people to, one, know about this and, two, undertake the tedious process of registering paths, in their spare time. This means reading a 316-page guide and gathering evidence like turnpike records, tithe maps, railway and canal plans, sales documents – it's a circus of bureaucracy and legalese. They know that no one has time for that. They're counting on it.

So, physical enclosure is still happening, but it's also about who is welcome in the countryside. We're told that the countryside is for straight, white, middle-class, middle-aged people to use for walking, not only by all these walls and laws, but by practically every branding or commodification of nature. But there's nothing inherent to the countryside itself that fits that image. Nature is queer as hell; mandarin ducks change gender! In saying the countryside isn't for everybody, we're systematically marginalizing people from being allowed to care for it. If they're being told they don't have rights to it, then of course the implication is they don't have responsibilities for it.

With no power comes no responsibility?

Exactly. When people grumble, "teenagers leave so much litter" or "the travelling community leave a mess", number one, those are stereotypes that do not apply by any means to the vast majority of those communities. There's no evidence of having left no trace, so of course all that people can point to is the anomalous energy drink jutting out of the hawthorn hedge. Second, if teenagers are disenfranchised from the countryside and looked at as vagabonds, if the travelling community are roundly unwelcome on a systemic level, then of course that breeds a sense of nihilism or a "screw you" perspective.

It's called the Pygmalion Effect: we act the way we are expected to, for better or worse. If you look around at the fields, the barbed wire, razor wire, fences and walls have become so normalized in our culture that we almost don't see them. But they're misanthropic, antisocial symbols. Our countryside has become militarized. Against what? People appreciating nature?

In 1947, a report proposing a full Right to Roam across England was shot down by landowning Members of Parliament, who saw the public as a threat to the countryside. Today, whenever we launch a campaign for greater access to nature, the arguments that come back are "the public would just trash it". But the people saying that don't refer to *themselves* as the public; there's this non-specific Other that's the target of distrust. This idea of the disrespectful Other ultimately becomes self-fulfilling because, when we then exclude – literally otherize – groups of people like working-class teenagers, we create the conditions for apathy and anger.

What's the solution? How do we break the cycle?

We need to educate our children in nature; they need to be in it to care about it. At the moment, education in nature is a privilege, but those that haven't got it are being blamed for not knowing the Countryside Code. We're told that the problem is human nature – that people are inherently bad or weak-willed – but it's really the architecture of our society and systemic inequality that creates this kind of outcome. We FOI'd the government and found that, since 2004, they'd spent £2,000 a year on promoting the Countryside Code. That's negligible.

The structure of the law also needs to be changed to encourage people to engage with nature: we need the rights to camp, swim, forage, build fires. The walk is an observation of it, you're looking at nature, like you might look at pictures in a gallery; what we need is to be in and amongst it. How can we care about the natural world unless we can immerse ourselves in it? There are no responsibilities without rights; and there are no rights without responsibilities. It's like walking: if you take one step with rights, to balance it, you have to take the other step with responsibilities.

It's ironic that the argument for private property is based on protecting nature from the public, because the rights to consume, abuse and destroy are legally part of the right to private ownership.

There are undoubtedly some concerned, dedicated landowners that see their job almost primarily as stewarding nature, but it's not the ramblers that have devastated and burnt moorland, it's not HS2 protesters chopping down ancient woodland, and it's not wild swimmers pouring tons of sewage into the rivers.

Property is this delusion that whatever lies on one side of a fence is entirely unconnected to the land and communities on the other side. The parcelling up or blocking off of "private entity" is a notion forced atop an ecology that doesn't work like that. Nature's "boundaries" – hedges, rivers, glades – are ecotones, places of transaction and interaction. You can't just bung a fence through a space and pretend that that makes two different things. The problems that follow are things like flooding and soil depletion, as well as the simple fact that a wall will stop animal migration. When landowners are burning fossil fuels and peat bogs, destroying habitats and spraying pesticides, the consequences don't stay neatly within their property lines. We don't get a say in how the land is used, yet we're all affected by it.

We've been lulled by the story that land is better off in the hands of private owners. The poster essay for this idea, Garrett Hardin's "Tragedy of the Commons", talked about an unregulated commons, in which individuals would take more than their fair share – essentially, neo-liberalism and unregulated market. This omits the absolute key to common's philosophy: there is no commons without collective, reciprocal, sustainable management. So, it's just an extremely pernicious misrepresentation.

If everyone has a vested interest in the land, then everyone will want to be part of how it's managed. Yesterday, I met a mountain biker, and we had a big old chat because they're allowed permissive access to these woods. I was like, "So how does it work?" Basically, they regulate themselves. There's a community of bikers who'll not just pick up other people's litter – because they see it as *their* space, which they have rights to, or belong to – but they'll also police themselves and create their own rules for sustainability, like not making loads of ramps.

Wild swimmers in Ilkley, West Yorkshire, recently ran a campaign to show that hundreds of locals use the River Wharfe as a resource for their mental and physical well-being, so it was granted bathing water status. For it to be clean enough for humans, it will be safe for beavers, otters, all the flora and fauna that thrive off it. It's a great case study of how, by engaging with the environment, humans can improve its resource.

Beyond the right to access the land, could we take this a step further to collective land management?

Scotland's Land Reform Act in 2003 introduced the Right to Roam and community land ownership in one go. For instance, when the Duke of Buccleuch (Scotland's largest landowner) decided to sell 5,000 acres (2,000 ha) of Langholm Moor, the community had the right to make an offer, and that offer was privileged over private individuals.

The idea of donating land to community land trusts was written into the Countryside and Rights of Way Act 2000. We FOI'd the government on how many people had done this and, when I asked about it, the person on the other end of the phone *snorted*, which suggests it's negligible at best. When people have historically tried to turn their land into common land, their decisions have been overruled in court on the premise that they were *mad* to do so. It was seen as evidence of actual insanity.

The legislation is there, but we need a cultural shift away from the idea that you'd be betraying your aristocratic family or class by opening up to "the oiks". You would be, in fact, doing something positive. In the same way that we want to heroize the act of picking up someone else's litter, because it can keep our rights of access alive, we can also frame the idea of dedicating land to public access as caring for the land.

Landed gentry will often say it's a full-time, stressful job looking after the land. First, could public access and engagement actually help them out? Second, are they even enjoying it? I doubt the Duke of So-and-So is reclining in a Fauvian fashion or climbing trees ...

If they stopped to think about it, from their perspective, they could get loads of people to come and help manage their land because they want to get involved in nature. I was kicked off the River Loddon, which rises in Basingstoke, Hampshire, recently because the Duke of Wellington owns a quarter of it. I was walking away thinking "As *if* the Duke of Wellington would be out on his kayak! So who's enjoying this?" There's over 100,000 people in Basingstoke – some of them could collectively manage the river. Collective management could extend to anything: community groups going coppicing, hedge laying, doing wildlife surveys or building bug hotels.

It's a win-win that might even allow us to have a nice relationship with the dude who's riverbank you swim in or woods you walk in. To be able to say "Morning" rather than "Oh shit". Then he could say, "Well if you're going to be here, could you keep an eye on those sheep or pull out those weeds over there."

So, how do we get there? Can we find common ground with landowners, or do we need an uprising?

Oh, I would love an uprising. Boringly, the practical solution is to maintain property ownership, but to override the privileges that it gives people with more equitable rules. If people start having to pay land value tax rather than receiving handouts, or if you ban land banking, then why the hell would a company in Singapore buy up land in Stroud? Farm subsidies are being reviewed at the moment; it's mainly environmentally focussed, but why can't public access be part of that? Paying landowners to allow public access is a practical and fair way to get them on board.

In terms of finding "common ground" with landowners, this idea exists in both metaphor and reality. To actually have common ground is to have a physical place where two people can meet without one being able to control the way the other person's day goes. We're sat here and, at any moment, the farmer could come along and very aggressively not just end our experience of this riverbank but also inject our bloodstreams with feelings of fear and guilt. How is that a good structure for human beings to exist within? The most fulfilling chats I've had with people from outside my "tribe" have been in the open countryside. When you're in a situation and place which isn't premised upon a hierarchy, you're actually able to find common ground on common ground. So there has to be a structural, architectural solution to division, we have to design ways for people to meet on a par.

When the Berlin Wall came down, Germans described a *Mauer im Kopf*, "a wall in the head" that the physical wall had implanted psychologically. Even as late as the 2000s, Germans were still estimating places across the ghost wall as being further away than they really were, because of this internalized mental divide. Borders buttress this feeling of division or opposition: if I'm on the other side of the fence to you, we're opposites. Whereas if you remove that fence – that glorious metaphor of common ground – our conversation and disagreement can move to different points without being limited to a tennis-like, binary interaction.

So walls really do have a psychological effect, they nest themselves in the way we think about our relationship to nature and to life. This idea of dividing nature is just denying reality. A wall is just cemented denial.

What else can people do to help reclaim our rights to engage with the land?

Andy Wightman, one of Scotland's key land rights campaigners, told me that one reason Right to Roam was possible in Scotland was that loads of people took their right to roam anyway – they were just going walking regardless – and so landowners were interested in regulating it. That's not the case yet in England. We need a generation of Benny Rothmans, out trespassing. If you do, just follow the Scottish Outdoor Access Code – I always do. It's where we want to be heading: a connection with nature that foregrounds respect for the countryside's ecologies and communities, human and non-human. This includes respecting people's privacy.

Obviously no one wants strangers camping in their garden, but surely allowing access to vast private property isn't home invasion?

This notion that we want to trespass on people's back gardens is just a reactionary, mad reframing of the issue. There are hundreds of thousands of acres of open spaces behind private walls. There's plenty of space in England for people to pitch a tent, leave no trace, enjoy the dawn chorus and disappear.

Every country that has a Right to Roam protects an area of privacy. There's an understanding that the curtilage of a private dwelling – the extent of its home, garden and drive – are personal sanctuaries that shouldn't be invaded. In Sweden, you can't walk or camp within 70m (76½ yards) of this curtilage. In Norway, it's 150m (164 yards). In Scotland, they let you use your common sense in allowing "reasonable measures of privacy".

For centuries, the Right to Roam has been deliberately conflated with home invasion. This is so lacking in nuance that it's absurd. Tort law, which governs trespass, doesn't distinguish between climbing into someone's back garden and taking a woodland stroll in a 13,000-acre (5,300-ha) estate. Of course people have a right to privacy in their home, but when an estate extends over tens of thousands of acres, we have to ask: how much land does one person need?

*

Throughout our conversation, I've been secretly hoping that the farmer who owns this field will stagger over, hurling outrage. He doesn't, though. Instead, a heron graces the Avon, skimming the glinting surface before gliding off into the cerulean. Just another intruder, enjoying someone else's river.

The streets we live by fall away.
Even the asphalt is tired
of this going and coming to work,
the chatter in cars,
and passengers crying on bad days.

Trucks with frail drivers
carry dangerous loads. Have care,
these holes are not just holes
but a million years of history
opening up, all our beautiful failures
and gains. The earth is breathing
through the streets.

Rain falls.
The lamps of earth switch on.
The potholes are full
of light and stars, the moon's many faces.

Mice drink there in the streets.
The skunks of night drift by.
They swallow the moon.
When morning comes,
workers pass this way again,
cars with lovely merchandise. Drivers,
take care, a hundred suns look out of earth
beneath circling tires.

DISABILITY IS NATURAL
Syren Nagakyrie

Nature has always had an important place in my life, but, until my late twenties, I didn't feel like I belonged in the outdoor recreation community. My family wasn't particularly "outdoorsy"—we didn't camp, hike, or go on vacations. I had one disabled parent and another who worked full time (and is now disabled) who struggled to make ends meet, and I was a sick kid. I spent much of my childhood at the doctor, recovering from an illness or injury or trying to prevent one, so outdoor recreation just didn't seem like an option. But I did spend as much time as I could sitting outside, watching the birds and plants and insects, or gazing at the moon on humid Florida nights, when the daytime temperatures were too high to venture out in. I created stories from what I observed, imagining the lives of frogs and hawks and honeybees, which provided great comfort as a lonely child. I learned to recognize the incredible diversity in nature; everyone had their role and their own way of living. This instilled a great sense of appreciation and belonging within nature, even as I felt disconnected from much of the rest of society. But at the time, I didn't know there were other environments and experiences available to me, so I didn't know I was being excluded from anything.

I was in my early twenties when I started exploring outdoor recreation. My early experiences inspired me to learn more about the natural world, so I enrolled in a few environmental science and biology courses at community college. Those classes brought me out into the Florida waters and marshlands and gave me the opportunity to take my first real trip—a visit to the Grand Canyon and the American Southwest. While the unfamiliar landscapes were inspiring, unfortunately, the instructors and students were not. They had so little understanding or acceptance of my needs and limitations, and I didn't have the language at the time to explain it. I was ridiculed and told that I should stay behind if I couldn't participate like everyone else. So I leaned into my connection with nature and the sense of belonging it provided. While everyone else rushed from site to site, exploring caverns and kivas, rocky cliffs and petrified forests, I sat. I watched and listened with all of my senses, taking in my surroundings and truly noticing the place I was in. I paid attention to where it felt okay to be and where it didn't—where the land seemed to welcome my presence and where it did not. When I discussed the trip with classmates a few years later, it turned out I remembered much more of the experience and felt a stronger connection with the landscape than they did.

After graduating with an associate degree in the mid-2000s, I moved to western North Carolina, where the ancient Appalachian Mountains sparked a new-old longing in my heart. I was determined to enjoy the beauty of the place and all of the outdoor opportunities that were available. But I quickly realized people still did not understand disability and chronic illness and didn't know how to provide the support and information that I needed. Sure, I could call a park about wheelchair accessible trails, but that wasn't always helpful. To be honest, I wasn't even entirely sure what I needed, because I had not had the opportunity to try new things and figure out what I could do. Because of this lack of opportunity and exposure, I still did not have the language to explain my experience or talk about outdoor recreation.

This is one of the ways that lack of accessibility perpetuates the exclusion of people who are disabled. When someone does not have access to a space, they miss out on the experiences and opportunities for learning that others enjoy. This results in a lack of knowledge that others may consider "common sense," which is then judged by people who have had many more opportunities to learn. This cycle of exclusion—a disabled person is refused access, which leads to lack of opportunity for learning, which leads to feeling more unwelcome in a space, which means that disabled folks aren't present to advocate for access—is one of the reasons it is important for people who have access to a space to advocate for accessibility and inclusion for people with disabilities.

Eventually, I enrolled in another educational program, this time to study herbalism. It felt like a perfect match between my attention to the ways that humans interact with nature, my love of plants, my interest in getting to know my new home, and my experience as someone with chronic illness. That program changed my life in many ways: I learned tools to sustainably care for myself and the environment, honed my skills at paying attention to nature, and learned how to share all of it with others. But I also continued to encounter a lot of misunderstanding, prejudice, and assumptions about my health and well-being—what I can now call ableism—in the herbal community. Some people told me that if I wanted to get better, I just needed to try harder—that, if I took the right herbs and developed the right "healing practice," I would be cured! Of course, that is not the case. It does not matter how many herbs I take, how much I meditate, or how many cleanses I put my body through—I will still be disabled. For this reason, many disabled and chronically ill people push back against the concept of "healing." Nondisabled people often assume that we want to be healed, but that is based on the concept of disability as inherently bad, of illness as something shameful that must be eradicated. "Health" is considered the normal experience, but who decides what "healthy" means?

Concepts of health are rooted in ableism, which in simplest terms is defined as discrimination against and social prejudice toward anyone who is, or is perceived to be, disabled. But ableism goes much deeper than that—it is tightly woven into all forms of oppression. Ableism is ultimately used as a tool of white supremacy, upholding all other forms of oppression; in conjunction with racism, classism, heteropatriarchy, imperialism, and colonialism, ableism creates classes of people whose bodies are determined to be more or less worthy. These societally constructed ideas around normality, desirability, productivity, and value place expectations on all people. As Talila "TL" Lewis explains in the January 2021 Working Definition of Ableism, you do not have to be disabled to experience ableism; we are all judged according to our language, appearance, and ability to [re]produce, excel, and behave. This is why many people strive for unattainable concepts of perfection and why disability is so feared— people intuitively know that their value to society is highly dependent on being an acceptably healthy, nondisabled person.

Disability discourse argues that we are all valuable exactly as we are. Of course, if given the unlikely opportunity, many people may choose not to be sick or disabled—I'm definitely not arguing that living with a disability or illness is fun—but that doesn't mean that we need to be "healed" to be valuable. Naomi Ortiz, a disabled artist, poet, and author, prefers the term "mending" as opposed to "healing." Healing connotes some kind of final resolution, the achievement of a state of being that is deemed whole and perfect. But we are already whole and perfect exactly as we are. Besides, aren't we constantly changing anyway? "Mending" allows space for this constant change without expecting a final resolution and implies that this work cannot be done alone. Mending requires interconnectedness, a weaving together of different pieces to create a whole.

The herbal program I enrolled in was also my first introduction to group hikes, or "plant walks." What would have been my favorite part of the program became a source of frustration: I faced numerous barriers and issues with the way the hikes were organized. The instructors didn't provide information on the length, elevation, or difficulty of where we would be hiking, and it was generally assumed that being out in more remote and wild areas was preferable to foraging in urban areas. The pace was determined by how many plants we saw along the way and how long the instructor wanted to lecture in each place. Since I never knew what to expect or when to reserve my energy for a hike, I often found myself unable to go on these trips. The instructors assumed I just didn't want to participate and questioned my dedication to the program. I couldn't respond since I didn't yet know how to advocate for myself.

But the hikes that I could go on were incredibly influential. It was so powerful to learn more about the ways each plant evolved to thrive in their place and the role their adaptation plays in the ecosystem. I noticed that the most unique plants often played vital roles in the ecosystem and had the rarest medicinal qualities. Other plants and animals depended on these plants for survival: if the plant disappeared, everyone else would be negatively impacted as well. Maybe if it was true for the plants, it could be true for people, too. Maybe I still had a unique and important place in the world, even with my unusual needs.

Interconnectedness is the central tenet of the natural world. No single animal or plant can survive on its own, and an ecosystem is never the same if you remove one of its members. We notice this in the decaying trees that are home to numerous animals, the mycelial networks that carry messages, and the first plants to regrow after a wildfire, which provide a source of food and return nutrients to the soil. Humans also depend on our more-than-human kin; we cannot survive without the bees that pollinate our food, the plants that provide oxygen, the oceans that stabilize our climate.

Interconnectedness is also a key to resilience. Disabled folks know this way of existing well—our lives are dependent on our connections with friends, family, caretakers, medical providers, and more. But this is true for all humans. We are all dependent on others for our survival; we wouldn't last very long without the people who grow food, make clothes, create medicines, or haul away the trash. Science is finally recognizing what so many marginalized people already know—that resilience is strongly associated with interpersonal relationships and interactions between social, economic, and ecological systems. It is not solely an individual trait. The adaptive ability of plants and animals does not exist independent of one another or their environment, and neither does humans'. The disability community mirrors this beautifully. It requires incredible creativity and adaptivity to exist as a disabled person in this world, and the community relies on each other for that knowledge. This brilliance has filtered out to affect much of daily life, and many of the things that nondisabled people use to make life a little easier come from adaptations that disabled people made.

My time in the Appalachians deepened my connection with nature and expanded my interest in outdoor recreation. I have moved often and have had the privilege of living in places with world-renowned outdoor recreation opportunities. Slowly, with much trial and error and the confidence that comes with age, I taught myself what I needed to know to enjoy the outdoors on my terms. I learned what kind of terrain I felt most comfortable on, the tools I needed to be safe, how to pack supplies, and when to plan for breaks. I eventually came to accept that I will probably never be able to do something like thru-hike a continental trail or climb a mountain, but that just makes what I can do even more meaningful. I have to focus on the quality of an experience rather than the quantity—instead of racing up a trail to a final destination, I move much more slowly and take the time to notice everything around me. Being more mindful in my approach to outdoor recreation gives me the opportunity to connect more meaningfully to a place, and I learn so much about myself in the process. Loving these places as they are has taught me how to love myself for all that I am. This love and sense of belonging is so critical to my sense of well-being. It gives me something to lean into during difficult times. Nature can hold my pain and sorrow and elation and joy when I can't.

Even as I came to accept my "limitations" (which don't

feel limiting at all) and learned how to hike as a disabled and chronically ill person, I continued to encounter barriers to hiking. Hiking gear, especially adaptive equipment, is incredibly expensive. Trails have historically not been designed for users with a variety of abilities, and the passage of the Americans with Disabilities Act did little to change that. It was impossible to find trail information that took into consideration a variety of users—most hiking guides assume that hikers are stereotypically fit, nondisabled people. It takes an incredibly long time for me to research, select, and prepare for a day hike, and I still encounter dangerous situations. For example, a few years ago I was planning a hike on a trail system in Olympic National Park, a remote area in north-west Washington State. I was already familiar with the area and previously hiked several segments of the trail system. I decided to try a different portion of the trail system and did my usual research to determine the trail conditions, elevation, surface, and any obstacles. Satisfied that it wouldn't be any more difficult than the rest of the trail, I started out only to immediately encounter several dangerous obstacles, including steep stairs, sharp drop-offs, and loose rocks. I couldn't turn back on the trail, so I continued on, hoping it would get easier. It did not. By the time I finished, I was exhausted, in pain, and dangerously close to passing out. This grueling and treacherous encounter inspired me to create my organization Disabled Hikers, to improve equity and access in the outdoors, help provide better information, and build community so that other disabled people can connect to nature and enjoy the great outdoors, without fear or danger.

As I hiked in urban and rural areas, I started to notice a perceived separation between the "natural environment" and the "built environment." When I hike in remote places, people are more likely to call me a "real hiker" who is out "braving the wild." When I share about hiking in urban parks, suddenly I'm not hiking at all—I am taking a walk in the city, removed from nature and not having a real "outdoor experience." Yet it is vital that we come to see urban environments—where the majority of humans reside, and essential hubs for people who depend on support networks of all kinds—as viable places for meaningful encounters with nature. We cannot continue to view "urban" and "wild" or "built" and "natural" as a binary, with wild spaces designated as pristine landscapes reserved for the few, while urban spaces are left to languish without access to green spaces. Wild and pristine spaces that are unimpacted by humans are often held up as the only way for nature to exist in perfection. But that has never been true—humans have always interacted with nature. It is a lie designed to ignore the history of the creation of those spaces; Indigenous peoples have lived on, worked with, and loved the land since time immemorial. The perceived separation between the natural and the built, the wild and the urban, leans on ideas of what is normal and beautiful and what is not. These same ideas are present in ableism and influence perceptions of disability.

Assumptions about the validity of built environments also impacts disabled people who want to enjoy the outdoors. I often get sarcastic comments from people who think that because I advocate for outdoor accessibility I just want to pave over the wilderness (I don't). But why is hiking in parks that have designated trail systems and more amenities less valid than backpacking the wilderness? Why are paved trails less important than rugged ones? Many disabled folks need built elements to be able to access the outdoors: well-designed trails; adaptive equipment; access to food, water, and toilets; benches and picnic tables; informational signage; cell phone service, and nearby medical facilities. These elements are all looked down on by the more stereotypical outdoorsy types. But that is what allows many people with disabilities to enjoy outdoor recreation. I often default to urban parks because they require less planning and it is less likely that the trails will be dangerous for me.

But urban areas aren't always accessible either. Across the US, 100 million American urbanites don't have any green space within at least a "10-minute" walk (meaning half a mile/0.8km) from home. This time, set by averaging nondisabled people's walking speeds, takes considerably longer for many disabled people and is a distance too far for many to comfortably make. There are more barriers to access green space for people with disabilities; green spaces are often not designed with accessibility in mind, and infrastructure is often in need of repair. A green space that is located on a city block without curb cuts, smooth sidewalks, or safe intersections, will not be accessible to many disabled people. We must advocate for urban green spaces that are welcoming and accessible for all, invest in infrastructure improvements, and create public transit options that bring green spaces to a disabled person's doorstep. But for some disabled and chronically ill folks, being outdoors can never be safe or accessible—there may be a number of reasons for this; a couple of examples include severe allergies, photosensitivity, or a very narrow window of temperatures that are safe for them to be outside. This does not mean they are disconnected from nature; they have as much of a right to nature as anyone else.

If the outdoors isn't safe or accessible, there are still many ways you can remind yourself of your connection to nature. Some of my favorites include caring for a houseplant or a pet, watching nature documentaries, and listening for birds outside the window. One year, as I was immobilized and recovering from surgery, I made a practice of noticing how the light changed through my bedroom window every day and kept notes in my journal. This practice grounded me into something other than the pain I felt; it reminded me that I was a part of something bigger, and that all of nature changes and cycles, myself included.

Disability is a natural and normal way to be embodied. Disabled people have always existed. Indeed, as humans age, most of us become disabled in some way. It is beyond time for disability to be recognized as the natural part of human experience that it is. It is not separate from nature, not separate from humanity, not better or worse than any other way to experience life. Through recognizing the interconnectedness of nature and the importance of all beings in the ecosystems, we may come to recognize the rights of all humans as well. We all belong to the Earth.

SHE'S THE CITY
Erin Rizzato Devlin

She hums and she sways, opens
her arms and offers her chest: it
is rash and carmine
as the grapes of angst that sprawl
in front of an unsought
traffic light or behind a bus,
losing sympathy in its haste.

A lone distillery sends its
fumes as offers to the sky,
reaching to the invisible gods
of man-made light,
pouring its desolate tendrils
of smoke and narcotic
as prayers upon the ungrateful
sons of the city.

The coil of sound, protesting
sirens and drills, races
into the shell of their ear,
survives as the eternal hum
of a great insect that never
allows for sleep; it stays
awake as a mother
taking care of her children.

It speaks of the carapace of
authority winding its spiral
around earthy nests of exclusion,
as cruel asphalt melts the roots
of being, killing every trace
of instinct, and breeds the
human silence.

She hums and she sways, locked
in a labyrinth of stone: the soul
of the city bears its wings
as sore scars of necessity.
She houses a chaotic procession
of life, scattered within the
spaces of concrete and feeling,
where the kindness
and the sunlight shine brighter
than they must.

CHANGE

CHANGE
Ellen Miles

"We've already lost too many trees, houses and people ... your community – you owe something to it."
Hattie Carthan (c.1968)

"If we do not do the impossible, we shall be faced with the unthinkable."
Murray Bookchin, *The Ecology of Freedom* (1982)

Change is in the air, hovering like a kestrel. It's time to strike. We must recognize and protect contact with nature as a universal right.

You might ask, "If forecasts are correct, and humanity's future is urban, is this realistic? Is it even possible?" Such doubts arise from the misconception that "urban" is the antithesis of "nature". Our zeitgeist pits these two concepts against one another, as if locked in a zero-sum game. In cinematic futures, one emerges as victor, the other vanquished; we're either treated to smoggy, post-nature cityscapes, or abandoned buildings, ravaged by overgrown plants. But, like these sci-fi dystopias, the urban–nature dichotomy is fictitious. The idea that urbanization entails ecocide is only a result of how it has worked to date – it is not an inevitability. As the two apocalyptic extremes illustrate, securing a viable future for mankind means finding ways for cities and nature to co-exist.

This isn't impossible, or even difficult. Analogies to the city are readily found in nature, from anthills to "Octlantis", and solarpunk visions of the future are becoming increasingly common. The best folding together of the imagined urban–nature spectrum that I've seen (and I'm as surprised about this as you are) is in the action-comedy *Free Guy* (2021). In the film's resolution, two game worlds – the gritty, *Grand Theft Auto*-inspired "Free City", and the wild, utopian landscape of "Life Itself" – combine to create "Free Life", a thriving biophilic metropolis. If Shawn Levy can see that "urban" and "nature" aren't opposites, surely policy-makers, developers and urban planners can too? Guerrilla geographer Dan Raven-Ellison saw it, and decided to make London the world's first National Park City. His essay sets out a framework for bringing National Park thinking to the world's cities (page 196).

Urban densification continues to be necessary to support growing populations and provide affordable housing close to communities and economic opportunities. But city governors are starting to innovate, finding ways to transform grey into green while accommodating other social and infrastructural needs. In Greece, Athens has begun installing "pocket parks", under a hectare (2½ acres) in size, across the city. In Colombia, Medellín has created 30 "green corridors", using 8,300 trees and 350,000 shrubs, in the inner-city's most nature-deprived areas. In Catalonia, Barcelona's 500 proposed "superblocks" (pedestrianized grids that only allow cars around the perimeter) could prevent 667 pollution-, stress- and heat-related deaths a year.

Existing street furniture can be used as a foundation for space-thrifty greening. In Leicester, England – where just 15 per cent of people currently live within the recommended 300m (330 yards) of green space – city authorities are transforming bus shelters into Bee Bus Stops by covering the roofs in pollinator-friendly plant life. Down in London, a 2021 pilot turned lamp posts into "living pillars" by adding vertical gardens, rigged with solar-powered irrigation systems, onto the poles.

Green walls are another ingenious solution to limited space. Counterintuitively, building up can actually provide even *more* room for nature than leaving land undeveloped. Here's the maths: if you take a perfectly square patch of land, and construct a cubic building on top of it, you end up with five times the original surface area. German engineer Rudi Scheuermann proposes a time- and cost-efficient way to cover these surfaces with plants: just roughen the surfaces and, over time, perfectly adapted species will naturally settle there and flourish, as they do on cliffs.

Ample opportunities for greening can also be found in abandoned urban land. About 17 per cent of land in large US cities lies vacant or abandoned – nearly one-sixth of each city's territory. Imagine the improvements to health, happiness and social harmony if all those spaces were transformed into green oases.

In some cases, we don't have to retrofit greenery, but can integrate nature as critical infrastructure from the outset. This is true in the context of urban sprawl, but also entirely new cities. More than 120 new metropolises are currently being built, in 40 nations around the world, including China, Nigeria and India. "We're in the midst of new cities fever," says Professor Sarah Moser, head of the new cities lab at McGill University. While starting a city from scratch poses many ecological dangers, it also provides opportunities for biophilic, community-centred architecture and urban planning.

The city of Putrajaya, Malaysia, was created in the mid-1990s to be an "intelligent garden city", with over a third of its land reserved for green spaces. Now fully up and running, Putrajaya is praised for its focus on community and environment. In the proposed "Forest City" in Liuzhou, China, every house, office, hospital, school and shop will be covered in plants of various shapes and sizes. Outnumbering its 30,000 residents, the city will also be home to 40,000 trees and over 1 million plants.

For governments and local authorities, investing in urban greening is a no-brainer. Not only is it the ethical thing to do but (to speak their language) it's financially sound. Every dollar spent on a community tree returns two to five times that investment, in benefits from cleaner air, cooler streets and flood control. UK charity Fields in Trust discovered that parks and green spaces save the NHS at least £111 million a year through reduced GP visits alone. They concluded, "any decision by a public body to remove a park or green space is completely short-sighted – and will in fact likely cost more money than is saved."

*

I'm often asked to define a minimum standard for satisfying the right to nature – the quantity, quality and proximity of green space required to meet this right. For this, I defer to Professor Cecil Konijnendijk of the Nature Based Solutions Institute, who has studied and analyzed huge volumes of data to arrive at such a standard. His principle, the 3-30-300 rule, states that everyone should be able to see three trees from their home, live in a neighbourhood with at least 30 per cent green cover, and be no more than 300m (330 yards) from the nearest green space. "At the neighbourhood level," Konijnendijk tells me, "30 per cent should be a minimum. In places where it's difficult for trees to grow and thrive (such as in arid climates) the target should be 30 per cent vegetation."

Connecting people to nature is not just about availability, but active inclusion and education. As well as funding their own ideas and interventions, those in power must invest in community-led greening initiatives, to bring people into the process and foster ownership and understanding. Journalist Sharlene Gandhi makes a compelling case for this idea, known as "placemaking", in her essay (page 232).

It's our right not only to have nature in our eyeline, but to understand what we are looking at. The call for educators to bring nature into children's lives is a major refrain throughout this chapter. In her column, writer Caitlin Moran once quipped, "Could my kid get a '9' [the highest GCSE exam grade] in bees? No, so bees are dead to me." A joke, but there's a serious message in there: our education system's failure to educate children about nature is resulting in a dangerous apathy. Bees really are dying.

Education can also help people to notice the abnormality of our situation. Psychologist Peter Kahn has highlighted the fact every new generation sees the environment they're born into – no matter how digital, urban or polluted – as what's "normal". "There's a shifting baseline of what we consider the environment, and as that baseline becomes impoverished, we don't even see it," he says. This phenomenon, which Khan calls "environmental generational amnesia", is preventing people from feeling incensed, a prerequisite for action. Among few examples of countermeasures, Sweden's "Factfulness" movement teaches children how to ask critical questions about the world around them.

We need to educate and equip people to take ownership of natural spaces. Parisians, for instance, can get a *permis de végétaliser* – a "permit to plant" anywhere in the city. In the UK, social enterprise Incredible Edible seeks to "build a bridge of positive actions, knowledge, and respect for nature through the Trojan horse of food; allowing us all to be advocates for a kinder prosperity where everyone, whatever their circumstances, can help nurture their community and benefit from being a part of a thriving and resilient natural world." For this book, rebel gardeners Ron Finley and Tayshan Hayden-Smith met to discuss how they're cultivating social justice through community gardening (page 212).

Helping everyone in society to meaningfully engage with nature won't just help them, it'll help the environment too. In our essay, climate researcher Clover Hogan and I explain how connection to nature is at the root of solving the climate crisis (page 258).

*

What can we each do, as individuals, to bring more nature to our neighbourhoods? If you have outside space, you can start at home. Siân Moxon, founder of project Rewild My Street, offers some simple, low-cost ideas for bringing nature into a small urban space (page 193).

Join me in becoming a "guerrilla gardener", planting in public places, with purpose. Take inspiration from the likes of Hattie Carthan, who founded the Bedford-Stuyvesant Neighborhood Tree Corps to fight back against the impacts of redlining in Brooklyn, or Liz Christy, leader of the Green Guerrillas, who set up New York City's first community garden.

Or, today, from Ron and Tayshan, who took urban greening into their own hands when their local authorities failed to. If you're not sure where to start, make some seed bombs using artist Ayesha Tan-Jones's recipe (page 226). They're potential-packed balls of seeds, clay and compost that you can pop in a pocket and leave on bare soil, to grow on the go.

Protest! In Sheffield, UK – a city in which just one-third of residents live within 300m (330 yards) of green space – local authorities planned to fell half its urban trees, in a bid to chop maintenance costs (a pattern of short-sighted behaviour sadly common across austerity-era Britain). Through peaceful direct action – standing under the condemned trees – Sheffield Tree Action Groups successfully saved thousands of healthy, mature trees from the chainsaw. Look out for organizations and protest camps (like the ones established in England's woodlands along the HS2 rail line) to join, to defend our rights and the rights of nature. From home, you can sign petitions, share information and write to those in power, calling for change. For an activist's guide on how to become one, look no further than climate activist Noga Levy-Rapoport's sharp tutorial (page 243).

*

Ancient Athenians had to swear an oath to leave the city greater than they found it. If each of us channelled that spirit, and did one thing to make our neighbourhoods greener, imagine what the world could look like in ten years' time. The authors of this chapter stand in fierce agreement: a nature-filled future is not only necessary, but possible – and each of us has the power to bring it about. Let's make Earth green again.

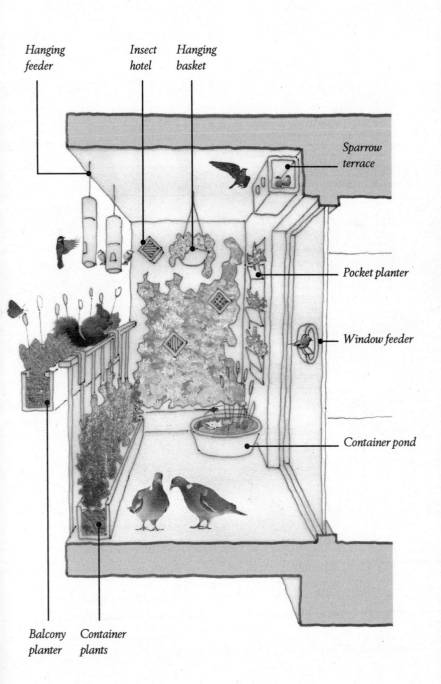

Hanging feeder

Insect hotel

Hanging basket

Sparrow terrace

Pocket planter

Window feeder

Container pond

Balcony planter

Container plants

FROM *ON LOVE AND BARLEY - HAIKU OF BASHO*

Translation by Lucien Stryk

WHAT IF YOUR CITY WAS A NATIONAL PARK?
Daniel Raven-Ellison

National Parks are amazing. They are simply one of humanity's best ideas. Without them, the ecological, climate and health crises would be far deeper, more widespread and more catastrophic than the ones we find ourselves facing today. In many cases, they have been the last line of defence against a tide of systematic violence inflicted by people against the rest of nature. At the heart of National Parks is a simple idea: we can designate and protect special places where people can have a better relationship with nature. National Parks are often rich cultural and spiritual places that are home to not only wildlife, but human communities too – and not least First Nations and Indigenous peoples who cared for nature in these places long before the idea of National Parks was ever invented. They are one of the few places where people have a right to nature and nature has a right to life – on the one hand, nature is better protected; on the other, people are able to experience, enjoy and benefit from it.

In 2013, to celebrate National Geographic's 125th anniversary, I visited all 15 of the United Kingdom's National Parks with my 10-year-old son. Our micro-adventures took us cliff climbing in Pembrokeshire, hiking in Loch Lomond and the Trossachs, and rock-pooling on the edge of Exmoor. This special journey created opportunities for my son and I to connect with each other, nature and the land. I too was privileged to grow up with adventurous parents. My father was in the military and we would regularly be posted to different countries around the world, meaning my brothers and I got to discover National Parks in Europe, Africa and the Americas. These experiences rooted, nourished and grew the love I have for nature today.

While travelling with my son and looking back at my own childhood experiences, I began to notice that something was missing from the world's family of National Parks. From the barren deserts of Death Valley, to the peat bogs of the Cairngorms, to the lush rainforest of Belize, every major kind of internationally recognized habitat and landscape is represented in the family of National Parks, apart from one: cities.

Despite all its remarkable benefits, nature has all too often – intentionally and unintentionally – been designed out of cities. We've learnt that city scenery means glass, tarmac, brick, concrete, plastic and metal. As a result, this idea of an urban area being a National Park may sound ridiculous to many people. After all, National Parks are the direct opposite of urban areas and the antithesis of cities, right? But the traditional principle that urban habitats and landscapes should be excluded from the world's family of National Parks didn't make sense to me, for three key reasons.

First, I don't believe that urban wildlife is worth less than rural wildlife. Urban nature should not be excluded from the National Park idea on the grounds that proximity to people and buildings somehow reduces its value. The red foxes and peregrine falcons in London – living among the city's glass canyons and preying on rats and parakeets – are just as beautiful, important and valuable as those that live in more rural and remote locations. As it happens, there are more breeding peregrine falcons in London than either Yosemite or the Peak District National Parks. The world's fastest animal loves the capital's cliff-like landmarks, including Tate Modern and the Houses of Parliament.

Second, it's important that we recognize urban areas as valuable habitats and landscapes. Just as deserts are different from rainforests, cities are different from other habitats – but they are no less significant. Indeed, given the rapid trend towards urbanization, we should be doing everything we can to make cities more habitable. It's estimated by Greenspace Information for Greater London (GiGL) that London's *Homo sapiens* are just one of 15,000 species in the city, and that our number is nearly matched by the capital's population of trees. According to one United Nations definition, London is, in fact, a forest because it has so many trees. While most Londoners are relatively privileged to have inherited such a green city from their predecessors, many of the world's fastest growing urban areas are designing nature out. Just as much of the world needs protection from humanity's insatiable appetite, it's also true that much of humanity – isolated in hostile urban environments – needs protection from a severe lack of nature. The protection these people and this nature requires cannot be served by classic National Park-style boundaries; a more creative and informal approach is required.

Third, National Parks are not just about protecting nature. They are also about creating places where people can spend time enjoying themselves, learning, healing and connecting. I love hiking across a savanna, moor or glacier, but I love exploring cities too. With their patchworks and mosaics of houses, gardens, streets, parks, peoples, cultures and ecologies, urban landscapes are often more diverse than rural ones. The fact that so many people and communities live in these areas makes urban habitats more inclusive and accessible than remote rural environments, meaning it's even more important that we protect, create and improve nature in these spaces.

Pragmatically, there are other good reasons to include urban areas in the family of National Parks. People in urban areas – who have the advantages of numbers, proximity and facilities – have extraordinary collective power to influence nature. From pollinator-friendly window boxes, to larger-scale community projects that make streets amazingly more green, urbanites often have the power (and the right) to create space for nature where they live. Not only that, through what we consume, who we invest in and how we vote, the urban majority shape and influence what nature looks like around the world.

What Makes a City a National Park City?

So, how does a city qualify as a "National Park City"? A National Park City is a place, a vision and a city-wide community that is acting together to make life better for people, wildlife and nature. A defining feature is the widespread commitment to act so people, culture and places work together to provide a better foundation for all forms of life. While London pioneered the National Park City idea, future National Park Cities must meet, or be making progress against, 23 different criteria to gain the status. These range from being a suitable place, and being visionary and inclusive, to having people, cultures and policies that can bring the National Park City to life.

Over time, I came to realize that the issue was not so much that cities are missing from National Parks – it is that National Park thinking is missing from cities. The National Park City idea set out to change this.

The National Park City idea starts with acknowledging the unique and significant challenges that cities and their inhabitants face. Just like rural National Parks need protection from various threats, city-dwellers (no matter how many legs they have) need protection from threats too. The threats Londoners face include: inequalities in life expectancy; stress, anxiety and depression; non-communicable diseases; air pollution, land pollution and water pollution; noise; flooding; extreme temperatures; over-development; crime; and species loss. This is the case not just within the city, but all the places that their voting, consuming and decision-making powers influence around the world. Just think of all those forest habitats that have been destroyed to feed urban appetites. All of these challenges can be alleviated or even resolved by people having a better relationship with the rest of nature. While recognizing this, the idea to make London a National Park City was also about realizing something important: many of the solutions to these problems already exist in the city.

You can see the impact and legacy of these solutions by simply exploring London on foot, or even looking at it on Google Maps. According to GiGL, nearly 50 per cent of the capital is green and blue; a third is made up of open space natural habitats; and a quarter is covered by the city's 3.8 million private gardens. There are also 1,602 designated Sites of Importance for Nature Conservation (SINCs), which cover 19 per cent of the capital, 37 Sites of Special Interest, 144 Local Nature Reserves, two Ramsar wetlands sites, three National Nature Reserves (including Richmond Park); 2,522 acres (1,020 ha) of allotments, community gardens and city farms, created and maintained by local residents; and Epping Forest, a great tongue of woodland extending into the city from the north-east, London's largest public open space, which still exists thanks to the work of Victorian activist Octavia Hill.

Since 1800, London's population has grown from 1 million to nearly 9 million people. Despite that growth (and the widespread industrial and development-led destruction of nature), the city and its residents have a long history of protecting and creating public green spaces. This includes both bottom-up, grassroots action – there are hundreds of thousands (if not millions) of people making their part of the city greener and wilder – to top-down policies, such as the greenbelt that restricts London from sprawling into the surrounding countryside. While top down and bottom up are often pitted against each other, the reality is both more simple and more complex. Policy-making institutions are driven by people and those people, in my experience, often want greener, healthier and wilder cities too. The National Park City idea is also about celebrating everything that has been done – and continues to be done – to make the city as green, wild and life-filled as it is today.

Around the world, you'll find an abundance of projects and policies that are focussed on making cities greener, healthier and wilder: Bogotá started closing its roads to cars every Sunday – now a quarter of the city's population turn out to walk, run, roll, cycle or hang out on the streets; Barcelona has introduced "superblocks", car-free areas that reduce traffic and allow for greater planting, making the city cleaner, cooler and even more beautiful; Singapore, the "City in a Garden", has a ferociously biophilic design.

The campaign to make London a National Park City started by simply asking the question, "What if London was a National Park City?" How might it change things in the future? How might it benefit people and places? How could it influence health, culture, art, nature, music, education, economics, relationships, hopes, dreams and futures? But that initial question led to more "what ifs" ...

- What if everybody could lose themselves in nature without leaving the city?
- What if all new buildings were designed for wildlife as well as people?
- What if we thought more about those who will be living in the city seven generations from now, whatever their species?

Asking the question "What if?" is about imagination. While imagination and vision is important, it is not enough on its own to bring about significant change. That's why, over time, the mantra of the campaign to make London a National Park City evolved into not just asking "What if?" but following that up with "Why not?" The "Why not?" is about power, culture, emotion and politics. It's a question that is about delivery catching up with hopes and dreams. I always write this with an interrobang. One of my favourite punctuation marks, it's designed to communicate the end of an exclamatory rhetorical question.

- What if streets were ten times greener? Why not?
- What if schools did more learning about, in and with nature? Why not?
- What if people had a right to nature? Why not?

Over years, and in some cases generations, the National Park City movement wants to build a critical mass of people, groups and organizations that move from simply asking "What if?" to daring to ask "Why not?" This process is not about being combative, but about challenging structures and systems that block those dreams.

Let's take schools and education as an example. Spending time being active and playful in nature can improve children's mental and physical health, reduce unhelpful behaviours, support creativity and relationship skills and, in the right settings, increase the likelihood of them caring for wildlife and the environment. Despite all these benefits, too many schools around the world do not provide sufficient opportunities for children to connect with nature. In my mind, this is a form of neglect, and something that could be rectified if schools had policies that recognized nature as a human right.

At one point in history, it was very normal for teachers to hit children. Sometimes this was done as a form of punishment, at other times it was simply an outlet for the teacher's anger. Over many decades, children, teachers and parents would ask themselves, "What if teachers didn't systemically abuse children in schools?" At a critical tipping point, when enough people asked "Why not?" and made the argument for its prohibition, corporal punishment was eventually banned in British state schools in 1986. What it took was enough dreamers to prompt enough people to ask the questions and challenge the systems to bring about the change.

Across London, there is a thriving community of teachers, forest school leaders, play workers, fieldwork instructors and other educationalists, who are doing outstanding work on a daily basis to connect children to nature. The problem in London is that far more of that good energy is needed, and it needs to be spread more equitably between the city's children and schools.

In the context of London being a National Park City, the fact that the majority of children are not sufficiently being taught about, in, or with nature feels like an obvious incongruence. After all, surely those opportunities and freedoms would be a central part of living in a National Park City? So, if they're not happening, why aren't they happening? Why not? To flip to a positive, active tone, it's about asking: "How can we?" How can we make sure that every child benefits from exploring, playing and learning in nature every day?

Greening from the Ground Up

Making the case that nature is a human right is a powerful argument that fits perfectly with the National Park City vision. If nature is a human right, then how can we ensure that high-quality and thriving nature is everywhere, so that everyone has contact with it every day? Securing our right to nature in a city is about policy, opportunity, availability and demand. We need initiatives that protect and deliver the availability of more high-quality nature, we need opportunities for people to sensitively experience that nature, we need people to demand and take up those opportunities, and we need family, institutional and governmental policies that create both that opportunity, delivery and demand. Looking around, there are plenty of great examples of things we can do to secure these.

Led by Friends of the Earth, in 2019 I helped set up an initiative called 10x Greener, with the aim to empower residents to make their neighbourhoods intensely greener – and keep them that way. We trialled the idea on a street in Hackney, East London. The diverse communities were already bubbling with inspiring activity, including community group Daubeney Fields Forever, which organizes local community gardens, and Eco-Active, a social enterprise that helps children connect to nature. Thanks to years of sustained effort by the brilliant gardener John Little, the area is also home to a local housing estate that is now so abundant with edible plants and beautiful flowers – in particular poppies – that it has become known locally as the Poppy Estate.

The project brought together all this existing community energy and added something extra: a crowdfunded "postcode gardener", called Kate Poland. Working on private, rented and social housing across terraced, low-rise and high-rise levels, Kate works across the postcode, helping people to make their gardens – front, back and shared – greener and wilder. She does this by gardening herself, passing on skills and materials, and working with the local groups. One of the insights for the initiative was that nature doesn't care who owns land, so what if there was someone who was funded to think about making the whole community greener and wilder?

The result has been people depaving their front gardens and replacing concrete with plants; wildlife street art, mini wildlife corridors, and wooden street planters; workshops to create bug hotels and bee-friendly window boxes; parents encouraging the local school to become greener; and the growth of a WhatsApp group that residents use to share ideas, seeds, tools, projects and support. As well as making the street greener and more supportive of people and ecology, the 10x Greener initiative has proven to be an important conduit for friendships, relationships and community that may not otherwise have existed.

The focus of activity led to additional investment by the local council: both by physically making the streets greener (through depaving and planting) but also through policy. In response to demand from local residents, the council is trialling a glyphosate-free area, which means that they have stopped spraying herbicides, weed-killing chemicals, on wildflowers that grow in pavements and other places where they've historically been unwanted. As well as benefiting the plants and improving air quality, this move will boost both the biodiversity and bio-abundance of local wildlife. For example, with insect-eating "Cockney Sparrows" in decline and sparrow hawks nearby, the decision could have a knock-on effect leading to a healthier population of the hawks, sparrows and insects.

10x Greener is an example of just one small greening initiative among many others – but it is unusual. Not many streets have layers of individuals and groups who are all focussed on the same purpose and are supported by a professional to help catalyze and spread good practices and ideas. What if every street in every city had a postcode gardener? What if every street, block and neighbourhood in every city wanted to be ten times greener?

How to Make Your City a National Park City

From conception, the campaign for London to be recognized as a National Park City lasted six years. Thousands of people got involved – attending events, joining workshops, responding to consultations, supporting crowdfunding campaigns, recruiting the support of over 1,000 local politicians, posting on social media, teaching sessions, creating news stories and building awareness. The challenge was to grow enough support for the idea that we could turn it into a reality. This culminated on 22 July 2019, when the London National Park City was launched with the help of a major festival that was funded by the Mayor of London, Sadiq Khan.

Led by the National Park City Foundation, a charity set up to help make National Park Cities a success, the London National Park City is doing a number of things to reframe the city, raise expectations and help good ideas and practices to spread more rapidly and equitably across the city. These have included collaborations to organize the festival, cross-sector gatherings, field trips to see exemplary projects, city-wide networks of groups, organizations and schools, alternative maps, and persuading the Mayor of London to support the initiative.

Inspired by Park Rangers of National Parks worldwide, we also have our own National Park City Rangers. While some of these volunteers are traditional rangers, with expertise in nature conservation, others are artists, makers, designers and influencers with skills that inspire and support people to help make London greener, healthier and wilder in new, creative ways. As I write, there are just over 100 National Park City Rangers in London, but the ambition is for there to be more than 2,000 across the city. What if your town or city had 100, 200 or 2,000 volunteer rangers, all working to increase the availability of nature and people's respectful access to it?

There are over 4,000 National Parks in the world, sharing expertise, science, knowledge, understanding, best practices, wisdom and a common purpose. At the same time there are over 10,000 cities that are collectively home to most of the world's population. What if, inspired by and learning from the international family of National Parks, there was a similar family of National Park Cities, securing people's right to nature in them?

While London is the world's first National Park City, lots of people are now working towards making their cities National Park Cities, including people in Berlin, Tokyo, Glasgow, Cardiff, Cape Town, Galway, Adelaide, Canberra, Auckland, Calgary, Breda, Louisville, Sacramento and more. Learning from one another, each campaign is following a journey of ten steps to become a National Park City. These steps are published in the *National Park City Journey Book* – a short guide to transforming your city into a National Park City. Steps include signing up to a unifying Universal Charter for National Park Cities, and demonstrating you have the right level of support, capacity and vision. While all efforts are about bringing people together, whatever their interest and background, some of the campaigns are being led by regional governments. Others, like London, are being spearheaded by grassroots campaigns by teachers, artists, health experts, sports leaders and environmentalists.

What if your city was a National Park City? What if *you* made your city a National Park City?

Why not?

SELF-PORTRAIT WITH A SWARM OF BEES

Jan Wagner

Translation by Iain Galbraith

a moment ago i wore at best a fuzz
around my chin and lips; but now my beard
is growing and seething i might even pass
for magdalena: all my face hirsute

with bees. how they come buzzing from every side,
and, ounce by ounce, how a person's being
slowly but steadily gains in weight and spread
to become the stone-still centre of song ...

my arms outstretched i bear a resemblance
to some ancient knight whom bustling varlets help
to fit his suit of armour, piece by piece –
first the helmet, then the harness, arms, legs, nape,

until he can hardly move – who does not tread,
just stands there gleaming, with barely a hint
of wind behind the lustre, lingering breath,
and only vanishing becomes distinct.

RESISTANCE IS FERTILE
Ron Finley and Tayshan Hayden-Smith in conversation

In 2010, Los Angeles fashion designer Ron Finley set out to fix two problems in his South-Central neighborhood: the lack of fresh food (he had to drive 45 minutes to get an organic tomato) and the neglected soil verges along the streets. After planting fresh herbs, fruit, and vegetables on his parkway, Ron was written up for "gardening without a permit" by the city's authorities. He fought back, and won. He's now known as the "Gangsta Gardener" and teaches communities how to transform food deserts into food sanctuaries.

Football (soccer) player Tayshan Hayden-Smith was born and raised in North Kensington's Lancaster West council estate. As a teenager, his coach nicknamed him the "English Neymar," but becoming a dad at 17, losing his mother, and the tragic Grenfell disaster of 2017, led him toward another, unexpected goal: empowering communities through gardening. After bringing residents together to co-create a peace garden, on their own terms, Tayshan has a new nickname: the Grenfell Guerrilla Gardener. He now runs a nonprofit, Grow2Know, helping young Londoners learn, grow, and heal through gardening.

In 2021, the two green-thumbed rebels met over video call to discuss how gardening can provide power and freedom to the communities that society is failing.

*

RON Why do I have to be first ... because I'm Black? I'm kidding! Look, I do gangsta gardening, because gardening is gangsta. I want to change what people consider as being badass as being dope. To change the whole vernacular of what a gangsta is—a gangsta protects, a gangsta provides, a gangsta understands the intrinsic contents of the soil and what soil represents to everybody around the world. And we're going against some true gangsters—politicians and corporations—who really don't want this to happen, because it's taking money out of their pockets. That's why this is gangsta. Because it's dangerous.

TAYSHAN I started off, similarly to you, Ron, going against what the "powers that be" would want and taking back our spaces without permission, because why do we need to ask permission if it's already land that's meant for us? Now that I've explored a few things, had a few conversations, I'm really passionate about placemaking, putting community at the forefront of urban design decisions. The typical "consultation" from the local authority is them putting out something really shabby, really half-hearted, and going, "Oh, no one really was interested, so we're going to go ahead anyways." Things are being imposed on us because of agendas that are beyond our control. We should be round the table, influencing and dictating what these spaces look like. That's how we revolutionize the way that we engage with our spaces, because at the moment it's like being done *to* us rather than done *with* us.

RON Yeah. It's real simple: if you're not at the table, you're on the menu. We've been on the menu for far too long. We've got to get to the point where people have a hand in what they're being served, rather than, "You people need this." I asked a group of mayors, "Why are underserved communities underserved?" They tried, "Oh, you know, that's a long answer and it's hard ..." and I said, actually, it's not hard and it's not long and it's not complicated. Underserved communities are underserved because you don't fucking serve them.

TAYSHAN One hundred per cent. And to add to that, the language they use is completely alien as well. And that's not by accident. These things are not by accident. Experiencing Grenfell opened my eyes to politics, but you go into these meetings, into these spaces, and they speak in a language that makes no sense to someone who has grown up in an environment like me. We've got to normalize these conversations and, like you say, make it cool, make it interesting. It already is interesting, but it's just about conveying it in the language of the people who actually need these spaces more than anyone else. Even the word "horticulture" is off-putting for me, because it doesn't sound like anything to do with what I'm doing.

RON Right! It's about shifting the narrative. You know, I've been to a few [community gardens] in the UK and here, and there's this idea that it's for old people, "Ladies that lunch," or grannies in their gardens. We have to put the value back into the soil. For young people, the latest iPhone, or the new Jordans, or whatever the hell it may be, are valued over life. Here, some of those things can get you killed if you have them, because we got people valuing that dumb shit instead of valuing air and the earth and each other. So yeah, how do we make gardening just as sexy as McDonald's?

That's what we need. All of this negative stuff—the tobacco companies, the alcohol companies—how do we take their marketing and apply it to this? Because their marketing works! We know that shit works. So how do we put another product in front of it?

TAYSHAN I mean, for me, I stumbled into gardening as a young, naive man, with no prior experience. As a city boy, the only reason I'd ever been outdoors and in gardens, so to speak, was playing football [soccer] in the park. When I started with the Grenfell garden—I was 19 at the time and trying to look cool, you know, trying to be trendy—I felt a bit embarrassed and ashamed; I felt uncomfortable because I don't really come across as your typical gardener. It's inspired me to change the way we see gardeners.

In the horticultural scene in the UK at the moment, there's a big focus on the aesthetics, the look of something. The flower shows are the pinnacle of that. They've got a section called the "community [garden]," but it's not the main thing. Why are the community spaces not the main focus of the horticultural show? For me, a garden tells a story of how it impacts people, rather than one person saying, "Oh, this is what a garden should look like." How did it change people? How did it empower people? The most inspiring thing to me is seeing when, like, 30 kids have built a garden—it might not look amazing, but it's impacted and inspired those children in so many ways.

RON And if we bring it to kids at a very early age, they're going to look at everything different. They're going to look at what truly has value, they're going to look at money different, because they're going to realize the soil is a resource. You know, it's not just dirt—life comes out of this. It's going to teach them that, "Oh, I put this one bean in and now I have 100? What about if I put 50 of those back in the ground, how many will I get?" From one tiny seed, you can get a tree that's going to give you fruit for 300 years. You want to talk about rate of return? That's power. Growing food is growing money.

These are the kinds of things that we need to be teaching in school. If that was taught in schools, it would just change everything, man. We would have a reverence for all the resources around us. But what happened in school—and I always tell this story—we had this petri dish with a wet paper towel and we put a seed in it, and we watched it grow on the side of the glass. We watched the seed totally destroy itself to create new life, sprout leaves, and start becoming a whole plant. And it's like, damn! But then we were told, "OK, next project." It was like, whoa, wait, where's the sexy part? You leaving out the sexy part in this? Why don't you tell us to get that plant and put it in the ground, so we can have a thousand more of these beans?

Imagine just going through your whole life without those lessons. And that's what they did to us. We didn't have nowhere to put that seed. We didn't have a garden. It was nothing but asphalt and fences and concrete. And it's like you said, that shit's by design, it's got to be, it's not happenstance.

TAYSHAN Definitely. It's mad because some of the most entrepreneurial people that I know are the ones that are trapped in, the ones that are gangstas, the ones that are on the roads. They'll make so much money out of, you know, obviously, whatever they're doing. But actually, if you just shift that conversation slightly to plants and soil and food, they've already got the intuition to turn that into something that they could make a massive amount of profit on. It's there, but it's just about the narrative change in that conversation—going, "Actually, you could do this, and not only are you empowering yourself, but you're taking power from the powers that be."

RON And you don't got to worry about going to prison doing it.

TAYSHAN Exactly. Although, that's debatable ... Can I tell you the maddest story? I was on the phone the other day with the Royal Horticultural Society (RHS), talking about the Chelsea Flower Show garden that we're looking to do in May, which is all about the Mangrove Nine, and raising awareness of their story and the police brutality that they faced, right. And, lo and behold, guess who comes up to my car, on foot, bangs on the window? A policeman. A policeman bangs on my window and says, "Routine traffic stop, can you pull aside?" Half an hour later, I'm still there. They've completely stripped my car out, taken everything out of my pockets and told me that I look like I'm on something. Meanwhile, the RHS are still wondering what the hell is going on.

It was mad because ... this story about the Mangrove Nine, I don't know if you're familiar with it? The Mangrove Restaurant was a Caribbean restaurant in Notting Hill where, when the Windrush generation migrated from the Caribbean to the UK after World War II, they would go. And the police would attack them. The Mangrove Nine were a group that stood up to the justice system and proved that the police institution was systemically racist at the time. So I'm talking to the RHS about racial inequality, a garden that we're building around racial inequality and—

RON And you get stopped.

TAYSHAN I get stopped. Right up the road from the restaurant, where the door was kicked in 100 times. It motivates me about what I want my kids to grow up in. I don't want them to feel how I feel. I don't want them to be afraid.

Going back to our roots, going back to the foundation of life—gardens, growing things, the environment, nature—I think that's the solution to so many different problems. And I don't think we need to go to anyone asking for permission to change these things. We just need to change them without relying on those systems, because they've let us down for how many years? Why is it going to change now?

RON It works perfectly; it's a well-oiled machine. I mean, and think, you're talking to the biggest organization probably in the world, as far as flowers go, and you get stopped by the cops.

TAYSHAN Whether I'm speaking about a garden or not, I'm still getting stopped, you know. And so for me, the problem doesn't go away. I don't think we need to go to anyone groveling desperately, saying, "Please, please, please, let's do this."

RON "Can I have more porridge, please, sir? Please?" No, get the hell out of here!

TAYSHAN We need to build from the ground up. We need to speak to people to our left and to our right. And actually, that in itself invokes a lot of change already. It changes perceptions; we're stronger together. Gardening and gardens are spaces that enable those conversations to happen. Not only that, but there's so much education you gain. I guess now there's loads of community gardening initiatives. There's still a lack of resources for those community gardening initiatives, but it's like everyone's trying to jump on it. I don't know how it is in the US, but in the UK—

RON Yeah, it's the same. All of a sudden, it's, "Ooh, this is new, and it's fun!" This ain't no damn fad—it ain't a fucking fad—that's what people got to realize. We're talking about people's lives here. For someone to be able to eat, for someone to be healthy, for someone not to have to worry about their next meal, to be self-sustaining—that's like right here in the bottom level of our needs.

What's highbrow is this shit is by design. The fact that people are sick, or poor, or homeless—somebody is benefiting from that. You think they can't fix that shit? You can send somebody to Mars, but you can't get people off the street? Stop!

TAYSHAN Exactly. There's a real conversation to be had about gardening and horticulture being a necessity to survive rather than a luxury. As a father of two young children, those are the lessons that I'm ensuring that my kids are fully aware of.

RON The empowerment that gives these kids, that they can take certain things into their own hands; it's going to make you look at life itself differently. What we're trained to do is be on a hamster wheel. It's like, you think you're successful? No, you're on a hamster wheel, dude. Get off that wheel and see what happens to you. I'm not doing none of that shit. I'm not hustling or grinding—I'm breathing and enjoying this beautiful space.

What I found is, a lot of times when you're in these communities, they don't appreciate beauty because it's not around them. They don't get to see it. That's for other people. So you get accustomed to things being, you know, ugly, gray, it becomes your normal—to see ugly shit. Just like if you're around violence all the time.

TAYSHAN So true. It's all about access, isn't it? If you don't have access to these things, then how will you even know that they exist? If you have no access to this information, then how are you going to use it and allow it to inspire you? A lot of my boys live in tower blocks [apartment blocks]. If you live on the 15th floor of a tower block [apartment block], and all your parents are worried about is how to put your next meal on the table, then how are you going to know about these things? Why are you going to be interested?

I was so blessed to have my mum. Through, you know, adverse circumstances—my mum was very ill for half my life—that's what inspired her to take a holistic view on the way that we lived, and bring nature into that. On reflection, because my mum's no longer with us, I kind of carry her in my legacy of gardens. My passion for gardening and horticulture, or whatever you want to call it—I call it nature—stems from my mum. Unless you have that influence, unless you have someone in your life that's going to say, "Actually, this is what you can do. This is interesting.

These are lessons that you can learn from this," then you won't know. We need more people that are not scared to say, look, I like flowers, I like growing shit.

RON Hell yes! Yes, without question. It's hard to bring people in because, with us Black folks here in the States, we had, um, what was that shit called? Oh, yeah. Slavery. We had that. And so Black people ain't trying to touch no soil. Why? Because it's seen as akin to slavery. And I'm like, no, no, buddy, that shit is akin to freedom. So that's a job that we have to do with people of color, period. They have a disdain for soil because of the trauma that was involved in the soil. So we got to say, no, no, no, no, no—that's where the gold comes from, that's where life comes from, that's where life goes ... back to the soil. Imagine, if you own the soil, all that you could have. Imagine yourself owning the soil. And that's hard.

TAYSHAN Even for myself personally, I had to ask some real deep questions about myself, about my masculinity, my area, my environment—everything that I'd been taught previously. When I stood in that garden for the first time and I had my hands in the soil, I had to ask myself, how did I get to this? How did I get here?

What's really funny is that a lot of my footballer [soccer player] friends (who, you know, live lives where it's all very materialistic and will never publicly want to be seen to ask me about what I'm doing), are slyly like, "Yo Taysh ... what's that gardening stuff about?" You know, like ... "How do I grow tomatoes?" It's never in front of everyone—it's almost like we're doing a little deal on the side. That's a first step, but what I want to get to eventually is everyone screaming and shouting about it because, like you said, gardening is sexy. It's just about the angle that you approach it.

With the pinnacle of horticulture being the flower shows, that's not really something for me to aspire to. That's not something for my mates to aspire to. It's very elitist and exclusive. And it's kind of all in, all out. At the moment, a lot of people I know are all out, and there's not much in between or there's not access to much in between, if that makes sense.

RON It makes total sense. I was invited to Chelsea once, but then I was disinvited for some reason.

TAYSHAN Yeah, I wonder why ... you might start just growing stuff there. You might sprinkle a few seeds here and species there. I mean, that's what needs to be done, though. It needs to be flipped on its head completely.

RON All of a sudden, they "didn't have the budget." Some bullshit, I don't know. Look—there's a dragonfly and a hummingbird literally right next to each other. Can you see that? It was like they were communicating with each other for a second—you see it?

TAYSHAN Ooh yeah, yeah, wow. I see it.

RON I mean this ... kids don't get to see that. Shit, I've never seen that! I've never seen a hummingbird and a dragonfly interacting, you know.

TAYSHAN That's beautiful; it is beautiful. That is the best office that anyone could ask for really.

RON It's really interesting how, if you design these spaces for nature, you're designing a space for so many things to thrive. I tell people, "We are nature," so you're designing the spaces for us, too. It's going to help the community, it's going to help humanity, but it's also going to help build this planet. I don't have plans to go, "OK, let's go trash another planet!" When you get there, you know you have to maintain that planet too, right? So ... why not just fix this? Again, people are making money from it. Corporations are making money from it.

People should have a right to live and they should be given the tools so they can live. If people can support themselves, and take the power away from those corporations, we save the planet and we save ourselves, too. But then, how do we get people involved? That's one of the hardest things, because we've been detached from it for most of our lives.

TAYSHAN It's difficult. It's like, that same family we're talking about, that lives on the 15th floor of an estate, how are they going to acquire land to grow? How are they going to acquire the resources? How are they going to find time? How are they going to keep their job while doing these things? We really do need to rock the boat a bit, because people aren't going to like it. They aren't going to engage, they're going to try and refute it. But actually, at the end of the day, gardens can save lives. I feel like I'm not meant to be here; I'm not meant to be talking about gardens. But gardens saved my life, and saved people I know.

And all of a sudden, the way that I see things is completely different. I used to just walk through life, down my street, where I live, and not take in what exactly was happening. This journey has allowed me to realize that nothing is by accident, nothing is by coincidence. There were several people, several layers of decision-making that led to me living in the council house, why my space looks like this, why there's no trees there, why I'm not able to grow food on my street. There's several barriers and limits that I wasn't meant to see. I'm not even meant to see that *that's* a barrier. I'm meant to just go along with it.

It's all about making people wake up to these things—that's when the conversation can happen. It's just about getting involved. It's not all or nothing—there's so much in between that we can explore. And, yeah, plant some shit.

RON Go plant some shit, for real. Take your health and your life into your own hands and realize that growing food is a life skill. Gardening is your pathway to freedom.

TAYSHAN It's a universal language.

RON And compost. Compost, compost, compost.

TAYSHAN Let's plan our Chelsea Flower Show takeover.

RON No doubt. Let's make it happen.

TAYSHAN Nice one brother. Be safe.

SEED BOMBS

by AYESHA TANJONES

you Will NEED:

~ ½ cup of RED powdered clay
~ 60ml of water
~ 1 cup of compost
~ 2 spoofuls of WildFlower seeds
~ a pinch of chilli powder (to keep the bugs from nibbling on the seedlings)
~ paper + pen

Why SEED BOMBS?

SEED BOMBS ARE A FUN WAY to HELP WILDLIFE, INSECTS & POLLINATORS in YOUR LOCAL AREA! LIKE A TRUE EARTH WARRIOR- YOU CAN ARM YOURELF with WEAPONS of LOVE, growth + BEAUTY!
MAKING THEM is REALLY THERAPUTIC ,+ a lil bit MESSY....

Step 1: think of an intention,
maybe a wish you want to SEE BLOSSOM, OR
a PRAYER FOR A PEACEFUL & HEALED EARTH,
& WRITE it ON the PAPER.
SOAK thE PAPER IN WATER WHILE YOU DO the
NEXT STEPS

Step 2: Mix the clay, compost + WATER TOGETHER
in a BOWL, with a WOODEN SPOON OR
YOUR HANDS if YOU DON't Mind the DIRT...
DID YOU KNOW: SOIL CONTAINS MICROBES
that stimulate the RELEASE OF SERETONIN iNOUR
BRAiNS! THE HAPPY HORMONE

Step 3 ADD the WILDFLOWER SEEDS
MAKE SURE THEY ARE EVENLY MiXED
+ add the Pinch of chilli powdER~ (2 keep the
bugs from
nibbling the
seedlings)

Step 4 the PAPER with YOUR iNTENTioN
WRiTTEN ON SHOULD BE READY to TEAR UP
iNto Bits & ADD TO the MiX
AS YOU MiX ALL the iNGREDiANTS TOGETHER,
SPEAK YOUR iNTENTioN OUT LOUD

Step 5 SHAPE THE MiXTURE iNto PALM SiZED, OR SMALLER
BALLS. IF its too WEt ADD A Bit MORE CLAY
YOU CAN ALSO GEt CREAtive & SCULPt YOUR FAVORITE
iNSECts OR ANiMALS!

STEP 6

ALLOW THEM to FULLY DRY, iN a ShaDED SPOT,
the SUN will MAKE the SEEDS SPROUT EARLY!

STEP 7 ONCE DRY, GO FOR TH & PLANT YOUR SEEDS
& AS tHE SEEDS GROW iNto BEAUTiFUL
FLOWERS, So will YOUR INTENTIONS!
its Best to plant them iN patches of grass which arent
populated with much other competition

the BEES, iNSects , & OtHer POLLiNAtORS ARE
gONNA BE SO gRAtEFUL FOR
YOUR HARD WOR K !

guide BY AYESHA TAN JONES of FERTiLE SOULS COLLECtiVE

PERMACULTURE
Dora Young

As the rambling runner-bean vine

Collects some cherished bind of vertices

So there is pattern here

In this random assembly

Folk who draw meaning up

From the depleted subsoil

Of our collective modernity

Here to learn

To plug it with faith

In our guild

And the delicate tendrils

Of our imaginations

That meet in a curling green reach

As radical as rising

From soil to sky

Gently

Slowly

Without end.

PLACEMAKING: PUTTING COMMUNITIES AT THE HEART OF URBAN GREENING
Sharlene Gandhi

In recent years, the need for greener cities has taken centre stage. While this is a much-needed perspective shift, there's a risk that councils, developers and businesses start taking action just for the sake of it, leading to vanity projects that tick the "green space" box, but do little for community well-being. It's a delicate balance: if we fail to act fast, unchecked urbanization could swallow remaining land; but we can't just build band-aid solutions that fail to have a real, lasting impact on communities' connection to nature.

To find that balance, we need to put communities at the heart of urban greening. This means engaging developers and policy-makers from the top down, and communities from the ground up. Only when both parties see eye to eye can green space development really be sustainable – both for the environment, and for local communities and economies. The goal, according to landscape architects Tom Armour and Andrew Tempany, should be "to create a sense of ownership" for communities, rather than making them feel alienated by top-down development from institutions and planners.

As it stands, however, those in positions of power often push ahead with urban greening projects without engaging the communities they profess to serve. The resulting ivory tower solutions miss the mark – think benches in places no one wants to sit, outdoor gyms that women feel unsafe in, and herb gardens totally wrong for local communities' eating patterns. As Tayshan Hayden-Smith, founder of nonprofit Grow2Know (and a contributor to this anthology) says: "The council will pay ridiculous money to create a space that no one knows about and no one needs. Communities – the beneficiaries of the space – should be automatically involved from the get-go, so that these spaces are purposeful. There's no point in building a new football pitch or garden if the community won't use it."

Fortunately, our understanding of biophilic design is evolving and alternative structures of people-first planning, known as "placemaking", are springing up. Placemaking ensures that communities are involved in designing public spaces from the beginning, ensuring that people's real needs are heard, understood and met, resulting in cost-effective infrastructure that will outlive us.

The Evolution of "Biophilic Design"

"Biophilic" design – from psychoanalyst Erich Fromm's concept of "biophilia", the "love of life and of all that is alive" – is an umbrella term for design that incorporates nature into the modern built environment. Singapore's Changi Airport and Milan's Bosco Verticale ("vertical forest") apartment tower are great examples of biophilic architecture; Mumbai's under-flyover gardens and New York's shrub-covered High Line of biophilic urban planning.

Though quickly gaining popularity, biophilic urbanism (incorporating nature into public urban spaces) has to be more than an aesthetic device or tick-box exercise. Given that humans are part of nature, and that our mutual survival depends on strengthening human–nature connection, biophilic design must also be community-philic design. It must also increase people's connection with, and understanding of, natural beings and systems, and how they intersect with our lives.

In practice, this means that urban greening initiatives must respond and adapt to real communities' diverse needs. That includes accessible spaces for people with visual or mobility impairments, safe spaces for women and girls, and culturally-relevant spaces that reflect local tastes. Horticulturist and Learning Through Landscapes charity worker Hafsah Hafeji points out: "If a new green space was to be created in my local South-Asian majority neighbourhood, I would imagine it having a larger seating area to accommodate for large gatherings with extended family."

Nobody can assess the viability of new green spaces better than local communities themselves. So, we need to bring communities into urban greening decision-making at every stage. Failure to do so can have embarrassing outcomes ...

*

In July 2021, London's Westminster City Council unveiled the hotly anticipated Marble Arch Mound, a temporary natural environment designed by Dutch architecture firm MVRDV. Throned at the top of the world-famous Oxford Street, the 82-ft (25-m) high artificial hill was meant to "create an experience of the 'great outdoors' right at the centre of the city." Early illustrations and architectural renderings of the Mound suggested that it would be a lush, flora-covered Eden, bringing a biodiverse ecosystem into Europe's busiest high street.

This Arcadian vision quickly dissipated when the attraction opened. The £2 million hill looked half-finished

– covered in patchy squares of dead-looking grass and a sparse smattering of trees. To add insult to injury, the Mound (overlooking the sprawling, freely accessible Hyde Park) charged a £4.50 fee – £6.50 at weekends – for the privilege of walking up it, to admire a view of scaffolding and cars. Two days after opening, amidst a social furore (one visitor called it "the worst thing I've ever done in London"), the council closed the gates and refunded visitors.

Two months previously, over in New York City, the state government had opened another high-concept public green space: the $260 million "Little Island". Jutting out from Manhattan's wealthy Chelsea neighbourhood, the artificial island (which covers less than 2½ acres/1 ha) spectacularly fails not only to bring plant life to the low-income neighbourhoods where it's most needed, but to bring nature into the city at all, instead, creating a new destination in itself (a literal island).

So, who is Little Island for? When we see an eight-figure sum for a new development, suspicion and cynicism are natural, and usually justified. The island was the brainchild of Barry Diller, a businessman who serves on Coca-Cola's board and is Senior Executive of travel booking site Expedia. The site, like the ill-fated Mound, seems crafted as a flashy tourist destination. Diller says his intention was to "build something for the people of New York and for *anyone who visits* — a space that *on first sight was dazzling*".

Other cases of navel-gazing greening initiatives are more everyday. In 2014, the city of Detroit, Michigan, decided to plant 1,000 to 5,000 new trees every year. This meant planting in historically underserved Black neighbourhoods, whose street trees had previously been cut down following the 1967 Detroit Riots (a move the city authorities attributed to Dutch elm disease). Despite understanding the benefits of having street trees near their homes, residents were wary of this new initiative, which had failed to meaningfully involve them. The reforestation project-leader, The Greening of Detroit, had decided which neighbourhoods to plant in, which tree species to plant, and how they'd be maintained – informing residents of all this through leaflets and poorly advertised community meetings.

Christine E. Carmichael, who led research into residents' kick-back, explained "they felt they should have a choice in this since they'll be the ones caring for the trees and raking up the leaves when the planters leave. They felt that the decisions regarding whether to cut down trees or plant new ones were being made by someone else, and they were going to have to deal with the consequences."

This trend isn't uncommon. As local and regional authorities feel pressure to create green spaces, projects that don't take community needs into account will increase. I call this phenomenon "forced greening". "Forced greening" happens when a local authority or developer approves and builds new green space that (despite having environmental or aesthetic benefits) negatively impacts local people's way of life. Such developments can not only interfere with people's daily routines, but can amount to gentrification – raising local real estate prices and pricing out resident communities. As Hafsah says, "retrofitting green spaces needs to be carried out collaboratively, so as to not cause green gentrification and result in the displacement of long-term residents."

As far as concerns about maintenance go (frequently cited by councils as a barrier to creating new green spaces), such collaboration can address this head on: engaging residents means enhanced desire to care for the co-created space; they feel it belongs to them, and they to it. As Tayshan says: "If you get people to take part in the space, designing and building it, they automatically respect it a lot more and it becomes more of a unified effort to ensure that it's maintained and gets passed down to the future generations."

In order to ensure long-term sustainability of new green space initiatives, our concept of "biophilic urbanism" must evolve to include community engagement. But what does this look like?

New Models for Engagement

Strong local democracy is central to enabling community-led urban greening. But participation in local democracy is dire: voter turnout for local elections is half that of general elections. Local councils need to proactively draw communities in. They need to go beyond creating a feedback portal that no one will look at, and posting letterbox leaflets that no one will read, to seeing the community as an essential co-creator and partner in any green space project.

Even for residents who are keen to get involved with local democracy, it isn't easy; it can be inaccessible and overly bureaucratic. For councillors, members of the local community who choose to represent their local areas, there is no salary (only expense reimbursement) and the responsibility can take up significant amounts of time. These factors conspire to make the role inaccessible and unattractive to low-income workers, parents and those with caregiving responsibilities (who, more often than not, are women). It's no surprise that the average age of England's local councillors is 59, or that 63 per cent are male. On top of this, 96 per cent of councillors are white. Can (and should) such a group really make decisions on behalf of diverse communities? What models could we adopt to represent communities more accurately and engage them more meaningfully?

One such model is the Citizens' Assembly, in which a representative group of citizens are invited to learn about, deliberate upon, and make recommendations in relation to a particular issue. In 2019, London's Camden Council hosted a Citizens' Assembly on the climate crisis, the first to be hosted by a local authority. They brought together a group of people who were broadly representative of the borough's population, providing them with top-level education on the climate crisis, and facilities to incentivize participation (small reimbursement, childcare and translation services). The group was presented with ideas from local schools, small businesses and residents, divided across three levels of responsibility (the home, the neighbourhood and the council) to feed back on. Members of the Assembly were invited to join optional follow-up meetings, as well as a scrutiny panel to hold the Council accountable for implementing agreed actions. Such Assemblies could perhaps develop into an ongoing, evolving dialogue between authorities and citizens, with a rotating panel of residents – like a "jury service" model, embedded into local civic duty.

Another strong model is third sector organizations (such as voluntary and community organizations, charities, social enterprises, mutuals and cooperatives) working closely with local authorities. Usually local and community-led, these organizations have an ear to the ground and know what communities really need. Tayshan's organization,

Grow2Know, acts as a mid-point between the resource provider (the council or developers) and the community. The team conducts an in-depth community consultation in an engaging, interactive way, designing the green space based on what they've heard. They then share this design with the community to get feedback, which they incorporate into the final design. When it comes to building, they sort out the hard landscaping – structural elements like digging the beds and constructing paths – but will run a day for the "soft landscaping" or planting, where the community can get stuck in.

As a third model, there are a growing number of ways that businesses can empower communities to own local green spaces. Urban Growth Learning Gardens is one such social enterprise, collaborating with Londoners to create and improve public green space. The team trains residents in how to maintain such spaces, and plant crops that require little-to-no maintenance. The enterprise's beneficiaries can also sign up to undergo formal horticultural training, and the team is always on the hunt for new freelancers who specialize in landscaping, carpentry and metalwork. Being able to pay people above the London Living Wage to transform underused public spaces through gardening strengthens communities in two ways: building more green spaces for community interaction, while making it financially viable for people to contribute to that too. It also shows that improving local democracy alone won't be enough – the private sector also needs to be involved in creating and filling jobs that create and maintain publicly owned natural space.

In 2021, Urban Growth created Gaia's Garden, a pop-up community garden in a "meanwhile site" (a site set aside for future development) in central London. The free, public space, funded by creative studio Play Nice and property developers Dominvs Group, was designed and created by five female creatives, with consultation from activist Noga Levy-Rapoport, and the support of over 200 volunteers. The garden aimed "to educate Londoners about sustainable practices – economic, environmental and social", and hosted a programme of events, talks, performances and workshops to actively draw people in, giving the space cultural significance and making it more accessible.

Letting the People Talk

The North London neighborhood of Tottenham is on the brink of being gentrified: the local marshes are at risk of being replaced by studios and one-bedroom homes for young professionals and commuters, which are not only unfit for families, but unaffordable for current low-income local communities. Seeing the mounting division and inequality this insidious process is causing, local resident Leyla Laksari started the local charity Living Under One Sun. To show the potential of reclaiming unused urban spaces for community benefit, she converted a disused bowling green into a community centre and café. The outdoor space is often rented out for events – bringing the community into the green space – and the café is open to locals. The attached allotment and greenhouse, where staff and volunteers grow vegetables and keep bees, provide a source of revenue. That revenue then funds free activities for local immigrant and refugee communities, including cycling lessons and walking groups. The cycling lessons have been a huge success, given that women – particularly isolated, unemployed mothers who sometimes don't speak

English – have found real sanctuary in them.

This proves the importance of putting money back into the hands of communities, and letting them choose their own priorities and outcomes, rather than declaring them from the top down. From 2017 to 2021, London mayor Sadiq Khan handed out nearly £5 million in grants to community tree planting and green space projects through the Greener City Fund. Grow Back Greener is a £1.2 million pot of funding for communities to control and maintain their own green spaces post-Covid.

One recipient of the funding, Wildlife Gardeners of Haggerston, received £15,000 to create a green corridor along the Regent's Canal in Haggerston. Floating islands of vegetation were installed along the canal to improve water quality and create habitat for wildlife. The project, carried out by a team of 25 volunteers, aims to be a pilot for improving the whole of the canal as a green corridor. Dayle, a volunteer, said: "My son Oskar is a keen gardener and relishes all opportunities to get his hands in mud. It's a delight for him to be invited each year to help the Wildlife Gardeners of Haggerston. It's a unique opportunity to spend a day working alongside one's neighbours. We look forward to it, and it feels very meaningful to be part of these projects."

On top of that, Khan announced in summer 2021 that an additional £4 million would be made available in the Green and Resilient Spaces Fund to support larger-scale greening projects. Crucially, the authorities handing out this funding already recognize that it needs to be strategically directed towards marginalized and low-income communities. The question now is: will those communities have a say in the spaces that are designed "for them"?

Rather than waiting for the systems to fix themselves, it's time to arm local communities with the means, knowledge and confidence to demand more from the institutions that serve them. As Tayshan says, "There's a misconception that residents aren't capable of doing things, but there's some real natural talent in our communities – people have every clue to what's going on and can influence decisions. It's just whether you give them the tools and the skills and the resources to be able to do that."

It's time to extend more funding for project and startup grants to those on the ground, who are closest to the solutions that benefit both people and the natural environment. And maybe then, the concept of climate justice – the equal balance of environmental, human, economic and cultural rights – can be the founding principle of all green space development.

REBEL WITH A CAUSE: HOW TO BECOME AN ACTIVIST
Noga Levy-Rapoport

"You are never too small to make a difference."
Greta Thunberg

"Never doubt that a small group of thoughtful, committed citizens can change the world; indeed, it's the only thing that ever has."
Margaret Mead

On 15 February 2019, aged 17, I turned up to Parliament Square in London to discover hundreds of young people, as terrified and angry about the climate crisis as I was, gathering and chanting. Just yards away, in the Houses of Parliament, politicians were making decisions that condemned our generation to a lifetime of volatile ecological chaos.

The immediate comradeship I felt with the total strangers around me strengthened my focus. I knew we had to be loud – loud enough for the MPs sitting comfortably inside to hear us. So, I turned to the crowd, riding the elation of our security in collective fury, and borrowed a cheap megaphone off a fellow protestor. I began desperately chanting that we had to take over the roads around us, to prove that young people were serious about change, that we would not slow down or step aside for the fossil fuel lobby and its complicit politicians. In that moment, I was ready to walk onto the road alone, at whatever risk, buffeted by the knowledge that, with so many other young people here, together we would make a difference. But I was not ignored; the crowd responded, pushing forwards as we spilled out onto the street, suddenly in absolute solidarity as we spoke, sang, shouted and marched together. That day, having arrived like everyone else – with no authority and no plan – I ended up leading 5,000 people through the streets of Westminster, swarming roads and standing firm against polluters and their enablers.

That protest – the UK's first school climate strike – was the beginning of an upsurge of youth climate activism in the UK. Now, at 19, I'm an award-winning climate justice activist. I've organized YouthStrike4Climate strikes across the UK, as part of Greta Thunberg's Fridays For Future movement, and played a leading role in organizing the record-breaking, 350,000-strong, September 2019 climate strike – the largest pro-climate mobilization the UK has ever seen. I've worked on, and led, campaigns for a global Green New Deal, educational reform and youth empowerment, as well as hyperlocal community initiatives. All because, at one moment, I decided to step up, enabling myself and those around me to find the courage to tap into our rage and transform it into revolutionary action.

*

The Strategic Blueprint: Mapping a Method for Change

Often, movements set on transforming our society seem overwhelmingly steeped in dense, traditional, historical and deeply political theories about social change. No matter how daunting this can seem to those starting out in activism, it's vital that would-be changemakers embrace these aspects of social theory. But armchair theorizing, without experience of action, means very little. Through my organizing and the people I've met, I've amassed theoretical and experiential knowledge of successful collective action, and have boiled this all down into a blueprint that can be reformatted and applied to a variety of campaigns and social issues.

First, to gain insight into the situation, we have to ask three key questions:

1 **Authority:** Who's in charge? (Generally, a government authority, or a corporate power where the political class or group is servile.)
2 **Incentives:** Why would they change what they're doing? (For example, monetary incentives, fear of international or domestic insecurity, fear of bad public image.)
3 **Threshold:** What would be the tipping point or the final threshold for the authority to make them change? (What will mean it is *no longer worth it* for them to continue on as before? What is the required level of threat to the incentives identified in #2?)

Second, to devise a strategy for action, we ask two more open questions:

1 **Actions:** What actions could bring about that level of threat to their incentives that's necessary for them to change their behaviour?
2 **People:** Who do we as activists and organizers need to reach, mobilize and convince in order to make that change happen?

Centring Activism in Community

In environmental activism, we face both corporate power and political opposition, often intertwined. For instance, in the UK, the oligopoly of the six major energy companies presents a complex obstacle of immense corporate strength. Demonstrations and our consumption choices must bring the government to the point where it is *no longer worth it* for them to implement policies that benefit corporate profit over people and planet. In order to build a mass movement, capable of protesting at the scale this kind of shift demands, we have to build from the ground up.

As poet and environmental activist Gary Snyder said:

> *"Stewardship means, for most of us, find your place on the planet, dig in, and take responsibility from there—the tiresome but tangible work of school boards, county supervisors, local foresters—local politics. Even while holding in mind the largest scale of potential change. Get a sense of workable territory, learn about it, and start acting point by point."*

Grassroots community organizing forms the basis of all movement building; the social theory of collective action and "people power" is at the heart of mass mobilization. It is community-building that enables us to support each other in achieving political and social goals, while recognizing the different struggles that marginalized and vulnerable groups experience, so we can build a stronger, more unified, kinder movement for the future. Therefore, the most necessary component of all activism is forming *community*.

Community brings with it connection, networks, mutual support, reliance and dependency, safety, and security; understanding and respect for one another in a comfortable, localized space. Communities are the basis of all organizing, the basis of the connections between all the Snyder-referenced stewardship roles – from councillors to teachers to those protecting our parks and nature reserves – we wish to see fulfilled in order to create change. Communities in their hundreds and thousands are the foundation of the hundreds of thousands at marches and protests; communities provide support for each other to go on strike; communities protect each other when one of us breaks down or burns out; communities entrust future generations with the knowledge of what brought change in the past, and preserve it for the future.

Young people have long been at the forefront of social justice movements. This isn't just a coincidence, it's the natural result of a symbiotic relationship based on a dependency on community: young people are dependent on the communities whose responsibility it is to raise and protect us; in return, we have a responsibility to give back by supporting and safeguarding our communities. From childcare settings to school groups, youth clubs to sports centres, support networks mark out our lives at every step of childhood. We have the closest, and perhaps most important, connection with community, because we require it in our youth more than we do at any other stage in our lives. We expect to see help provided in the form of collective mutual support throughout the early stages of our lives, so we understand communal, grassroots forms of organizing intricately. This results in a *youth to community to activism* pipeline.

The collective comradeship I felt at my first climate strike, so overwhelming that it still provides a source for me to draw inspiration and motivation from, wasn't a coincidence or a one-off. It was a natural pull towards community that young people feel more acutely than anyone else. So, of course, we end up among the cogs of change – collective power is second nature to young people, and the empathy-rooted enfranchisement that every social movement desperately needs can only come from such an understanding of community.

The Powers and Pitfalls of Digital Activism

Whilst my generation actively seeks to break down stereotypes, the archetype of the "digital generation" is one that we neither want to, nor can, shake. Though digital and social media-led activism are often derided as "slacktivism" or "clicktivism", utilizing social networks is an incredibly powerful tool for movement building, empowering you to spread your reach – not only in volume and geography, but also by facilitating the inclusion of vulnerable or marginalized individuals (who may otherwise be unable to join in).

For leadership and mobilizations to be effective across any social justice movement they have to be delegated and spread out across the collective. The importance of regional networks and decentralization in organizing climate protests has never been clearer. Currently, over 150 countries are registered for monthly or weekly strikes around the world, and we have grown from one teenager to a global network within the space of almost two years – none of which would have been possible without digital work and grassroots organizing.

Volunteer organizers are immediately welcomed onto online community spaces. These spaces join national and regional working groups (groups of people tasked with coming up with plans and ideas for a particular issue, and sometimes executing those plans) to focus on areas such as funding, press, social media, local coordination, community engagement, and arts and graphics.

The constant adaptation and development of digital content creation also allows us to keep up with changing attention spans and the wants of a rapidly growing, demanding global audience. We know that social sharing can make a serious difference, through the power of cases like the video exposing the murder of George Floyd, which set off a new wave of record-breaking Black Lives Matter protests, and forced people and institutions worldwide to reckon with their biases, privileges and actions. The archival aspect of the internet, however, is so often underestimated. The ability to delve into the online world and retrieve moments from several protests or demonstrations at once can inspire and mobilize more people than we may realize. Through digging into the past with these immense photo and video libraries, we can, in seconds, draw attention to the incredible work others have done before us, inspiring and driving ourselves forwards in the process, while inviting collaboration in the same breath.

It is impossible to discuss how much of an asset social media is without highlighting the very real risks including: performativity; the limitations of cancel culture, the constant need for purity in progressivism; and the pitfalls of "slacktivism". There are, however, flipsides.

"Performative activism" culture, where users are accused of sharing posts only to prove they too care about an all-important issue "for clout", can result, and often does, in *useful* information being shared, reaching and educating audiences who might otherwise remain unexposed.

"Cancel culture" serves to highlight the collective power

of centuries-strong protesting traditions and delineates that it *is* possible to translate collective action and activism to the digital sphere. Even where "cancellations" arguably nitpick at faults or mistakes, and disallow for change and apology, online discourse opens up about what can or should be forgiven in political spaces as progressivist ideas become more accessible through this very discourse, introducing users to past and present political disputes and debates. As model and Black trans activist Munroe Bergdorf explained, after accepting an apology from L'Oréal and returning after being fired for speaking out on racial violence, "accountability and progress, not cancellation and grudges" are crucial where improvement is possible.

Finally, it cannot be forgotten that there is not always a need to "justify" the use of social media or digital spaces in activism. There is nothing wrong with online campaigning; for many people, particularly disabled people, physical spaces to organize in are significantly less accessible. "Slacktivism" – a portmanteau of "slacker" and "activism" – refers to the practice of supporting a cause by means such as social media or online petitions, which are framed as involving little effort or commitment. This is ultimately about the ability to connect online, to reach contacts and co-organizers across the country (or even the world), and mobilize people en masse.

Action Plans to Get You Started

While there are infinite ways to be an activist, here are three classic examples of how to take action. I've given them a spike rating: the larger the reach of the plan, the scale of the action, and the greater difficulty of its execution, the higher the spike rating.

CREATE A COMMUNITY FORUM ⚡

Communities are the foundation of activism and campaigning, but simply throwing around a vague idea of what community actually looks like is a trap that many risk falling into. Campaigners have to actually build and establish human connections.

As an activist, it's vital to understand that change starts small. A great way to implement change locally is by reaching out to the people around you, and coming forward with what you think can be done in your neighbourhood. You can discuss and create creative local solutions specific to your area, whilst also bringing people together in preparation for larger mobilizations, through a community or town forum.

How to run an effective community forum:

- **Find a local place and a time.** Your town hall is perfect for this, otherwise any open space will do, and invite everyone in your neighbourhood and school by:
  - Printing invites to slip under doors and into letterboxes.
  - Utilizing existing networks. Mailing lists, WhatsApp groups or other neighbourhood groups for your street probably already exist that you can tap into.
  - Making sure you invite everyone in the community. It's easy to overlook groups like young people, or assume that people you haven't had much contact with aren't interested – but you never know who might end up being helpful or passionate.
- **Lay out your plan.** What exactly are you looking to

change? Who will this affect? What suggestions can you offer or encourage to avoid the change disrupting people's lives in the area negatively? How can you show that this is both positive for the environment and for the community? Who will oversee these changes? Who will fund the changes and what needs to be done to ensure it happens smoothly and effectively? What amendments can you make to improve on your plan together with the community? Make sure you have a council or other local representative present to ensure these needs can be met and questions can be answered.

- **Convince your community!** Get vocal active support and a written list of names of people who would like your plan to go ahead, as well as support from local schools and independent businesses if you can, or similar important pillars in your community, so that you can bring this to the local authority.

- **Be prepared for setbacks ...** Not everyone may agree with your ideas; some people just don't want to see change happen, or could take issue with a number of obstacles in your plan that you may not have noticed. Encourage as much civil, open and constructive discussion as possible in the forum – and ask for help from your supporters to overcome structural or personal setbacks!

- **Make sure to stay involved and follow up after your win.** Stay in touch with everyone – maybe now you can even establish regular community meetings. Are people happy with the changes you managed to make? What kind of new sustainability initiatives can you continue to implement now that you've built this network of supportive people in the community? You have a network and a community now. That gives you the power to keep going.

PROMOTE AN ONLINE PETITION OR CAMPAIGN ⚡⚡
Petitions and similar campaigns are ultimately about ensuring a groundswell of support that is too loud and abrasive for the antagonist to ignore. It says to your opposition: there are not only enough people that support this motion that it is morally right to follow through with it, but also enough people who are willing to follow through with an even "spikier" action if this campaign fails to secure a win.

What's key about petitioning in particular is the reach. This is where social media and outreach skills really start to come in handy.

How to run an effective campaign online:

- **Actively reach out.** Use group texts, emails and mass DMs to ask people to share and support. Don't be afraid to ask anyone and everyone!

- **Widen your reach.** People tend to mass follow those with similar interests. For example, Twitter's "Lists" function allows users to follow curated groups of selected accounts around a common factor – for example, people interested or working in the environmental sector. You can also engage with users who follow accounts that share your message.

- **Never stop resharing.** There's no guarantee that everyone will see one post, or be online in time to see a story. Share on as many platforms in as many formats as you can, consistently, with repeated explanations as to what you're doing and why people should support you.

- **Put a social media "pack" together.** This is a set of templates for resharing on social media and online platforms so that your supporters can easily support and take part in your campaign, including visual assets, links and text. You can attach this in a public, accessible place, such as your Instagram bio, and pile all the information and blueprinted posts into a Google document or another collaborative platform for easy copy and paste!

- **Catch people's attention.** Often, long captions don't quite cut it. Grab a friend and film a catchy and engaging video that you can widely share on quick-video platforms.

- **Utilize everything online platforms have to offer.** Play the algorithms – the save, share and comment buttons are your best friends. Put together a "hype group" of friends and supporters who will mass share, save and comment on every post you make to ensure the highest possible level of engagement. Use hashtags, and allocate a small budget for boosting and promoting posts.

- **Launch it on as many socials at once,** with a clear visual "identity" so people can recognize your campaign. As the days and weeks go on, put together a "content calendar" so you know what you need to create and share in order to keep people's attention and support. This is a great way of maintaining traction on your campaign.

ORGANIZE A MARCH, DEMONSTRATION, OR SIT-IN ϟ ϟ ϟ

Change on a national – or even international – level builds on community work to create protests on a scale impossible to ignore. The community you are able to build through localized, grassroots work can form a blueprint for a march, demonstration or sit-in occupation (for example, the occupations by Extinction Rebellion in 2019, or Black Lives Matter and Kill the Bill protests throughout 2020 and 2021). Laying out the roles and jobs in your network enables you to open up more discussions around the action itself and how exactly you can make it happen (see pages 256–257 for more information).

*

Activism is ultimately about people power: taking the achievements of communities who take care of each other to new heights, embracing collective organizing, reclaiming the shared spaces around us (both physical and online), and securing the future relationships we deserve to have with nature, the Earth, and each other.

ACTIVIST NETWORKS
ROLES AND REQUIREMENTS

ENGAGEMENT
Rally the crowd at the protest or event for your campaign or actions.

COMMUNITY
Reach out to local events and ask to give a talk or a speech about the importance of attending your event or supporting your campaign.

MEDIA
Go on record on the press release; speak to the media; get interviewed about your campaign.

Contact local and national media to let them know about your campaign or action.

↑
└ *ON THE GROUND* ──────────

ADMIN
Arrange and minute meetings, send out emails and speak to new volunteers – internal admin roles are often understated but they're incredibly significant to ensure everything in the network or organization runs smoothly before or when organizing the action.

DIGITAL
Manage social media and online outreach, through mass emailing, leafleting, creating photo and video hype, and social media posts.

CONTINGENCY

Be ready to make an emergency or last-minute decision if something goes wrong on the day of action, and assign a small and specific group of people to this role – in conjunction with your legal and welfare teams!

ACTION

Someone has to *do the action*: the rank-and-file, who know the risks and can carry out the demonstration.

LOGISTICS

Organize logistics for a major event: you might need stewards, route-planning, the logistics and order of events on the day, and will need to know where all your megaphones and first aid kits are kept, for example.

BEHIND THE SCENES

LEGAL

Ensure your action is legally "sound" – and if it's not strictly above board, as many protests are not, what are the risks? People well-versed in protest law and tradition can communicate these risks – not everyone is equipped to take on this role, so it's always worth contacting organizations whose job it is to help, such as independent grassroots project Green & Black Cross.

WELFARE

Protecting welfare and making sure that before, during, and after any action or event, everyone's mental and physical health is at its best – burnout is a real risk, especially with eco-anxiety ravaging many environmental campaigns, and similar emotional difficulties across a range of social issues.

THE POWER OF LOVE: WHY NATURE CONNECTION IS AT THE ROOT OF SOLVING THE CLIMATE CRISIS
Ellen Miles and Clover Hogan

"If we make life multiplanetary, there may come a day when some plants & animals die out on Earth, but are still alive on Mars."
@ElonMusk · 17 April 2021 · Twitter

"The love of wilderness is ... an expression of loyalty to the earth, the earth which bore us and sustains us, the only home we shall ever know, the only paradise we ever need – if only we had the eyes to see."
Edward Abbey, *Desert Solitaire* (1968)

What comes to mind when you hear the phrase "climate solutions"? In 2021, Elon Musk tweeted that he'd be "donating $100 million towards a prize for best carbon capture technology" (as if trees didn't already exist); Bill Gates's book *How to Avoid a Climate Disaster* urged technological breakthroughs; and US climate envoy, John Kerry, claimed that "50 per cent of the carbon reductions needed to get to net zero will come from technologies that *have not yet been invented*." The climate solutions at the forefront of global discourse are the stuff of science fiction. We're told that techno-utopianism will "save us" from the climate crisis – that we can geoengineer ourselves out of this mess (or, better yet, sack Earth altogether and colonize Mars).

This technocentric tunnel vision is a symptom of the belief that "progress" means conquering nature. We're so fixated on being above the rest of earthly life that our "solution" to climate collapse is to double down on this divorce, rather than address the real threat: the disconnect itself. But seeing – let alone addressing – this root cause is all but impossible within an anthropocentric society that tells us a tree is worth more dead than alive; a society predicated on limitless growth within finite resources, which rewards competition, comparison and consumption over connection and community. As Mark Fisher noted in *Capitalist Realism*, "it is easier to imagine the end of the world than the end of capitalism". Talk of terraforming proves this.

Rebuilding our relationship with nature doesn't mean abandoning technological achievements altogether – many innovations can help us treat the symptoms of the environmental multi-crisis. But addressing its *causes* means abandoning some of the assumptions on which our society is currently built: infinite growth, the commodification of nature and speciesism. Climate action must start with the one thing we can all control: our mindset. As environmental anthropologist Peter Sutoris summarizes:

"Even if the technologies on which we pin our hopes for the future deliver as expected and do not lead to much collateral damage – both of which are huge assumptions – they will not have fixed our mindsets. This is a crisis of culture and politics, not of science and technology. To believe that we can innovate and engineer ourselves out of this mess is to miss the key lesson of the Anthropocene – that dealing with planetary-scale processes calls for humility, not arrogance."

There has never been a greater need for more environmental champions in industry, policy and civil society. Yet apathy abounds. How can we galvanize the disinterested, and burst the bubble of anthropocentrism, technocentrism and extractivism? Connecting to nature holds the key.

Nature connection is a radical solution in the purest sense. Though often mischaracterized as wacky, controversial or unfeasible, what "radical" (from the Latin *radix*, meaning "root") really means is addressing the root causes, not the symptoms, of an issue. In fostering a connection to nature, we address the root causes of climate apathy, inertia and hostility. Here's how.

Nature Makes Us Care

You cannot love what you do not know. It might seem obvious, but this is the root of climate inaction. For much of the world, habitat loss and species decline are abstract matters. Without a personal experience of this loss, it doesn't feel quite so real or painful. We are plagued by widespread blindness: a blindness to the *loss* of nature and a blindness to *nature* itself.

As society urbanizes and digitizes, fewer people are connecting with nature; our children will experience even less. Conservationist Dr Robert Pyle captures the spirit of this generational attenuation in what he calls the "extinction of experience":

"[As] citizens grow more removed from personal contact with nature, awareness and appreciation retreat. This breeds apathy toward environmental concerns and, inevitably, further degradation of the common habitat ... So it goes, on and on, the

extinction of experience sucking the life from the land, the intimacy from our connections ... What is the extinction of the condor to a child who has never known a wren?"

Helping people in industrialized societies to connect with nature can break this cycle. After experiencing nature's quiet, dauntless balm for the soul first-hand – accepting the forest's embrace, tending a garden – you'll naturally feel more connected to, grateful for, and so inclined to protect these places, and the beings that call them home. Masses of research shows that people are more likely to behave in pro-environmental ways if they have experienced a personal connection to nature. A 2020 study of over 24,000 people found that those with greater connection to natural environments were more likely to behave in ways that benefit the Earth, including recycling, walking or cycling (rather than driving), and environmental volunteering.

Nature's pro-environmental influence seems to be particularly important for children – adults frequently associate their care for the environment with a childhood connection to nature. George Eliot said it best: "We could never have loved the earth so well if we had no childhood in it". Pre-teen years are vital; if a child is introduced to the natural world before the age of 12, they'll most likely continue this relationship – with all the benefits it brings – into adulthood. Conversely, without exposure to nature (particularly wild nature) as a child, people are less likely to look after and protect natural areas as adults. A 2012 resolution by the International Union for Conservation of Nature World Conservation Congress concluded that: "... connecting children with nature is of such a fundamental importance for both children and the (future of) the conservation of nature and the protection of the environment, that it should be recognized and codified internationally as a human right".

Anti-environmental behaviour – from everyday actions to the callous, wide-reaching decisions made by oil executives – can be put down to a lack of empathy. How can we supercharge our empathetic tendencies, and become kinder and more compassionate? Surprise, surprise: nature connection. In one experiment, subjects were more likely to pick up a stranger's dropped glove and return it to them if they'd spent time in an urban green space. In a series of studies conducted by the University of Rochester, researchers found that contact with nature leads people to value more prosocial, less self-focussed aspirations. When participants were exposed to natural environments, they reported prioritizing more intrinsic values (like intimacy, personal growth and community), orienting them to greater connection with, and focus on, others. In contrast, exposure to urban and artificial environments elicited more extrinsic, selfish goals (such as fame and wealth).

This supercharged empathy helps us to look more kindly on ourselves too: nature contact has been shown to boost our self-esteem and body image. Social psychologist Viren Swami, an expert on this phenomenon, believes these feelings of self-acceptance come from nature's provision of an outlook "based on compassion and harmony, rather than competition or selfishness". This self-love, in turn, makes us better environmentalists, as we're less likely to fall prey to consumerist pressures that tell us we're not enough without [insert product you don't need].

Green behaviours are often viewed through the lens of sacrifice; we focus on the extrinsic things we're losing (a holiday abroad, a cool new outfit), rather than the intrinsic things we can gain (a sense of belonging and contentment). By connecting to nature, your priorities naturally shift – away from extrinsic wants, and towards more altruistic visions – to make you a better environmentalist, without feeling like you're sacrificing anything.

Appreciating nature can also help us see the value of nature-based climate solutions: protecting, restoring and creating natural environments. Currently, such solutions are woefully overlooked. Conserving tropical forests (huge carbon sinks and biodiversity hotspots) is one of the most effective climate solutions we have today, providing at least a third of the carbon capture needed to avoid the worst climate tipping points. Yet nature-based solutions receive only 3 per cent of all climate funding. Learning to respect nature more may help us to see trees, soil, moss and algae as valuable "technologies" in the fight against climate change – rather than looking to invent costly, resource-draining, carbon-intensive new machinery.

We're Not Robots

One of the reasons we have struggled to mobilize en masse in response to the climate crisis (beyond the decades-long efforts of fossil fuel giants to obfuscate the science, and discredit the scientists) is because the best communication tools in our arsenal have often been graphs and spreadsheets. Climate scientists are brilliant, brainy, but by no means the best communicators – particularly when their audience are non-rational, loss-averse humans. Numerical imperatives like "limit warming to 1.5°C" fail to ring alarm bells in our brains. We're wired for fight or flight, not "this is an enormous yet largely long-term, complex threat ... which requires our immediate action". We're more aware (and afraid) of losing things in the short-term (e.g. forgoing the holiday and the outfit) than we are in the long-term (e.g. losing every comfort of the 21st century when we annihilate much of life on Earth, including ourselves).

While there's growing intellectual acknowledgement of the issues, viscerally, the problem of climate change to many still feels remote – belonging to far-flung corners of the globe, and a dystopian imagined future. Of course, the crisis is not abstract – many people (including communities in climate privileged countries like the UK) are already living on its frontline, suffering through heatwaves, droughts, floods, crop failure, bushfires and forced migration. But the clinical, analytical framing of the discussion makes the issue feel intangible, which risks inertia.

This emotionless, number-heavy framing is rooted in patriarchy. While understanding the facts and figures is undoubtedly necessary, deeming this the only respectable way to discuss climate change is a symptom of the archaic view that emotions (associated with the feminine) are, at best, frivolous and, at worst, dangerous. While rationality is not itself inherently "masculine" (as Laboria Cuboniks notes: "There is no 'feminine' rationality, nor is there a 'masculine' one. Science is not an expression but a suspension of gender") quashing the validity and value of emotions reeks of internalized misogyny. Additionally, fewer than one-fifth of the UK's tech workforce are women, meaning that technocentric solutions are inevitably lacking female perspectives.

Talk of love for nature is often passed over as "hippy, tree-hugger" wish-wash, but emotions are our most powerful tool for galvanizing action. Humans are irrational creatures – we're driven by emotions, not statistics. We've seen that emotion-led narratives can drive real change: the UK's "War on Plastic" was triggered when *Blue Planet* aired scenes of a grieving mother whale, whose calf had been suffocated by ocean plastics. Seemingly overnight, plastic straws were a headline news item, and a flurry of legislation followed (to some extent misguided: the EU's mandate against plastic included 23 of the most *disliked* plastics – including straws – rather than those disproportionately contributing to the waste crisis, such as discarded fishing gear).

The lesson here is that we need to marry the cold, hard facts with compelling, heart-pulling stories. In *21 Lessons for the 21st Century*, historian Yuval Noah Harari explains that our capacity for telling, and being led by, stories is the reason that humans wield so much power: "Humans control the world because they can cooperate better than any other animal, and they can cooperate better than any other animal because they believe fictions." These shared fictions include what the future can, or will, look like.

Harari continues that, though few people read the latest scientific articles, millions watch films and television programmes about what the future could look like. This, he says, "means that science fiction needs to be far more responsible in the way it depicts scientific realities". In order to share reality-grounded stories about nature, we first need to know enough about it. We are unable to see or notice plants that we can't name – a psychological quirk that botanists Elisabeth Schussler and James Wandersee call "plant blindness". The prevalent "climate apocalypse" and techno-futurist mentalities stem from our collective inability to imagine a verdant, nature connection-led future

– a result of our dearth of knowledge and experience. Through connecting everyone to nature, we will be better equipped as a society to write and understand stories of what a nature-filled future can look like – the first step to realizing it.

Love Over Fear

When we *do* talk about emotions in the climate arena, the pervasive tone is one of angst. The emotions associated with driving climate action are typically negative: fear, guilt, anxiety. There was a 4,290 per cent increase in the use of the term "eco-anxiety" – persistent worry about the future of Earth and the life it shelters – in 2019 alone. The negative impacts of climate change on our mental health are so widespread that they have their own name: Australian philosopher Glenn Albrecht coined the word "psychoterratic" to describe emotions, feelings and conditions that relate our mind (*psyche*) to the earth (*terra*), including eco-anxiety, solastalgia (the existential distress caused by a change in environment) and ecophobia (the feeling of powerlessness to prevent cataclysmic ecological change).

This mental suffering loops back into destructive behaviours. Ecopsychology pioneer Chellis Glendinning diagnosed Western culture's "original trauma" as being our severance from nature. The symptoms of this severance include inappropriate outbursts of anger, mental numbing, emotional repression and a sense of lack of control; not the mindset we need to drive positive change. In 2021, youth-led climate action nonprofit Force of Nature found a concurrence between negative emotional states and a sense of powerlessness in relation to climate change: 70 per cent of the young people surveyed said that the climate crisis negatively contributes to their mental health; the same number felt hopeless in response to this crisis.

As ecologist and peace activist Satish Kumar notes: "Much of the current environmental movement is driven by a fear of doom and disaster. That cannot be the right motivation for a truly sustainable future. Love and reverence for the Earth will automatically result in sustainability, coherence and harmony." We need to know not only what we're fighting against, but what we're fighting for. In her talk show *All of The Above* (co-hosted with designer and activist Céline Semaan) self-proclaimed "climate optimist" Sophia Li asks:

"Is your relationship to the climate crisis rooted in fear and scarcity, or abundance and love? Mother Nature is the ultimate source of abundance and love. The climate apocalypse mentality is based on fear. They are completely different energetic frequencies. Acting for love is sustainable. Energy from fear leads to burnout."

Of course, feeling fear, anxiety and grief is an unavoidable aspect of truly understanding the crisis we are in. But cultivating positive emotions can help us to deal with the inevitable negative ones. It isn't just important that we cultivate "ecophilia" (love and awe for nature), but connect to the loss of it, too. Force of Nature's students often speak of a "bittersweet" sensation when out in nature. The bliss of being submerged in trees, or diving in the sea, coupled with the pain of seeing stray plastic pollution, or knowing that much of the world's underwater life is estimated to disappear due to warming waters and overfishing. These feelings are difficult, but healthy. Indeed, many climate psychologists would argue that they're *essential*. This "feeling soup" is evidence of our humanity. It shows that we're awake to the crisis, rather than blindly numbing ourselves to it. The problem isn't the feelings – it's how we *feel* about the feelings. It's the judgement we place on them. Fear, uncertainty and anxiety are inevitable feelings in response to the climate and ecological crisis. Yet we can't allow these feelings to exclusively define our relationship with nature and the future of our planet, as this binary will cause us to shut down. In any case, we must learn to couple feelings of anxiety with agency, so that we can channel our emotions into fighting for all that's left, and restoring all that has already been lost.

System Thinking: Kincentricism and the Rights of Nature

We need to take nature connection seriously as a climate solution. As a 2018 report concluded: "The importance of meaningful personal connections with nature should be considered and integrated, along with scientific knowledge, into public policies related to the environment and sustainable development." But what does this look like? Even once we've seen through the techno-utopian miasma, to recognize that nature is what we're fighting for, it can feel difficult to *truly* connect with it in an economy built on its commodification, and a culture indoctrinated by the mythology of separation. How do we rekindle nature connection on a system-wide level?

The good news is, we're not having to draft the blueprint from scratch: there is so much to learn from the world's Indigenous cultures, who to this day protect over 80 per cent of the planet's biodiversity. This powerful conservation success is due to a "kincentric ecology": "an awareness that life in any environment is only viable when humans view the life surrounding them as kin ... part of an extended ecological family that shares ancestry and origins".

Conservation and climate mitigation efforts are struggling because, as American conservationist Aldo Leopold reflected in the 1940s, we regard land as a *commodity* belonging to us, rather than a *community* to which we belong. In the present day, Indian scholar and activist Dr Vandana Shiva affirms that our climate and conservation efforts must begin with dismantling (the illusion of) our separateness from nature – what she terms "the ecological apartheid" – including the "colonial idea of the wild" as being a place "where there are no humans".

Extrapolating the lessons of kincentric ecology to global systems requires two things: humans must be given a first-hand understanding of nature, so that we can learn how and why to care for it; and nature must be legally protected as inherently valuable, so that humans are impelled to carry out that care. How we can achieve the former (including changes to our education system, community empowerment and urban planning policy) has been set out by our allies in this anthology of ideas. Let's briefly consider the latter – the rights of nature, a blossoming legal and cultural revolution, rooted in ecology and ethics, that is not only inspired, but spearheaded, by Indigenous communities.

The case for the rights of nature is grounded in the same truth as the case that nature is a human right: we are part of nature. Environmental lawyer and the United Nations' Special Rapporteur on Human Rights and the Environment, David R. Boyd, explains that present Western legal systems

– at odds with the most basic biology – regard humans as distinct from other animals. In his book *The Rights of Nature: A Legal Revolution That Could Save the World*, Boyd makes the case that:

"Humans are but one species among millions, as biologically dependent as any other on the ecosystems that produce water, air, food, and a stable climate. We are part of nature: not independent, but interdependent …."

And that, to halt multi-species extinction and environmental collapse:

"… we urgently need to establish and enforce a new set of rights and responsibilities. The rights belong to non-human animals, other species, and ecosystems. The responsibilities rest with humans."

By granting environmental features and non-human species legal rights, not only can we start to overhaul the self-destructive legal, political and cultural systems that class elements of nature as "things" for our use and abuse, we can also start a trickle-down effect (one that actually works) that will begin to repair the mental rift – the illusion of separateness – between humans and the rest of nature.

Where does this leave industry? Just 100 companies are responsible for 71 per cent of global greenhouse gas emissions. Do we simply need to take these companies' CEOs and stakeholders on a forest-bathing excursion? Or make business districts so green that avoiding nature – and its empathy-boosting effects – is impossible? Though we'd love to see what would happen if we did (it's alluring to picture a teary Jeff Bezos, in a moment of epiphany in the actual Amazon), the impacts on corporations will happen naturally by this two-pronged approach. By connecting people (the so-called "consumers" on whose custom these businesses depend) to nature from the ground up, and enforcing the rights of nature from the top down, corporations will have no option but to act in pro-environmental ways.

While thinking about climate solutions at a systemic level can feel daunting and alienating, systems are ultimately made up of institutions, which are made up of organizations, which are made up of individuals. As individuals, we subscribe to stories about the world and about ourselves. Through developing our individual relationships with nature – reorienting our internal narratives towards love and reverence for earthly life – each of us can help to usher in a world in which humans live in harmony with the planet.

LOOK DOWN, LOOK UP
Olafur Eliasson

Look down
Notice how the earth is holding you up
Be down to earth
Make a garden
The garden is also the gardener
And you are the garden
Swing back and forth
Extend your senses into the garden
Become with your local environment
Commit compassionately
Stay with the trouble – our garden planet
No need to hurry to Mars
Now look up again
And notice the intensity with which the earth holds you

WHAT IF?
Dan Raven-Ellison and Ellen Miles

Based on ideas shared by London National Park City supporters

1   What if all cities were more green than grey?

2   What if everyone felt at home in nature?

3   What if a tree was planted for every child born?

4   What if every area code had its own community gardener?

5   What if city rivers and canals were clean and safe to swim in, for humans, otters and other wildlife?

6   What if half of all urban walls were covered in plants?

7   What if it was safe and easy to cycle everywhere?

8   What if public ponds were created in every urban ward?

9   What if, like Business Improvement Districts, we created Green Improvement Districts?

10 What if no one had to breathe poisonous air?

11 What if we really gave residents a say in how their neighbourhoods are developed?

12 What if any citizen could get a licence to plant in public places?

13 What if everywhere was herbicide- and pesticide-free?

14 What if there was an app for connecting communities to available land?

15 What if people were paid to rewild their lawns and depave their driveways?

16 What if more golf courses became public parks?

17 What if all homes and offices included habitat-making and habitat-connecting features for birds and pollinators, and knew how to maintain them?

18 What if part of every park's grassed area was given to the local community to plant up and maintain?

19 What if every borough had a car-free street that residents could use for sports, workshops and performances?

20 What if everyone could confidently identify 10 trees, 10 birds, 10 wildflowers and 10 insects?

21 What if fruit-bearing trees were planted in public streets?

22 What if everyone could see three thriving trees from their window?

23 What if every new home stored rainwater for gardening and ran on clean, green energy?

24 What if social housing grounds created spaces for community food growing?

25 What if cities were designed so we could hear the sounds of nature?

26 What if there were more "Do this" signs, instead of "No ball games" signs?

27 What if all parks were linked by a "quiet way" for walking, cycling and gardening?

28 What if all busy roads were lined with pollution-absorbing hedging?

29 What if we gave nature more rights in the city and beyond?

30 What if we invested in teaching and employing thousands of people in urban gardening?

31 What if all banked land and "brownfield" sites were made available for meanwhile use, for community gardens, gatherings and recreation?

32 What if learning in nature was a part of every child's education?

33 What if contact with nature was a human right?

ENDNOTES

Pages

11   "… like lemmings on hoverchairs": Hoverchairs are the primary mode of transport for passengers of the Axiom spaceship in Pixar's *WALL•E* (2008). The animated film, set in the year 2805, is a cautionary tale about consumerism, techno-utopianism and severance from nature.

13   "Now … the natural world will depend": From the final scene of BBC's *Planet Earth II*, Episode 6, "Cities", first broadcast 11 December 2016.

INTRODUCTION

14   "While other species … solve problems": Godfrey-Smith, P., *Other Minds: The Octopus and the Evolution of Intelligent Life*, William Collins, 2017. *Other Minds* is a fascinating investigation into non-human intelligence and the nature of consciousness.

14   "although humans … all living things on Earth": Bar-On, Y.M., Phillips, R., and Milo, R., "The biomass distribution on Earth," *PNAS*, National Academy of Sciences of the United States of America, 2018. In: H. Ritchie, "Humans make up just 0.01% of Earth's life – what's the rest?" Our World in Data, 2019.

14   "we're now the planet's dominant influence … 'the age of humanity'": This is not something to be proud of. Put another way, if life on Earth is a finely-tuned symphony, with every species playing its part, then *Homo sapiens* is currently thrashing an off-key guitar solo.

15   "'the phenomena … human creations'": Definition from lexico.com, 2021. My emphasis.

15   "We *are* 'products of the earth' … Atlantic Ocean": Dartnell, L., *Origins: How the Earth Made Us*, Bodley Head, 2019.

15   "all life … single-celled organism": Theobald, D.L., "A formal test of the theory of universal common ancestry," *Nature*, 2010.

15   "you share DNA … amoeba to zebra": There are three "domains" of life on Earth: bacteria, archaea (which are similar to bacteria) and eukarya (the group that includes all multicellular species). All three share one type of DNA, made up of a combination of four bases: adenine (A), thymine (T), cytosine (C) and guanine (G).

15   "Human history": Refers here to the time since humans have existed, not just the time that has elapsed since the invention of writing (which is considered the start of the academic pursuit of "history").

15   "the 300,000 years that humans have existed": The oldest *Homo sapiens* fossils that anthropologists have discovered, the Jebel Irhoud bones, are 315,000 years old. See Hublin, JJ. et al., "New fossils from Jebel Irhoud, Morocco and the pan-African origin of *Homo sapiens*," *Nature*, 2017.

16   "At 11:30pm, … rise up from the dust": "Where was the first city in the world?", *New Scientist*, 10 February 2021.

16   "Today, … urban environments": In 2018, 55% of the world's population lived in urban areas. This figure will now be even higher. "2018 Revision of World Urbanization Prospects", United Nations, 2018.

ENDNOTES

16   "Genetic variations ... to emerge": Our species' fastest genetic adaptation was thought to have taken place over the "rapid" period of 3,000 years. Scientists then realized that the gene variant in question, which allows Tibetans to thrive at high altitudes, had actually been present in the group for around 40,000 years. Gibbons, A., "Tibetans inherited high-altitude gene from ancient human," *Science*, 2014.

16   Professor Kaye Reed: Personal interview with Professor Kaye Reed, President's Professor and Director of the School of Human Evolution and Social Change, Arizona State University, 1 June 2021.

17   Edward O. Wilson: Wilson, E.O., *Biophilia*, Harvard University Press, 1986.

17   "Although it might feel ... stubbornly anchor us to it": Many studies suggest that individuals' desire for contact with nature is an important adaptive process, which appears to aid optimum functioning. See, for example, Van Den Berg, A.E., Hartig, T., and Staats, H., "Preference for Nature in Urbanized Societies: Stress, Restoration, and the Pursuit of Sustainability," *Journal of Social Issues*, Wiley-Blackwell, 2007.

17   "Transhumanism ... gaining momentum": Transhumanism is a movement that predicts and advocates for the technological advancement of human beings so as to end physical decline, enhance our mental capacities and attain immortality. A key goal of transhumanism is consciousness transference: extracting the "mind" into an immortal vessel.

17   "For now, ... carbon-based apes": We don't just share a common ancestor *with* apes, nor did we simply evolve *from* apes, we *are* apes. Great Apes, to be precise.

17   "civilization's achievements ... quality of life": Matthews, D., "23 charts and maps that show the world is getting much, much better," Vox, 2018.

17   "At present, ... or taming, nature": This dogma has its roots in 15th-century colonialism. As Rupa Marya and Raj Patel explain, "The psychic technology crucial to justifying the expansion of empire was the invention of the diametrically opposed concepts of 'society' and 'nature'." The distinction rested on the fact that the brains of Western humans ("society") had the capacity for rational thought, while everything else on the planet ("nature") did not, and thus lacked inherent value. Marya, R. and Patel, R., *Inflamed: Deep Medicine and the Anatomy of Injustice*, Allen Lane, 2021.

18   "As proof of this, ... or even 'barbaric'": Cunneen, C., "Assimilation and the Re-invention of Barbarism," *Australian Indigenous Law Review*, 2007.

18   "extinction of keystone species": Keystone species (such as bees) are ones that play a vital role in holding an ecosystem together.

18   "toxic air, land and water": In 2012, a quarter of all human deaths were traceable to environmental factors in the air, water, and soil. Prüss-Ustün et al., "Preventing disease through healthy environments: a global assessment of the environmental burden of disease," World Health Organization, 2016.

18   "the sixth mass extinction": A mass extinction is a widespread and rapid decrease in the biodiversity on Earth. The current rate of extinction of species is estimated at 100 to 1,000 times higher than natural background extinction rates. Human action is now widely understood to be the driver of this sixth mass extinction event, which scientists warn may be a tipping point for the collapse of civilization. Aldhous, P., "We are killing species at 1000 times the natural rate," *New Scientist*, 2014.

19   "Definitions of 'nature' ... mercurial": For a history and analysis, see Ducarme, F. and Couvet, D., "What does 'nature' mean?", *Palgrave Communications*, Palgrave Macmillan, 2020.

20   "'deep ecology' ... human needs": Naess, A., "The shallow and the deep,

long-range ecology movement. A summary," *Inquiry: An Interdisciplinary Journal of Philosophy*, 1973.

21   Jeremy Bentham: Bentham, J., *The Works of Jeremy Bentham, Volume II*, William Tait, 1843.

21   "The text enshrined … arbitrary arrest": United Nations, "Universal Declaration of Human Rights," 1948.

21   "The declaration … global humanitarian concern": Climate change is a major driver of humanitarian need and human suffering, particularly for economically deprived countries and the Global South. In addition to deepening existing inequalities, climate change is creating new problems, such as climate displacement, as its effects (including drought, sea level rise and extreme weather) render millions of homes uninhabitable.

21   "In 1948, a time … lived rurally": United Nations, "Growth of the World's Urban and Rural Population, 1920–2000," 1969.

22   "If work, … any of this": If you're not convinced of this, Amelia Horgan sharply picks apart work's pitfalls. Horgan, A., *Lost in Work: Escaping Capitalism*, Pluto Press, 2021.

23   "the calamitous Biosphere 2 project": The $200 million Biosphere 2 project, which ran in Arizona in the early 1990s, was the largest closed ecological system ever created. It was intended to test the viability of such systems to support and maintain human life in outer space. The closed-system experiment ran twice, with both attempts running into problems, including the "desert" being too wet, population explosions of greenhouse ants and cockroaches, invasive "morning glories" overgrowing the rainforest area, only half the amount of sunlight entering the facility than was anticipated, and breathtakingly low amounts of oxygen.

23   "protected by resident Indigenous communities": Jones, B., "Indigenous people are the world's biggest conservationists, but they rarely get credit for it," Vox, 2021.

WELFARE

28   "We learn in school … plants clean the air": In one year, an acre of trees absorbs the same amount of carbon dioxide as a 26,000-mile (41,000-km) car journey produces; roadside trees reduce nearby indoor air pollution by more than 50 per cent, Lancaster University, UK, 2013. Find out more at arborday.org/trees/treefacts/

28   "vitamin D": Our increasing disconnect from nature is leading to a "Vitamin D deficiency pandemic". Cashman, K.D. et al., "Vitamin D deficiency in Europe: pandemic?," *The American Journal of Clinical Nutrition*, American Society for Nutrition, 2016.

28   "sharpens eyesight": Davis, N., "Children urged to play outdoors to cut risk of shortsightedness," *Guardian*, 2018. Study referenced: Williams, K.M. et al., "Early life factors for myopia in the British Twins Early Development Study," *British Journal of Ophthalmology*, BMJ, 2019.

28   "As recently as 2005, … on the subject": Louv, R. In: J. Robbins, "Ecopsychology: How Immersion in Nature Benefits Your Health," Yale Environment 360, 2020.

28   Richard Louv: Author Richard Louv is known for coining the phrase "nature deficit disorder", an umbrella term to describe the costs of our alienation from nature. Louv, R., *Last Child in the Woods*, Atlantic Books, 2005.

28   "Nature … is a 'have-to-have'": Louv, R. In: J. Robbins, "Ecopsychology: How Immersion in Nature Benefits Your Health," Yale Environment 360, 2020.

ENDNOTES

29   "banishing stress": See Professor Qing Li's essay in this anthology for an in-depth look at how nature contact reduces stress (page 36).

29   "alleviating anxiety": In studies funded by the Wellcome Trust, a 15-minute walk in a forest reduces anxiety by 23% to 31% compared to a street with traffic. "Exposure to green spaces is key to preventing anxiety and depression in young people, study finds," UWE Bristol, 2021.

29   "The emerging evidence ... supports this intuition": Kaplan, S. and Talbot, J.F., "Psychological Benefits of a Wilderness Experience." In: I. Altman and J.F. Wohlwill (eds.), *Behavior and the Natural Environment*, Plenum Press, 1983.

29   "can even relieve and prevent debilitating psychiatric disorders": Engemann, K. et al., "Residential green space in childhood is associated with lower risk of psychiatric disorders from adolescence into adulthood," *PNAS*, National Academy of Sciences of the United States of America, 2019.

29   "including ... schizophrenia'": Chang, H.-T. et al., "Green space structures and schizophrenia incidence in Taiwan: is there an association?", *Environmental Research Letters*, IOP Publishing, 2020.

29   "'accessible natural areas ... vital for mental health.'": Bratman, G.N. et al. "Nature experience reduces rumination and subgenual prefrontal cortex activation," *PNAS*, National Academy of Sciences of the United States of America, 2015.

29   "works its magic ... more resilient to illness": For study references on the physical and cognitive boosts nature provides, look no further than Professor Qing Li's illuminating essay in this anthology (page 36).

29   "We now know ... surrounded by plants": Hermans, T. (Red) et al., "Planten voor een prima binnenklimaat," ["Plants for a healthy indoor climate"], Wageningen Environmental Research, Wageningen University & Research, 2019.

29   "hospital patients ... can see foliage from their beds": Ulrich, R.S., "View through a window may influence recovery from surgery," *Science*, 1984.

30   Paul Shepherd: Shepherd, P., "Ecology and Man—A Viewpoint." In: L.J. Forstner and J.H. Todd, *The Everlasting Universe, Readings on the Ecological Revolution*, Heath and Company, 1971.

30   "you assimilate ... move, think and heal": Schrivjer, K. and Schrivjer, I., *Living With The Stars*, Oxford University Press, 2015.

30   "Moreover, ... outnumber human cells three to one": Sender, R., Fuchs, S., and Milo, R., "Revised Estimates for the Number of Human and Bacteria Cells in the Body," *PLoS Biology*, PLOS, 2016.

31   Rupa Marya and Raj Patel: Marya, R. and Patel, R., *Inflamed: Deep Medicine and the Anatomy of Injustice*, Allen Lane, 2021.

31   "Healthy microbiota ... reduce inflammation": This study found that just two hours in a forest significantly reduced participants' cytokine levels (cytokines are biomarkers for inflammation). Im, S.G. et al., "Comparison of Effect of Two-Hour Exposure to Forest and Urban Environments on Cytokine, Anti-Oxidant, and Stress Levels in Young Adults," *International Journal of Environmental Research and Public Health*, 2016.

31   Rupa Marya and Raj Patel: Marya, R. and Patel, R., *Inflamed: Deep Medicine and the Anatomy of Injustice*, Allen Lane, 2021.

31   "Green spaces ... to hang out in": Coley, R.L., Kuo, F.E., and Sullivan, W.C., "Where Does Community Grow? The Social Context Created by Nature in Urban Public Housing," *Environment and Behavior*, 1997.

31   "A Zurich study ... from different cultures": Seeland, K., Dübendorfer, S., and Hansmann, R., "Making friends in Zurich's urban forests and parks: The role of public

green space for social inclusion of youths from different cultures," *Forest Policy and Economics*, Elsevier, 2009.

31 "A study in New Haven ... in property crime (theft and arson)": Gilstad-Hayden, K. et al., "Research note: Greater tree canopy cover is associated with lower rates of both violent and property crime in New Haven, CT," *Landscape and Urban Planning*, Elsevier, 2015.

31–32 "Other research ... comparable plantless spaces": Brunson, L., Kuo, F.E., and Sullivan, W.C. "Resident appropriation of defensible space in public housing: Implications for safety and community," *Environment and Behavior*, 2001.

32 "A study of the ... Robert Taylor Homes public housing project in Chicago, Illinois": Kuo, F.E. and Sullivan, W.C., "Environment and crime in the inner city: Does vegetation reduce crime?" *Environment and Behavior*, 2001.

32 Frances E. Kuo: Kuo, F.E. In: T. Prow, "The Power of Trees," *The Illinois Steward*, 1999.

32 "Spending time ... improves our self-esteem": Blackwell, S., "Impacts of Long Term Forest school programmes on children's resilience, confidence and well-being," Get Children Outdoors, 2015.

32 "body image": Swami, V. et al., "Visits to Natural Environments Improve State Body Appreciation: Evidence from Malaysia, Romania, and Spain," *Ecopsychology*, Mary Ann Liebert, Inc., 2019.

32 Robin Wall Kimmerer: Kimmerer, R.W., *Braiding Sweetgrass*, Milkweed Editions, 2013.

THE SECRET POWER OF THE FOREST: FROM A FEELING TO A SCIENCE

37 "a lower likelihood of cardiovascular disease": Kardan, O. et al., "Neighborhood greenspace and health in a large urban center," *Scientific Reports* 5, Nature, 2015.

37 "obesity": Halonen, J.I. et al., "Green and blue areas as predictors of overweight and obesity in an 8-year follow-up study," *Obesity*, Silver Spring, 2014; Wood, S.L. et al., "Exploring the relationship between childhood obesity and proximity to the coast: A rural/urban perspective," *Health & Place*, Elsevier, 2016.

37 "diabetes": Astell-Burt, T., Feng, X., and Kolt, G.S., "Is neighborhood green space associated with a lower risk of type 2 diabetes? Evidence from 267,072 Australians," *Diabetes Care*, American Diabetes Association, 2014.

37 "asthma hospitalization": Alcock, I. et al., "Land cover and air pollution are associated with asthma hospitalisations: A cross-sectional study," *Environmental International*, Elsevier, 2017.

37 "mental ill-health": Mitchell, R.J. et al., "Neighborhood Environments and Socioeconomic Inequalities in Mental Well-Being," *American Journal of Preventive Medicine*, Elsevier, 2015.

37 "childhood myopia": Dadvand, P. et al., "Green spaces and spectacles use in schoolchildren in Barcelona," *Environmental Research*, Elsevier, 2017.

37 "ultimately, death": Of course, contact with nature cannot make you immortal! But it can help you live longer. Gascon, M. et al., "Residential green spaces and mortality: A systematic review," *Environmental International*, Elsevier, 2016.

37 "In an eight-year study ... socioeconomic status)": James, P. et al., "Exposure to Greenness and Mortality in a Nationwide Prospective Cohort Study of Women," *Environmental Health Perspectives*, National Institute of Environmental Health Sciences (United States), 2016.

ENDNOTES

37   "In a study of Tokyo residents … little nearby greenery": Takano, T., Nakamura, K., and Watanabe, M., "Urban residential environments and senior citizens' longevity in megacity areas: the importance of walkable green spaces," *Journal of Epidemiology and Community Health*, BMJ, 2002.

38   "Stress is often called 'the health epidemic of the 21st century'": Fink, G., "Stress: concepts, definition and history," *Reference Module in Neuroscience and Biobehavioral Psychology*, Elsevier, 2017.

38   "I have proven … can reduce all three": Li, Q. (ed.), *Forest Medicine*, Nova Science Publishers, 2012.

38   "After walking in the forest … in very little time at all": Li, Q. et al., "Acute effects of walking in forest environments on cardiovascular and metabolic parameters," *European Journal of Applied Physiology*, Springer, 2011.

39   "This further indicates … preventative effect on heart disease": Li, Q., *Shinrin-Yoku*, Penguin, 2018.

39   "In Japan … six hours a night": Ibid.

39   "we sleep better … even without a significant increase in physical activity": Li, Q. (ed.), *Forest Medicine*, Nova Science Publishers, 2012.

40   "forest-bathing … improved sleep quality": Li, Q., *Shinrin-Yoku* (in Japanese), Mamukai Books Gallery, 2020.

41   "I found that … where there is a good density of trees": Li, Q., Kobayashi, M., and Kawada T., "Relationships between percentage of forest coverage and standardized mortality ratios (SMR) of cancers in all prefectures in Japan," *The Open Public Health Journal*, 2008.

41   The sounds of … strong link to stress recovery": Annerstedt, M. et al., "Inducing physiological stress recovery with sounds of nature in a virtual reality forest — Results from a pilot study," *Physiology & Behavior*, Elsevier, 2013.

42   "Looking at natural patterns … 60 per cent": Taylor, R., "Fractal patterns in nature and art are aesthetically pleasing and stress-reducing," The Conversation, 2017.

42   "One of the ways … POMS … test": Li, Q. (ed.), *Forest Medicine*, Nova Science Publishers, 2012.

42   "In my studies … positive feelings such as vigor": Ibid

42–43   "several short visits … one long visit": White, M.P. et al., "Spending at least 120 minutes a week in nature is associated with good health and wellbeing," *Scientific Reports* **9**, Nature, 2019.

43   "A study in London … per 1,000 people": Taylor, M.S. et al., "Research note: Urban street tree density and antidepressant prescription rates—A cross-sectional study in London, UK," *Landscape and Urban Planning*, Elsevier, 2015.

43   "A German study … around their home": Marselle, M.R. et al. "Urban street tree biodiversity and antidepressant prescriptions," *Scientific Reports* **10**, Nature, 2020.

44   "The warmer it is … 30°C (86°F)": Li, Q. (ed.), *Forest Medicine*, Nova Science Publishers, 2012.

45   "Researchers at Brown University … in 2007": "Brown chemists explain the origin of soil-scented Geosmin," News from Brown, 2007.

45   "a South Korean team … particularly in women": Kim, M. et al., "Gender Differences in Electroencephalographic Activity in Response to Earthy Odorants Geosmin and 2-Methylisoborneol," *Applied Sciences*, MDPI, 2017.

45   "We've also since learned … sharks are to blood": Campbell, H., "Geosmin: Why We Like The Smell Of Air After A Storm," American Council on Science and Health, 2018.

46   "*Mycobacterium vaccae* ... fear and stress responses": Lowry, C.A. et al., "Identification of an immune-responsive mesolimbocortical serotonergic system: Potential role in regulation of emotional behavior," *Neuroscience*, Elsevier, 2007.

46   "Spending just one hour ... by 20 per cent": Berman, M.G., Jonides, J., and Kaplan, S., "The Cognitive Benefits of Interacting With Nature," *Psychological Science*, SAGE Publications, 2008.

46   "a four-day trip ... 50 per cent": Atchley, R.A., Strayer, D.L., and Atchley, P., "Creativity in the Wild: Improving Creative Reasoning through Immersion in Natural Settings," *PLoS ONE*, PLOS, 2012.

46   "Growing up ... cognitive development": Dadvand, P. et al., "Green spaces and cognitive development in primary schoolchildren," *PNAS*, National Academy of Sciences of the United States of America, 2015.

46   "A Belgian study ... by 2.6 points": Bijnens, E.M. et al., "Residential green space and child intelligence and behavior across urban, suburban, and rural areas in Belgium: A longitudinal birth cohort study of twins," *PLoS Medicine*, PLOS, 2020.

47   "green outdoor settings ... and diagnoses": Kuo, F.E. and Taylor, A.F., "A Potential Natural Treatment for Attention-Deficit/Hyperactivity Disorder: Evidence From a National Study," *American Journal of Public Health*, American Public Health Association, 2004.

47   "Researchers performed ... greener neighborhoods": de Keijzer, C. et al., "Residential Surrounding Greenness and Cognitive Decline: A 10-Year Follow-up of the Whitehall II Cohort," *Environmental Health Perspectives*, National Institute of Environmental Health Sciences (United States), 2018.

47   "With its astounding benefits ... attention in Japan": Li, Q. (ed.), *Forest Medicine*, Nova Science Publishers, 2012.

47   "The 'Nature Prescriptions' calendar ... 'Really look at a lichen'": The Royal Society for the Protection of Birds (RSPB) Scotland created the "Nature Prescriptions" calendar in conjunction with the National Health Service (NHS) Shetland.

47   "Forests occupy 68 per cent": Watson, C., "Tokyo strives to build resilience with city trees and healthy farmlands around it," World Agroforestry, 2020.

THE NECESSARY MEDICINE

54   "research shows that those who 'move to greener areas have ... improvements in mental health'": University of Exeter, "Green spaces deliver lasting mental health benefits," exeter.ac.uk, 2014.

59   "Songlines": Lines of music criss-cross the land making invisible paths ... These paths are memorized in the form of songs which describe the land, providing a map in music so you can find your way for hundreds of miles.

See Griffiths, J., *Wild: An Elemental Journey*, Penguin, 2008.

ANIMISM(S) AND OUR NEED FOR BEYOND-HUMAN KINSHIP

66   "It has been ... well-being, and survival": Gable, S.L. and Bromberg, C., "Healthy social bonds: A necessary condition for well-being." In: E. Diener, S. Oishi and L. Tay (eds.), *Handbook of Well-Being*, DEF Publishers, 2018.

66   Graham Harvey: Harvey, G., *Animism: Respecting the Living World*, Hurst, 2005.

66   Linda Hogan: Hogan, L., "We Call It Tradition." In: G. Harvey (ed.), *The Handbook of Contemporary Animism*, Routledge, 2014.

67   "Based on this observation … normative consciousness'": Schrei, J.M., "Animism is Normative Consciousness," The Emerald podcast, 2020.

RESTOR(Y)ING PLACE: TRACKING AND THE NECESSITY OF ECOLOGICAL INTIMACY

68   "When a bird watcher … is activated": Gauthier, I. et al., "Expertise for cars and birds recruits brain areas involved in face recognition," *Nature Neuroscience* **3**, Nature, 2000.

68   Richard Prum: Prum, R.O., *The Evolution of Beauty*, Doubleday, 2017.

69   "a project connecting young Heiltsuk people … within the community": Macdonald, N., "Bella Bella, B.C.: The town that solved suicide," Maclean's, 2016.

74   Naveh and Bird-David: Naveh, D. and Bird-David, N., "Animism, Conservation and Immediacy." In: G. Harvey (ed.), *The Handbook of Contemporary Animism*, Routledge, 2014.

76   Mary Oliver: Oliver, M., *Upstream: Selected Essays*, Penguin, 2016.

WHEN SEEING THE WORLD AS ALIVE IS CALLED MADNESS

79–80   "so much of the pain … trauma and memory": Studies suggest that trauma can be inherited—that our ancestors' experiences can alter our DNA. See Yehuda, R. and Lehrner, A., "Intergenerational transmission of trauma effects: putative role of epigenetic mechanisms." *World Psychiatry*, Wiley-Blackwell, 2018.

THE ANCIENT ALCHEMY OF COMPOSTING

86   "transforms potentially pollutant waste": When food rots in landfill, it produces methane (a greenhouse gas that contributes to climate change) and pollutes our waters. Composting creates a valuable resource out of this potentially toxic "waste".

IS NATURE CAFFEINE FOR CREATIVITY?

92   "when *Homo sapiens* … 45,000 years ago": The oldest cave art known to man is a painting of a wild pig discovered on Sulawesi, an Indonesian island. Researchers believe the painting is at least 45,500 years old. See Brumm, A. et al., "Oldest cave art found in Sulawesi," *Science Advances*, AAAS, 2021.

92   "let alone NFTs": Non-Fungible Tokens, or NFTs, are digital data units that certify digital assets as one-of-a-kind. NFTs are increasingly being used to represent (and sell) photos, videos, audio, and other types of digital artwork.

93   "After a few days … umbrella links": Atchley, R.A., Strayer, D.L., and Atchley, P., "Creativity in the Wild: Improving Creative Reasoning through Immersion in Natural Settings," *PLoS ONE*, PLOS, 2012.

93   "In another study … leafy colour beforehand": Lichtenfeld, S. et al., "Fertile Green: Green Facilitates Creative Performance," *Personality and Social Psychology Bulletin*, SAGE Publications, 2012.

93   "According to Prospect-Refuge ... shelter (refuge)": Appleton, J., *The Experience of Landscape*, John Wiley & Sons, 1975.

93   "When the world ... we can relax": Li, Q., *Into the Forest*, Penguin Life, 2019.

94   Richard Mabey: Mabey, R., *Nature Cure*, Chatto & Windus, 2005.

94   "Attention Restoration Theory (ART) ... nature can renew our focus and mental energy": Kaplan, R. and Kaplan, S., *The Experience of Nature: A Psychological Perspective*, Cambridge University Press, 1989.

95   Daniel Goleman: Goleman, D., "The Pros and Cons of Mind Wandering," Korn Ferry.com, 2021.

96   "'To sit in the shade ... is the most perfect refreshment.'" Austen, J., *Mansfield Park* (first published 1814), rev. ed., Penguin Classics, 2003.

96   Richard Taylor: Taylor, R., Micolich, A., and Jonas, D., "Fractal analysis of Pollock's drip paintings," *Nature*, Nature, 1999.

97   Doctors Eva Selhub and Alan C. Logan: Selhub, E.M. and Logan, A.C., *Your Brain on Nature*, Collins, 2014.

98   "Nature's beauty ... comfort and joy": In *The Fight for Beauty*, former Director-General of the National Trust, Fiona Reynolds, argues that beauty is essential to our well-being, and should not be considered a luxury. In: F. Reynolds, *The Fight for Beauty*, Oneworld, 2016.

98   Doctor Chanuki Illushka Seresinhe: Personal interview with Chanuki Illushka Seresinhe by Ellen Miles. See also: Seresinhe, C., Preis, T., and Moat, H., "Quantifying the Impact of Scenic Environments on Health," *Scientific Reports* **5**, Nature, 2015.

99   Psychologists Stacker Keltner and Jonathan Haidt: Dacher, K. and Haidt, J. "Approaching awe, a moral, spiritual, and aesthetic emotion," *Cognition & Emotion*, Routledge, 2003.

102   "Metzger said the artist's task ... the good of the universe": Metzger, G., "Remember Nature," readingdesign.org, 2015.

103   Satish Kumar: Kumar, S., *Soil Soul Society*, Ivy Press, 2013.

INJUSTICE

106   "By 2050, it'll be more than four in six": In 1900, just 15% of the global population was urban. The United Nations predicts that, by 2050, it will be 68%. See United Nations, "2018 Revision of World Urbanization Prospects," 2018.

106   "Concrete is the ... after water": Gagg, C.R, "Cement and concrete as an engineering material: An historic appraisal and case study analysis," *Engineering Failure Analysis*, Elsevier, 2014.

106   "it already outweighs ... on the planet": Resnick, B. and Zarracina, J., "All life on Earth, in one staggering chart," Vox, 2018; Watts, J., "Concrete: the most destructive material on Earth," *The Guardian*, 2019.

106   "39 per cent more likely ... anxiety (*tick*)": Peen, J. et al. "The current status of urban-rural differences in psychiatric disorders," Acta Psychiatrica Scandinavica, Wiley-Blackwell, 2010.

106   "my life expectancy ... (*I guess we'll see*)": People born in rural areas are expected to live two years longer than people born in urban areas. See assets. publishing.service.gov.uk/government/uploads/system/uploads/attachment_data/file/834244/Health_September_2019.pdf; Bauwelinck, M. et al., "Residing in urban areas with higher green space is associated with lower mortality risk: A census-

based cohort study with ten years of follow-up," *Environment International*, Elsevier, 2021.

107 "neoliberal urbanization": Neoliberal urbanism is "a form of urbanism subordinated to the dictates of capital ... in which competitiveness is the key." Vives-Miró, S., "Producing a 'Successful City': Neoliberal Urbanism and Gentrification in the Tourist City—The Case of Palma (Majorca)", *Urban Studies Research*, 2011.

107 "In the United States ... half-mile (0.8km) radius from home": The Trust for Public Land, "Imagine you were never more than a 10-minute walk from a great place to get outside," tpl.org, accessed 10 August 2021. I've amended the "10-minute walk" metric – both here and in the upcoming statistic relating to England on page 108 – to relate to the half-mile measure it actually denotes, as this distance takes many people significantly longer.

107 "In England ... nature-devoid neighbourhoods": Around 10 million people in England (out of 56 million) live in the 1,108 neighbourhoods which are the most deprived of green space. Friends of the Earth, "England's green space gap – How to end green space deprivation in England," 2020.

107 "It's an injustice ... biases towards income": Americans earning $100,000 or more enjoy almost 50% more local greenery than those whose annual salary is under $30,000. Leahy, I. and Serkez, Y., "Since When Have Trees Existed Only for Rich Americans?" *The New York Times*, 2021.

107 "'race'": Following Louisa's lead (and academic best practice), these inverted commas demonstrate that "race" is a construct, invented by colonizers and enslavers during the 15th century, and not an actual biological classification.

107 "In the United States, people of colour ... nature-deprived neighbourhoods": Landau, V.A., McClure, M.L., and Dickson, B.G., "Analysis of the Disparities in Nature Loss and Access to Nature," Conservation Science Partners, 2020.

107 "England's most affluent ... are taken into consideration": CABE Space, "Urban green nation: Building the evidence base," Commission for Architecture and the Built Environment, 2010.

107 "a Portuguese review ... well-to-do areas": Hoffimann, E., Barros, H., and Ribeiro, A.I., "Socioeconomic Inequalities in Green Space Quality and Accessibility-Evidence from a Southern European City." *International Journal of Environmental Research and Public Health*, 2017.

108 "Across England ... half-mile (0.8km) walk from home": Fields in Trust, "Green Space Index 2020."

108 "London ... only 0.44 per cent of the 2.7 million": At the time of writing, London's population was 9.5 million, and England's population was 56 million.

108 "Moving north, towards underfunded": the North of England is underfunded by £6 billion per year compared to London. IPPR, "North '£6 billion a year underfunded compared to London', investigation finds," ippr.org, 2017.

109 "'redlining'": Redlining was a discriminatory practice implemented in cities across the United States from the 1930s to the 1970s. Colour-coded maps dissuaded mortgage, healthcare and infrastructure investments based on the area's demographic make up. Literal red blocks were drawn around areas deemed "D" grade: predominantly Black neighbourhoods, as well as Jewish, Catholic and immigrant communities. Areas filled with US-born white people in new houses were given an "A" grade and were blocked in green. This "green" legacy lives on tangibly: today, "A"-rated neighbourhoods have double the tree coverage of formerly "redlined" ones. See Locke, D.H. et al., "Residential housing segregation and urban tree canopy in 37 US Cities," *npj Urban Sustainability*, Nature, 2021.

109 "'reflects structural racism ... The Trust for Public Land": Patino, M. and Poon,

L., "The Inequality of American Parks," Bloomberg CityLab, 2021.

109 "Chestnut Hill ... in the city'": Leahy, I. and Serkez, Y., "Since When Have Trees Existed Only for Rich Americans?" *The New York Times*, 2021.

109 "The average temperature ... just 5 miles (8km) apart": Temperature can vary up to 10 degrees between places with trees and those without. Ziter, C.D. et al. "Scale-dependent interactions between tree canopy cover and impervious surfaces reduce daytime urban heat during summer," *PNAS*, National Academy of Sciences of the United States of America, 2019.

109 "If Americans ... this figure would almost double": Trees prevent 1,200 heat-related deaths a year in the US. Mcdonald, R., "Trees in the US Annually Prevent 1,200 Deaths During Heat Waves," Cool Green Science, The Nature Conservancy, 2019.

109 "The problem is even worse ... killed 1,500": Haider, K. and Anis, K. "Heat Wave Death Toll Rises to 2000 in Pakistan's Financial Hub," Bloomberg.com, 2015.

109 "Increased outdoor air pollution ... over 4 million deaths worldwide every year": Find out more at who.int/health-topics/air-pollution

109 "In the UK ... more lethal than car crashes": Royal College of Physicians, "Every breath we take: the lifelong impact of air pollution," RCP, 2016; Centre for Cities, "More than one in 19 deaths in the UK's largest cities and towns now linked to air pollution – and the south is worse off," centreforcities.org, 2020.

109 "And your income and ethnicity ... you are subject to": Aether, "Updated Analysis of Air Pollution Exposure in London," ether-uk.com, 2016; Wong. S., "Ethnic minorities and deprived communities hardest hit by air pollution," Imperial College London, 2015.

109 Ella Adoo-Kissi-Debrah: The Ella Roberta Family Foundation was set up in Ella's memory as a way of remembering her life, and leads research and education into the dangers of asthma and air pollution. Learn more at ellaroberta.org

110 "In December 2020 ... official cause of death": Laville, S., "Air pollution a cause in girl's death, coroner rules in landmark case," *The Guardian*, 2020.

110 "Simply by being Black ... illegal levels of air pollution": Despite only accounting for 13% of the city's population, Black Londoners make up 15% of the group exposed to illegal levels of air pollution in the city. Aether, "Updated Analysis of Air Pollution Exposure in London," ether-uk.com, 2016.

110 "Simply by living in a borough ... are people of colour": Find out more at lewishamjsna.org.uk/a-profile-of-lewisham/social-and-environmental-context/ethnicity#:~:text=Lewisham%20is%20the%2015th%20most,the%20total%20population%20of%20Lewisham

110 "Ella had 11 times ... overwhelmingly white neighbourhoods": Cabe Space, "Community green: using local spaces to tackle inequality and improve health," Commission for Architecture and the Built Environment, 2010.

110 "As sociologist Dr Adam Elliott-Cooper ... all over the world ...'": Elliott-Cooper, A. In: *Death By Pollution*, a documentary by Novara Media, 2021.

110 "This is due to a web of factors ... biased towards white bodies": Brathwaite, B., "Black Mothers Are Disproportionately More Likely To Die In Childbirth – We Need To Address The Race Gap In Motherhood," Huffington Post, 2018.

110 "in addition to their body-wide benefits ... healthy fetal growth": Dadvand, P. et al., "Surrounding greenness and pregnancy outcomes in four Spanish birth cohorts," *Environmental Health Perspectives*, National Institute of Environmental Health Sciences (United States), 2012.

THE ENCLOSED PLACE

113   "Numerous studies ... working class people and people of colour have less access to nature": See, for instance, Wolch, J.R., Byrne, J., and Newell, J.P., "Urban green space, public health, and environmental justice: The challenge of making cities 'just green enough,'" *Landscape and Urban Planning*, Elsevier, 2014. "This paper reviews the Anglo-American literature on urban green space ... Most studies reveal that the distribution of such space often disproportionately benefits predominantly White and more affluent communities."

113   "categorized as an E-rated 'red zone'": Friends of the Earth, "Access to green space in England: Are you missing out?", friendsoftheearth.uk, 2020.

121   "In Philadelphia an inexpensive project ... in those neighbourhoods": Branas, C.C. et al., "Citywide cluster randomized trial to restore blighted vacant land and its effects on violence, crime, and fear," *PNAS*, National Academy of Sciences of the United States of America, 2018.

121   "Residents began to ... their greener, safer streets": The project saw a 76% increase in use of outdoor spaces.

CROSSFIRE: GLOBAL INTERSECTIONS

126   "a busy junction of injustices": The World Counts, "US$ earned by low-wage sweatshop worker," theworldcounts.com/challenges/consumption/clothing/sweatshop-facts/story; Amnesty International, "Americas: Governments must halt dangerous and discriminatory detention of migrants and asylum seekers," 2020; Trilling, D., "'It's a place where they try to destroy you': why concentration camps are still with us," *The Guardian*, 2020.

NATURE'S OUTCASTES

128   Ravikumar: Ravikumar, *Venomous Touch: Notes on Caste, Culture and Politics*, trans. from Tamil by R. Azhagarasan, Bhatkal & Sen, 2005.

128   Joel Lee: Lee, J., "Odor and Order: How Caste is Inscribed in Space and Sensoria", *Comparative Studies of South Asia, Africa and the Middle East*, Duke University Press, 2017.

128   "India's biggest cities ... highly segregated based on caste": Sriharsha, D., "Geography of caste in urban India," livemint.com, 2019.

130   340 Dalit men have died in sewers 2015–2020: "340 sewer cleaning deaths in past 5 years: Government," thehindu.com, 2021.

130   "71 per cent of Dalits in agriculture are landless labourers": Stevens, H., "Seven decades after independence, most Dalit farmers still landless," hindustantimes.com, 2018.

131   Bama: Bama, *Sangati*, trans. from Tamil by L. Holmström, OUP India, 2005.

AFTER APARTHEID, GREEN SPACES ARE STILL WHITE SPACES

132   "my family finally ... refugees in 2001": UNHCR, the UN Refugee Agency, is a global organization dedicated to saving lives, protecting rights and building a better future for refugees, forcibly displaced communities and stateless people.

132   "along with two million others": Cutts, M., "Chapter 10: The Rwandan genocide and its aftermath." In: Office of the United Nations High Commissioner for Refugees,

The State of the World's Refugees 2000: Fifty Years of Humanitarian Action, Oxford University Press, 2000.

133 "'The archetypal "Apartheid city" ... in public space'": Davies, R. J., "The spatial formation of the South African city," *GeoJournal* **2**, Springer, 1981; Simon, D., and Christopher, A.J., "The apartheid city," *Area*, The Royal Geographical Society (with the Institute of British Geographers), 1984. In: Z.S. Venter et al., "Green Apartheid: Urban green infrastructure remains unequally distributed across income and race geographies in South Africa," *Landscape and Urban Planning*, Elsevier, 2020.

133 Henri Lefebvre: Lefebvre, H., *The Production of Space*, Wiley-Blackwell, 1991.

133–134 "'The inequity ... across the country'": Venter, Z.S. et al., "Green Apartheid: Urban green infrastructure remains unequally distributed across income and race geographies in South Africa", *Landscape and Urban Planning*, Elsevier, 2020. My emphasis.

135 "Today's solutions ... in the Khayelitsha community)": Hogg, C., "Meet Khayelitsha's guerilla gardeners," timeslive.co.za, 2017.

LATVIA'S SOVIET HOUSING: A GREY LEGACY IN A GREEN NATION

137 "Besides ... covered in forest": Eurostat, "Agriculture, forestry and fishery statistics 2020 edition," Publications Office of the European Union, 2020.

137 "Latvia was occupied ... Soviets in 1944": Latvia had formerly gained independence from Russian Tsarist authorities and German barons in the Russian Revolution of 1905.

137 "Today, ... the capital, Riga": O'Neill, A., "Latvia: Urbanization from 2010 to 2020," Statista.com, 2021.

137 "Nikita Khrushchev ... by state architects": Tompson, W.J., *Khrushchev: A Political Life*, St. Martin's Press, 1995.

138 "The mass housing ... than a commodity": Morton, H.W., "Housing in the Soviet Union," *Proceedings of the Academy of Political Science*, 1984.

138 "International onlookers ... large scale'": *Chicago Tribune* (1967). In: M. Byrnes, "The Disappearing Mass Housing of the Soviet Union," Bloomberg.com, 2017.

138 "In 1995, ... still lived in these buildings": Tompson, W.J., *Khrushchev: A Political Life*, St. Martin's Press, 1995.

139 "To rebuild is costly ... thousands of people": Displacement seems to be the trend. In East Germany, many blocks have been demolished because reconstruction was deemed too expensive. In 2017, the mayor of Moscow, Russia, set forth controversial plans to demolish 8,000 *Khrushchyovkas*, as part of a major programme to rehouse some 1.6 million Muscovites. See: Byrnes, M., "The Disappearing Mass Housing of the Soviet Union," Bloomberg.com, 2017.

140 "In Tartu, Estonia, ... class A energy efficiency": Wright, H., "Estonia's Soviet-era housing finds new eco-friendly future," DW.com, 2019.

HOW CAN WE END RURAL RACISM? IT'S TIME TO REIMAGINE THE COUNTRYSIDE

141 "'*race*'": I use inverted commas (as many academics have done for some time) to demonstrate that "race" is a construct, invented during times of colonialism and slavery, and not an actual biological classification.

141   "The vast majority … overwhelmingly likely to live in urban locations": "Regional ethnic diversity," England and Wales 2011 Census, Office for National Statistics, 2020. (The most recent census data available at time of publication.)

141   "a total Black and minority ethnic population … of 242,506": See: derivation. esd.org.uk/?area=E12000009&period=cen_2011&metricType=3294

141   "out of a total population of 5,288,935": Nomis, "South West Region Local Area Report," nomisweb.co.uk. Figures sourced from the 2011 Census key statistics.

141   "For instance, 93 per cent … get there in their own car": National Parks UK, "Tourism in National Parks Information Sheet," 2020.

141–142   "In the US, … 95 per cent of visitors": Vaske, J.J. and Lyon, K.M., "Linking the 2010 census to national park visitors," Natural Resource Technical Report, National Park Service, 2014.

142   "a widely criticized report": Commission on Race and Ethnic Disparities, "The report of the Commission on Race and Ethnic Disparities", UK government, 2021.

144   "a 'race map' illustrating … victim of racist assault in rural areas than in cities": Rayner, J., "The hidden truth behind race crimes in Britain," *The Guardian*, 2001.

144   Neil Chakrabarti: Chakrabarti, N. and Garland, J. (eds.), *Rural Racism*, Routledge, 2004.

144   "'experiences of racism … than is generally thought'": "'Rural racism more common and more disturbing than generally thought' say Leicester experts," University of Leicester Press Release, 2004.

145   "Fin from Cornwall": Adjoa Parker, L., "Meet Fin, from Cornwall," Where Are You Really From?, 2019.

145   Marli McNab: Aspirations Academies Trust, "'Marli Keep Your Head Up, You Are Strong & Powerful': Budmouth Student Films Moving BBC Racism Report After Hit School Project," 2021.

146   Benjamin Zephaniah: Zephaniah, B. In: R. Prasad, "Countryside retreat," *The Guardian*, 2004.

THE ROAD TO COMMON GROUND: TRESPASSING WITH NICK HAYES

154   Right to Roam campaign poster: "Everybody Welcome" sign, Right to Roam, 2021.

155   "a third … don't own a home at all: Just 65.5% of people in the UK are homeowners. See "Distribution of home owners in England from 2019 to 2020, by age," statista.com, 2021.

155   "one in every 200 people in England are homeless": Shelter England, "280,000 people in England are homeless, with thousands more at risk," 2019.

155   "The Diggers … sought to make 'the Earth a Common Treasury for All … fed by the Earth'": Winstanley, G., *The True Levellers Standard Advanced*, 1649.

155   "St George's Hill … THE most exclusive private residential address outside of London'": Grant, A., "What's it like to live on St George's Hill, Weybridge, England," Curchods, 2017.

158   "And it was this exploitation … Africa, the Caribbean and India": Fowler, C., *Green Unpleasant Land*, Peepal Tree Press, 2020.

159   "Nature is queer … mandarin ducks change gender!": Galloway, R., "How does a duck change its sex?", BBC News, 2017.

160 "the Pygmalion Effect": This refers to the phenomenon where high expectations can bring about high performance. Rosenthal, R. and Jacobson, L., "Pygmalion in the classroom," *The Urban Review* **3**, 1968.

161 "FOI": "Freedom of information (with reference to the public's legal right of access to information held by government agencies and public authorities)." Definition from lexico.com, 2021.

161 "It's ironic ... right to private ownership": Spranking, J.G., "The Right to Destroy," *The International Law of Property*, Oxford University Press, 2014.

162 Garrett Hardin: Hardin, G., "The Tragedy of the Commons," *Science*, American Association for the Advancement of Science, 1968.

163 "Countryside and Rights of Way Act 2000": See legislation.gov.uk/ukpga/2000/37/contents

163 "It was seen ... actual insanity": When eccentric landowner Richard Norton died childless in 1732, he left a detailed and unambiguous will bequeathing his entire estate to the poor of Southwick, his district in Hampshire. At total odds with the norms of society, the will caused a great deal of consternation and was hotly contested by his relatives. Eventually, it was declared null and void by a jury of Hampshire gentlemen, on the grounds of his insanity.

165 "If people start ... land value tax": Land value tax is a tax on landowners, based on the value of their land. Throughout history, economists have advocated such a tax: Adam Smith said "nothing [could] be more reasonable"; Milton Friedman said it was the "least bad tax"; the *Financial Times* has even described it as "the perfect tax". Economists favour land tax as, unlike other taxes, it does not cause economic inefficiency, and it tends to reduce inequality. Yet there are only a handful of real-world examples of land value taxes.

165 "ban land banking": Land banking is the practice of buying up land purely as an investment, with no specific plans to live there or develop it. A 2015 investigation on land banking by *The Guardian*, revealed that the UK's biggest housebuilders are sitting on 600,000 plots of undeveloped land.

165 "Germans were still ... internalized mental divide": Carbon, C.C. and Leder, H., "The Wall inside the brain: Overestimation of distances crossing the former Iron Curtain," *Psychonomic Bulletin & Review*, Springer, 2005.

166 "a generation of Benny Rothmans": Benny Rothman was an activist known for leading the mass trespass of Kinder Scout in 1932.

166 "Scottish Outdoor Access Code": Find out more about the Scottish Outdoor Access Code at www.outdooraccess-scotland.scot

167 "In Scotland ... 'reasonable measures of privacy'": Ibid.

167 "Tort law": English tort law concerns compensating people for harm done to their rights to health and safety, a clean environment, property, their economic interests, or their reputations. A "tort" is a wrong in civil (rather than criminal) law.

DISABILITY IS NATURAL

173 Talila "TL" Lewis: Lewis, T., "January 2021 Working Definition of Ableism," 2021.

177 "Americans with Disabilities Act": Also known as the ADA. The ADA became law in 1990 and is a civil rights law that prohibits discrimination based on disability.

177 "my organization Disabled Hikers": Find out more about Disabled Hikers at disabledhikers.com

179 "Across the US ... (meaning half a mile/0.8km)": Merriam, D. et al., "Improving Public Health through Public Parks and Trails: Eight Common Measures," US

Department of Health and Human Services, Centers for Disease Control and Prevention and US Department of the Interior, National Park Service, 2017.

179 "from home": Find out more about the 10-minute walk at The Trust for Public Land, tpl.org/10minutewalk

CHANGE

186 "'Octlantis'": *Octopus tetricus*, a species found at a site in Jervis Bay, Sydney, Australia, sculpt underwater dens and construct walls from shells, creating community sites that marine biologists have called "Octlantis" and "Octopolis". Marine behavioural ecologist Stephanie Chancellor has called the octopuses "true environmental engineers" and Peter Godfrey-Smith, author of *Other Minds: The Octopus and the Evolution of Intelligent Life*, describes Octopolis as an "artificial reef".

187 *"Free Guy* (2021) ... a thriving, biophilic metropolis": The original natural world was there all along, but banished to a space outside the city, as well as being encoded in every person. (The more I think about it, the more I want to write a thesis about this film.)

187 "In Colombia ... nature-deprived areas": Nelson, R., "Medellin returns to its tropical modernist roots," wallpaper.com, 2021.

187 "In Catalonia ... heat-related deaths a year": Mueller, N. et al., "Changing the urban design of cities for health: The superblock model," *Environment International*, Elsevier, 2020.

187 "In Leicester, England ... 300m (330 yards) of green space": Sotoudehnia, F. and Comber, L., "Measuring Perceived Accessibility to Urban Green Apace: An Integration of GIS and Participatory Map," 2011. In: S. Geertman, W. Reinhardt and F. Toppen (eds.), *Advancing Geoinformation Science for a Changing World*, Springer, 2011.

188 "Down in London ... onto the poles": Find out more at scotscape.co.uk/services/living-pillar

188 German engineer, Rudi Scheuermann ... as they do on cliffs": *Fixing City Noise, Stress, and Pollution Using Only Plants*, Mashable. 2021. Find out more at youtu.be/wcdkiBk8FU0

188 "About 17 per cent ... vacant or abandoned": Newman, G.D. et al., "A current inventory of vacant urban land in America", *Journal of Urban Design*, 2016.

188 "Professor Sarah Moser": Voce, A. and Van Mead, N., "Cities from Scratch," *The Guardian*, 2019.

189 "The city of Putrajaya ... 'intelligent garden city'": "The Intelligent Garden City of Putrajaya," newcities.org

189 "proposed 'Forest City' in Liuzhou, China, ... over 1 million plants": Withey, J., "China is building first 'forest city' of 40,000 trees to fight air pollution," indy100.com, 2017.

189 "Every dollar spent on a community tree ... cleaner air, cooler streets and flood control": Pacific Southwest Research Station, "Trees Pay Us Back – Urban trees make a good investment," US Forest Service, 2011; In New York City, public trees provide $5.60 in benefits for every dollar spent on planting and maintenance. Randall, D.K., "Maybe Only God Can Make a Tree, but Only People Can Put a Price on It," *The New York Times*, 2007.

189 "UK charity Fields in Trust ... reduced GP visits alone": Fields in Trust, "Revaluing Parks and Green Spaces," 2018.

189 "They concluded ... more money than is saved'": Helen Griffiths, Chief Executive, Fields in Trust. Find out more at fieldsintrust.org/revaluing

189 "His principle, ... from their home": Research demonstrates the importance of nearby, visible foliage for mental health and well-being. Rugel, E.J., "Connecting natural space exposure to mental health outcomes across Vancouver, Canada,". University of British Columbia, 2019; Velarde, M.D., Fry, G., and Tveit, M., "Health effects of viewing landscapes – Landscape types in environmental psychology," *Urban Forestry & Urban Greening*, Elsevier, 2007.

190 "'At the neighbourhood level ... 30 per cent vegetation'": Personal correspondence with Cecil Konijnendijk, July 2021.

190 Caitlin Moran: Moran, C., "Caitlin Moran: how to survive school – as a parent," thetimes.co.uk, 28 May 2021.

190 Peter Kahn: Kahn, Jr., P.H. and Weiss, T., "The Importance of Children Interacting with Big Nature," *Children, Youth and Environments*, University of Cincinnati, 2017.

190 "Among few examples ... Sweden's 'Factfulness' movement": Pioneered by Hans Rosling's Gapminder Foundation. Find out more at gapminder.org

191 "social enterprise Incredible Edible ... a thriving and resilient natural world'": Personal correspondence with Pam Warhurst, co-founder of Incredible Edible, July 2021.

191 "Join me in becoming a 'guerrilla gardener'": Not sure where to start? My social enterprise, Dream Green, exists specifically to help people become guerrilla gardeners! Get educated, equipped and empowered at www.dreamgreen.earth and @dreamgreen.earth

192 "In Sheffield, UK ... within 300m (330 yards) of green space": Barbosa, O. et al., "Who benefits from access to green space? A case study from Sheffield, UK," Landscape and Urban Planning, Elsevier, 2007.

192 "From home, you can sign petitions": Sign ours! Go to change.org/natureisahumanright to sign the petition to make contact with nature a recognized human right.

WHAT IF YOUR CITY WAS A NATIONAL PARK?

197 "there are more breeding peregrine falcons in London": See Davies, E. and Hendry, L., "Peregrine falcons are the top birds in town," nhm.ac.uk; Yosemite Conservancy, "Peregrine Falcon Protection," yosemite.org/projects/peregrine-falcon-protection-2021/; Peak District National Park, "Encouraging year for peregrines in Peak District uplands," peakdistrict.gov.uk, 2021.

198 "London is, in fact, a forest": Barkham, P., "London is a forest – who knew?", *The Guardian*, 2015.

200 "According to GiGL, ... 3.8 million private gardens": Find out more on the Greenspace Information for Greater London website, gigl.org.uk

201 "Barcelona has introduced ... reduce traffic": Barcelona's superblocks are projected to reduce private vehicle journeys by 230,000 a week as people switch to walking, cycling or public transport. See: Mueller, N. et al., "Changing the urban design of cities for health: The superblock model," *Environment International*, Elsevier, 2020.

208 "a National Park City": National Park City Foundation, "How to make your city a national park city," National Park City Foundation, 2021. Find out more and download the book at nationalparkcity.org/journey

RESISTANCE IS FERTILE

212 "food deserts": A food desert is an area where access to healthy food is extremely limited or non-existent. There are currently 23.5 million people living in food deserts in the United States.

PLACEMAKING: PUTTING COMMUNITIES AT THE HEART OF URBAN GREENING

232 "if we fail … swallow remaining land": According to the Committee for Climate Change, urban green space in England shrunk from 63% to 56% between 2001 and 2016. Find out more at theccc.org.uk

232 Tom Armour and Andrew Tempany: Amour, A. and Tempany, T., *Nature of the City*, RIBA, 2020.

233 "'The council will pay … community won't use it'": Hayden-Smith, T. [discussion with Ellen Miles], 6 May 2021.

234 "'create an experience … the centre of the city'": "Visit Marble Arch Mound," osd.london

235 "'the worst thing … in London'": @emmabethwright, Twitter, 27 July 2021, twitter.com/emmabethwright/status/1419932605449969665?ref_, accessed 20 October 2021.

235 "brainchild of Barry Diller": Find out more about the directors of the Diller-Von Furstenberg Family Foundation at dvfff.org/directors/

235 "Diller says … '*on first sight was dazzling*'": littleisland.org/vision-and-design

236 "The reforestation project-leader … poorly advertised community meetings": Mock, B., "Why Detroit Residents Pushed Back Against Tree-Planting," Bloomberg CityLab, 2019.

236 Christine E. Carmichael: Carmichael, C. and McDonough, M.H., "Community Stories: Explaining Resistance to Street Tree-Planting Programs in Detroit, Michigan, USA," *Society & Natural Resources*, IASNR, 2019.

237 "But participation … of general elections": 67.3% of the UK's voting population turned up for the 2019 general elections, while only 34.6% voted in the 2018 local elections. Uberoi, E., "Turnout at Elections," House of Commons Library, 2021.

237–238 "It's no surprise … are white": National census of local authority councillors 2018, Local Government Association. See: local.gov.uk/sites/default/files/documents/Councillors%27%20Census%202018%20-%20report%20FINAL.pdf

240 "The garden aimed … economic, environmental and social'": Find out more about Gaia's Garden at gaiasgarden.london

241 "Greener City Fund": Find out more about the Greener City Fund at london.gov.uk/what-we-do/environment/parks-green-spaces-and-biodiversity/greener-city-fund

241 "Grow Back Greener … green spaces post-Covid": Find out more about Grow Back Greener at london.gov.uk/what-we-do/environment/parks-green-spaces-and-biodiversity/grow-back-greener

REBEL WITH A CAUSE: HOW TO BECOME AN ACTIVIST

244 "a global Green New Deal": The Green New Deal, first designed in 2008, is an economic plan for decarbonization that includes a "just transition" (i.e. one that

reduces socioeconomic inequalities) to renewable energy. Find out more at greennewdealuk.org

246 "in the UK ... six major energy companies": Kuzemko, C., "Energy Depoliticisation in the UK: Destroying Political Capacity," *The British Journal of Politics and International Relations*, 2016.

246 Gary Snyder: Snyder, G., *Turtle Island*, New Directions Books, 1974.

248 "Currently, over 150 countries ... almost two years": Following Greta Thunberg's first "School Strike For Climate" on 20 August 2018, groups of schoolchildren and teenagers have taken part in climate strikes around the world, forming the international organization Fridays For Future. Find out more at fridaysforfuture.org

249 "murder of George Floyd ... biases, privileges and actions": The George Floyd Memorial Foundation honours George Floyd's legacy by uniting and activating communities to challenge the root causes of racial inequity and end the systemic violence affecting Black Americans. Learn more at georgefloydmemorialfoundation.org

250 Munroe Bergdorf: PA Media, "'It Feels Good To Have Closure': Munroe Bergdorf Working With L'Oréal Again After Apology," Huffington Post, 2020.

253 "Twitter's 'Lists' function": For more on how to use Twitter Lists, go to help.twitter.com/en/using-twitter/twitter-lists

255 "occupations by Extinction Rebellion in 2019": Taylor, M., "The evolution of Extinction Rebellion," *The Guardian*, 2020.

255 "Black Lives Matter": Smoke, B., "2020: The year in UK activism," *Huck*, 2020.

255 "Kill the Bill protests": "What are the Kill the Bill protests?", *The Big Issue*, 2021.

257 Find out more about legal support in regards to protest and action at greenandblackcross.org

THE POWER OF LOVE: WHY NATURE CONNECTION IS AT THE ROOT OF SOLVING THE CLIMATE CRISIS

258 John Kerry: Kerry, J., *The Andrew Marr Show*, BBC One, 16 April 2021.

259 Mark Fischer: Fischer attributes this quote to both Fredric Jameson and Slavoj Žižek. See Fischer, M., *Capitalist Realism*, Zero Books, 2009.

259 Peter Sutoris: Sutoris, P., "*The climate crisis requires a new culture and politics, not just new tech*," The Guardian, 2021.

260–261 Dr Robert Pyle: Pyle, R.M., *The Thunder Tree*, Oregon State University Press, 2011.

261 "A 2020 study ... and environmental volunteering": Alcock, I. et al., "Associations between pro-environmental behaviour and neighbourhood nature, nature visit frequency and nature appreciation: Evidence from a nationally representative survey in England," *Environment International*, Elsevier, 2020.

261 "adults frequently associate ... childhood connection to nature": Chawla, L., "Childhood Experiences Associated with Care for the Natural World: A Theoretical Framework for Empirical Results," *Children, Youth and Environments*, University of Cincinnati, 2007.

261 George Eliot: Eliot, G., *The Mill on the Floss* (first published 1860), new ed., Wordsworth Editions, 1993.

261 "Pre-teen years ... into adulthood": Bird, Dr W., *Outdoor Nation Interview*. In: S. Moss, "Natural Childhood" report, National Trust, 2012.

ENDNOTES

261 "Conversely ... protect natural areas as adults": Bird, W., "Natural Thinking" report, Royal Society for the Protection of Birds, 2007.

261–262 "A 2012 resolution ... as a human right'": "Child's right to connect with nature and to a healthy environment," World Conservation Congress, 2012.

262 "In one experiment ... urban green space": Guéguen, N. and Stefan, J., "'Green Altruism': Short Immersion in Natural Green Environments and Helping Behavior," *Environment and Behavior*, 2014.

262 "In contrast, exposure to ... fame and wealth)": Weinstein, N., Przybylski, A.K., and Ryan, R.M., "Can Nature Make Us More Caring? Effects of immersion in Nature on Intrinsic Aspirations and Generosity," *Personality and Social Psychology Bulletin*, SAGE Publications, 2009.

262 "nature contact ... shown to boost boost our self-esteem and body image": Swami, V. et al., "Visits to Natural Environments Improve State Body Appreciation: Evidence from Malaysia, Romania, and Spain," *Ecopsychology*, Mary Ann Liebert, Inc., 2020.

262 Viren Swami: Anglia Ruskin University, "Nature makes us happier about our bodies," aru.ac.uk, 2016.

262 "This self-love, ... product you don't need]": Stuppy, A., Mead, N.L., and Osselaer, S.M.J., "I am, therefore I buy: Low self-esteem and the pursuit of self-verifying consumption," *Journal of Consumer Research*, Oxford University Press, 2020.

262 "Green behaviours are often viewed through the lens of sacrifice": Xiao, J.J. and Li, H., "Sustainable Consumption and Life Satisfaction," *Social Indicators Research*, Springer, 2011.

263 "Conserving tropical forests ... climate tipping points": "Correction to Supporting Information for Griscom et al., "Natural climate solutions," *PNAS*, National Academy of Sciences of the United States of America, 2019.

263 "nature-based solutions ... only 3 per cent of all climate funding": Buchner, B. et al., "Global landscape of climate finance 2019," Climate Policy Initiative, 2019.

264 "emotions (associated with the feminine)": The belief that women are more emotional than men is one of the strongest gender stereotypes held in Western cultures. See Shields, S.A., *Speaking from the Heart*, Cambridge University Press, 2002.

264 "Science is not ... suspension of gender')": Cuboniks, L., *The Xenofeminist Manifesto*, Verso, 2018.

264 "fewer than one-fifth ... lacking female perspectives": 19% of tech workers are women. Find out more at technation.io/insights/diversity-and-inclusion-in-uk-tech-companies

265 "Humans are irrational creatures": Nobel Prize Winner Daniel Kahneman's *Thinking, Fast and Slow* is widely regarded as the defining text on human irrationality. See Kahneman, D., *Thinking, Fast and Slow*, Penguin, 2011.

265 "we're driven by emotions, not statistics": Morris, B.S. et al., "Stories vs. facts: triggering emotion and action-taking on climate change," *Climatic Change*, Springer, 2019 – "The central proposition of this research is that climate change narratives structured as stories will facilitate higher levels of pro-environmental behavior than their analytical counterparts."

265 "the UK's 'War on Plastic' ... suffocated by ocean plastics": Thompson, R., "Has *Blue Planet II* had an impact on plastic pollution," Science Focus, 2019; Calderwood, I., "88% of People Who Saw 'Blue Planet II' Changed Their Lifestyle," Global Citizen, 2018.

265 "the EU's mandate … discarded fishing gear)": Macfadyen, G., Huntington, T., and Cappell, R., "Abandoned, lost or otherwise discarded fishing gear," UNEP Regional Seas Reports and Studies No.185; FAO Fisheries and Aquaculture Technical Paper, No. 523., UNEP/FAO, 2009; Lebreton, L. et al., "Evidence that the Great Pacific Garbage Patch is rapidly accumulating plastic," *Scientific Reports* **8**, Nature, 2018.

265 Yuval Noah Harari: Harari, Y.N., *21 Lessons for the 21st Century*, Jonathan Cape, 2018.

265 "Harari … depicts scientific realities'": Ibid.

265 Elisabeth Schussler and James Wandersee: Wandersee, J.H. and Schussler, E.E., "Preventing Plant Blindness," *The American Biology Teacher*, 1999.

266 "use of the term 'eco-anxiety' … in 2019 alone": "Word of the Year 2019," Oxford Languages, 2019.

266 Glenn Albrecht: Albrecht, G., "Chronic Environmental Change: Emerging 'Psychoterratic' Syndromes." In: I. Weissbecker (ed.), *Climate Change and Human Well-Being*, Springer, 2011.

266 Chellis Glendinning: Glendinning, C., *My Name is Chellis and I'm in Recovery from Western Civilization*, Shambhala, 1994.

266–267 "In 2021 … Force of Nature … in response to this crisis": "The Rise of Eco-Anxiety March 2021 Report," Force of Nature, 2021.

267 Satish Kumar: Kumar, S., *Soil Soul Society*, Ivy Press, 2013.

267 "In her talk show … *leads to burnout*": Find out more about Sophia Li, Céline Semaan and *All Of The Above* at alloftheabove.tv

268 "As a 2018 report concluded … sustainable development'": Charles, C. et al., "Home to Us All: How Connecting with Nature Helps Us Care for Ourselves and the Earth," Children & Nature Network, 2018.

268–269 "Indigenous cultures … of the planet's biodiversity": Raygorodetsky, G., "Indigenous peoples defend Earth's biodiversity—but they're in danger," National Geographic, 2018.

269 "'kincentric ecology … shares ancestry and origins'": Salmón, E., "Kincentric Ecology: Indigenous Perceptions of the Human-Nature Relationship," *Ecological Applications*, Ecological Society of America, 2000.

269 Aldo Leopold: Leopold, A., *A Sand County Almanac* (first published in 1949), Penguin Classics, 2020.

269 Dr Vandana Shiva: Speaking at Advaya's Guardians of the Forest colloquium in 2021 (from transcript).

269 "the rights of nature … by Indigenous communities": For example, in 2003, the Navajo Tribal Council amended the Navajo Nation Code to formally recognize certain "fundamental laws", including the rights of nature. In 2015, the Ho-Chunk Nation added a clause to the bill of rights portion of its constitution that acknowledged the rights of nature. In 2017, New Zealand granted the Whanganui River rights of personhood. The river now has a legal standing, and representatives: including the Indigenous community that fought for these rights.

270 David R. Boyd: Boyd, D.R., *The Rights of Nature: A Legal Revolution That Could Save the World*, ECW Press, 2017.

270 "Just 100 companies … global greenhouse gas emissions": Griffin, P., "The Carbon Majors Database: CDP Carbon Majors report 2017," CDP and Climate Accountability Institute, 2017.

WHAT IF?

274 "What If?": Questions inspired by and adapted from the "99 What If's for the
Next Mayor of London?"; based on ideas shared by London National Park City
supporters. Find out more at nationalparkcity.london/ideas

INDEX

Note: page numbers in **bold** refer to diagrams.

INDEX

INDEX

CONTRIBUTORS

Louisa Adjoa Parker (she/her)

Louisa Adjoa Parker is a writer and poet of English-Ghanaian heritage who lives in South West England. Louisa's poetry and prose has been widely published. She has been highly commended by the Forward Prize; twice shortlisted by the Bridport Prize; and her grief poem, 'Kindness', was commended by the National Poetry Competition 2019. She has performed her work in her local area and beyond, and has run many writing workshops. Louisa has written extensively about ethnically diverse history and rural racism, and as well as writing, works as an Equality, Diversity and Inclusion consultant. She is a sought-after speaker and trainer on racism, Black history and mental health, among other topics.

Michelle Barrett (she/her)

Michelle Barrett lives in Liverpool with her partner Will. She works for a national charity and has spent ten years delivering shared reading groups in community settings. Michelle loves to explore nature writing and poetry with her group members and believes that access to nature and literature supports people to live well. Her favourite book is *The Living Mountain* by Nan Shepherd – she hopes to visit the Cairngorms soon. When she's not reading or planning trips to the mountains, Michelle spends most of her free time cycling the Sefton coastline or park hopping with her dad and their dog Sky.

Shareefa Energy (she/her)

Shareefa Energy is a poet, activist and author of *Galaxy Walk*. She is a creative writing workshop practitioner. Her poetry is raw, honest and consistent against injustice. Witnessing her performing has been described as an almost religious experience. She draws inspiration from hip-hop, politics, Muay Thai, theatre and nature. Shareefa won the UK Entertainment Best Poet 2017 Award and was a nominee for the Eastern Eye Arts, Culture & Theatre 2019 award by the Arts Council. Her poetry has featured on BBC's *The One Show*, Channel 4 and ITV.

Ron Finley (he/him)

Ron Finley is a rebel with a green thumb and a vision to rejuvenate communities worldwide through gardening and community spirit. In 2010, Ron decided to plant fresh herbs, fruit and vegetables on his parkway in his South-Central neighbourhood, an act that was deemed illegal by the City of Los Angeles. Ron pushed back against the ruling and, determined to provide accessible gardening to his community, organized a petition with fellow green activists. Ron demanded the right to garden and grow food in his neighbourhood and successfully overturned the law. Since then Ron has helped to create dozens of community gardens in unused spaces around the world.

Sharlene Gandhi (she/her)

Sharlene Gandhi is a journalist working at the intersection of business and sustainability. She began her climate journey at the Pentland Centre for Sustainability in Business at Lancaster University, attending the World Business Council for Sustainable Development and running sustainability communication workshops. She has written for the likes of the *Stanford Social Innovation Review*, AIGA *Eye on Design*, *Ours to Save* and *gal-dem*, and has spoken at the Welcome Kitchen, Almeida Theatre and Global Action Plan. She has also been a climate editor at *shado* magazine. Sharlene is currently a reporter at Courier Media, a media platform for modern business and entrepreneurship.

Jay Griffiths (she/her)

Jay Griffiths is a writer who explores themes of rebellion and human connection with nature. She has written seven books, including *Wild: An Elemental Journey*, that took her seven years to research and write. Based on her long journeys among Indigenous cultures, the book explores the concept of wildness, arguing that it is intrinsic to the health of the human spirit. Jay has also written for publications including *The Guardian*, *Orion* magazine, *The Observer*, *The Ecologist* and the *London Review of Books*. She has contributed to radio programmes including Radio 4's *Start the Week*, *Woman's Hour* and the World Service. She has written for the Royal Shakespeare Company and for Radiohead's newspaper *The Universal Sigh*.

Tayshan Hayden-Smith (he/him)

Tayshan Hayden-Smith is the Founder and Director of Grow2Know, a nonprofit that aims to heal, inspire, empower and educate using horticulture while reconnecting people with the environment and their surroundings. Born and raised in North Kensington, he breathed life into his community through gardening in the wake of the Grenfell Tower fire in 2017. He initiated the Grenfell Garden of Peace – among several other green spaces in the local area

– as a means of therapy for the community. He hopes to change the narrative of what it is like to be a gardener and what a gardener may look like, in turn empowering young people through nature and creating a more inclusive and diverse horticultural community.

Nick Hayes (he/him)

Nick Hayes is an author, illustrator, printmaker and political cartoonist who has published four highly acclaimed graphic novels, all of which explore humanity's relationship with the environment. Nick's debut narrative book, *The Book of Trespass*, is a call to arms for greater public access to nature and became a *Sunday Times* Bestseller in 2020. He is also co-founder of the Right to Roam campaign, which seeks to make nature more accessible for all. He has produced numerous book covers, including that for *Lark* by Anthony McGowan, which won the Carnegie Medal in 2020. His political cartoons on topics such as the fox hunting ban have appeared in *The Guardian* and *New Statesman*.

Clover Hogan (she/her)

Clover Hogan is a climate activist, eco-anxiety researcher and the Founder and Executive Director of Force of Nature, a youth nonprofit mobilizing mindsets for climate action. Her expertise has led her to work alongside the world's leading authorities on sustainability and she has consulted within the boardrooms of Fortune 500 companies. Her recent TED talk "What to do when climate change feels unstoppable" has reached over 1 million views. She has also launched the "Force of Nature" podcast, serves as a trustee to Global Action Plan, and is on the advisory boards of the National Lottery Community's Climate Action Fund and the Teach the Future campaign.

Celine Isimbi (she/her)

Celine Isimbi is a student of the Earth interested in reconciling the relationships between people and their environments – through Black geographies, Afro-environmentalism, Indigenous knowledge systems and ways of being. Her ancestral and familiar roots are in Rwanda and the Democratic Republic of the Congo, and she grew up in South Africa. Celine is now grateful to live and learn on the Haldimand Tract, Turtle Island – otherwise known as Canada. These intersecting identities and experiences have influenced the lens through which she approaches her work. Celine hopes to be intentional and unapologetic in her stance for environmental liberation and work with her community to realize this dream.

Daisy Kennedy (she/her)

Daisy Kennedy is a writer and playwright from Wakefield, West Yorkshire, who now lives in Bristol. Since graduating from the University of the West of England with a degree in Drama and Creative Writing, she has had various plays produced with her theatre company Mismatch Theatre. Daisy was a finalist at the 2018 Wicked Young Writers Awards with her short story *Tickets*, she was awarded runner up in the Bristol Playwright Festival with her play *Tic Tac Toes*; and her most recent play, *BLOOMERS* was awarded first place in the 2020 Bristol One Act Festival. Daisy has been environmentally conscious since she was an eco-warrior in Year 6, she loves the outdoors and is passionate about creating work that advocates making green spaces accessible for everyone.

Noga Levy-Rapoport (they/them)

Noga Levy-Rapoport, 19, is a student, organizer, speaker and award-winning climate justice activist, known for their work as a campaigner for the Green New Deal; as a lead organizer of the student climate strikes under Fridays For Future; and as a mentor and organizer behind Gaia's Garden, an urban regenerative community and sustainability project. They have been recognized as a leading environmental activist by *Forbes* and the *Evening Standard*, among others, focusing their work on the intersections of social and youth enfranchisement and climate advocacy and justice. Their writing and editing has been featured across numerous media platforms including *The Guardian*, It's Nice That, Fabian Society, Local Call and Reuters.

Professor Qing Li, MD, PhD (he/him)

Professor Qing Li is a medical doctor and clinical professor at Nippon Medical School Hospital, Nippon Medical School in Tokyo. He is a firm believer in the potential health benefits of *shinrin-yoku* (forest-bathing) and is involved with many organizations exploring the connections between the two. He is a founding member and President of the Japanese Society of Forest Medicine, a leading member of the Task Force of Forests and Human Health of IUFRO, the Vice President and Secretary-General of the International Society of Nature and Forest Medicine, as well as a Director of the Forest Therapy Society in Japan. He is also the Managing Vice Chairperson of Forest Health Maintenance Research of the World Federation of Chinese Medicine Societies. His book,

Shinrin-Yoku: The Art and Science of Forest Bathing (Penguin, 2018) has been translated into 26 languages.

Linda Ludbarza (she/her)

Linda Ludbarza is a Latvian-born designer, educated and currently based in the Netherlands. Many of her design projects centre around the governing themes of her native country – the pagan traditions, the close bond with nature and the impact of Soviet rule. These themes resonate within her writing. She writes about her observations through a political lens, taking in the impact made by history on the socioeconomic landscape of today.

Syren Nagakyrie (they/them)

Syren Nagakyrie is an activist, writer, community organizer and outdoor enthusiast. They have become a leading advocate and expert voice in making the outdoors more inclusive and accessible for the disabled community and other underrepresented groups. Syren grew up with multiple disabilities and chronic illnesses, including Ehlers-Danlos Syndrome and Postural Orthostatic Tachycardia Syndrome. When they started hiking, they found a severe lack of infrastructure, support and resources for the disabled community. Syren founded Disabled Hikers in 2018 to tackle these issues. They are now working on hiking guidebooks for disabled hikers with Falcon Guides and are also a Community Leader for the Eddie Bauer One Outside Program and shares valuable insight through a number of platforms to help create a more inclusive outdoor community.

Poppy Okotcha (she/her)

Poppy Okotcha is a trained horticulturist and regenerative

grower. She teaches people how to grow and forage for their food while living and eating consciously and advocates for the underrepresented and marginalized in the world of horticulture and environmentalism. Following a career as a model, in 2016 Poppy's focus turned to her garden, and she began to think more deeply about the connection between healthy environments, food and people. She went on to study at the Royal Horticultural Society and qualified as a Permaculture Designer in 2019. Since then her work has featured in *The Times* and *House Beautiful*, she has appeared on BBC Two's *Gardeners' World*, is a regular contributor to the RHS "The Garden" podcast and co-presented the Channel 4 series *Ronseal Presents ... The Great Garden Revolution*.

Hila Perry (she/her)

Hila Perry, aka "Hila the Killa", is an environmental educator and entertainer. She raps as Planet Earth about ecological topics such as: tree canopies, vegetables, compost, soil health, water, etc. Despite being born in the concrete jungle with very little access to nature, she has blossomed into a well-known eco-activist and artist. Hila has worked with House of Yes, Little Cinema, Meow Wolf, and more! She also performs in the duo "Nate and Hila" with her partner Nathan Dufour. Hila is committed to bringing joy, music, and comedy to the environmental space with her poems and performances.

Daniel Raven-Ellison (he/him)

Dan Raven-Ellison is a parent, guerrilla geographer, National Geographic Explorer, former geography teacher and led the campaign to make London the world's first National Park City. Dan's work focuses on challenging himself and others to see the world in new ways. He does this by combining creative exploration, geography and communication to tackle social and environmental challenges. He has walked across all of the UK's National Parks and cities while wearing a mind-reading device, makes innovative 100-second films on land use and is the founder of Slow Ways, a grassroots initiative to create a network of walking routes that connect all of Great Britain's towns and cities.

Pınar Sinopoulos-Lloyd (they/them)

Pınar Sinopoulos-Lloyd is a Quechua and Turkish multi-species futurist, mentor, wildlife tracker and ecophilosopher. They, along with their spouse So, founded Queer Nature, a transdisciplinary "organism" stewarding Earth-based queer community through ancestral skills, interspecies kinship and rites of passage. Their personal relationships with transness, hybridity, neurodivergence, indigeneity and belonging guided their work in developing queer ecopsychology through a decolonial lens. They are a founding Council Member of Intersectional Environmentalist, trans ambassador of Native Womens Wilderness and a founding member of Diversify Outdoors coalition.

Sophia "So" Sinopoulos-Lloyd (they/them)

Sophia "So" Sinopoulos-Lloyd is a non-binary Greek-American whose work explores the confluences of ecology, identity, and mysticism from queer and animistic perspectives. So is the co-founder of Queer Nature, an ecophilosophical project devoted to creating spaces for LGBTQ2IA people to learn place-based skills and re-story their relationships to the natural world. So holds an MA in Religious Studies from Claremont Graduate University in

California and a BA in Religious Studies and Animal Sciences from the University of Vermont. Their writing has appeared in *Written River, Loam* magazine and *The Wayfarer*.

Elizabeth Soumya (she/her)

Elizabeth Soumya is a writer and gardener based in Bengaluru, India. She loves foraging, going on nature walks and observing urban wildlife go about their city life. She spends a lot of time in her small space garden, where she grows vegetables and pollinator plants. She believes that gardening and green spaces must be accessible to all. She has contributed articles and pictures for both online and print media, including Al Jazeera English, *The Guardian, The Christian Science Monitor*, Daily News & Analysis (DNA) and *Hakai Magazine*.

Ayesha Tan-Jones (they/them)

Ayesha Tan-Jones is a creative artist who uses pop music, sculpture, alter egos, digital image and video to tell eco-conscious narratives that aim to connect, enthral and encourage audiences to think more sustainably and ethically. Their work is a spiritual practice that seeks to present an alternative, queer, optimistic dystopia. In 2019 they founded Fertile Souls, a community apothecary and survival skillshare community, which began planting seeds to bioremediate polluted soil in North London in 2021. Ayesha is also the co-founder of Shadow Sistxrs Fight Club, a physical and metaphysical self-defence class for women, non-binary people and QTIPoC, which combines Brazilian jiu-jitsu and medicinal herbalism to create a holistic approach to self-defence. They also write protest music through their musical alter ego YaYa Bones.

A NOTE FROM THE EDITOR

I'm often asked about my personal connection to nature. People expect me to declare a sublime intoxication – a heady bewitchment with soul-sunk claws.

The truth is, my relationship to the natural world is far from poetic. While other environmentalists may be rugged sprites with an encyclopedic knowledge of flora and fauna and green in their veins (let alone thumbs), I'm new to all this. Growing up, I was the kid squirrelled away indoors during the summer holidays, trying to keep the glare off my Gameboy. I can probably still identify more Pokémon than wildflowers. Far from being an "earth child", I've never quite felt at home in natural spaces.

I didn't start this campaign because I feel an innate sense of belonging and kinship with nature; I started it because I don't. Because I – *we* – have been robbed. And because we have a duty to ensure the next generation isn't.

ACKNOWLEDGMENTS

Creating this book was hands down the hardest thing I've ever done. And the best. Of course, it's not something I've done, it's something *we've* done. With long Covid's claws in me, and my mental health frayed from a year of plague and lockdowns, making the object you're holding would have been impossible without a host of beautiful and brilliant people.

First, hats off to all the contributors. I mean, really. I'm still buzzing that you responded to my emails, DMs and voice notes asking you to please, *please* write for this anthology. Thank you for your intelligence, wit and radical kindness, and for allowing me to throw countless questions, facts and ideas to you through the chaotic plane of Google Docs. It was a joy and an honour to work with each and every one of you as individuals, and I loved being the conductor to this global orchestra. I also want to acknowledge that several contributors managed to not only speak about intimate, raw and traumatic subjects, but did so with disarming grace and deftness. Thank you all – I can't wait to work with you again. And to the gifted poets who gave permission for their work to be reprinted in this volume, thank you for lending such a soulful dimension to our collective call to action.

Second, immense thanks is due to all the team at DK. This book wouldn't have existed without Stephanie Milner, who took a leap of faith on a first-time author and an unknown environmental justice campaign. Ruth O'Rourke, a steady force of nature, who survived a literal car crash and still checked into our fortnightly catch-up. Bess Daly, designer extraordinaire, who elevated my scrappy idea for the jacket to its current dazzling glory. Thank you all for bending over backwards to accommodate my madcap plans and ambitions. I am also hugely grateful to the rest of the team: Kiron Gill, Lottie Chesterman, Charlotte Beauchamp, Isabelle Holton, Megan Lea and Katie Hewett.

I am eternally indebted to Krissy Mallett, without whom I physically could not have done this. A true ray of light, the yin to my yangst, Krissy was my steadfast backstop throughout this process, bringing calm, compassion and unshakable competence to everything she touched. Thank you, Krissy.

Thank you to all the experts who generously gave up their time to answer my questions: Dr David R. Boyd, Professor Kaye Reed, Pam Warhurst, Dr Chanuki Illushka Seresinhe, Tayshan Hayden-Smith and Professor Cecil Konijnendijk. And to those who permitted me to print their pre-existing wisdom, in particular Hafsah Hafeji, Peter Sutoris and Sophia Li.

A big thank you to Wendy Muruli and Tony Stevens for your invaluable support helping ensure that this book was inclusive of, and accessible to, as many people as possible.

I also owe a debt of gratitude to the friends and family who offered feedback on my drafts. Lucy Crane, Kit Miles, David Papineau, Amelia Horgan, Sue Phillips, Nikita Montlake and Sophie Imber – you provided the perfect balance of reassurance and critique. Special thanks go to my father, Roger Miles, who read every word I wrote, twice. And to Matthew Janney, for your expert editorial eye throughout.

And to all the friends and family who offered emotional support, and dealt with me being a stressed-out hermit for the majority of 2021 (the year that wasn't). I daren't try and name everyone here, but you know who you are. Thank you to my mother, Deirdra, who in one sense did absolutely nothing to help with this book (apart from trying to introduce me to every gardener she met), but without whose lifelong support I would not – and could not – be doing what I'm doing today.

Nick Hayes, thank you for the beautiful cover illustration. Emma Latham-Phillips, for keeping Dream Green growing. Cara Armstrong and Lawrence Harrison, for your counsel. Valerie McConville, for keeping me sane. Thank you to the Year Here family, especially my all-star cohort, for your faith and friendship.

Finally, thank you to everyone who's ever supported the campaign. Those who've signed the petition, partnered with us, or simply shared a social post – I am so grateful to you all. Here's to the future.

RESOURCES

There are many places, both on- and offline, that can provide help and guidance when you need it. Here are just some resources that offer information and support on topics discussed in this book:

Anti-racism

Center for Racial Justice in Education, https://centerracialjustice.org/resources/resources-for-talking-about-race-racism-and-racialized-violence-with-kids/

Emma Dabiri, *What White People Can Do Next: From Allyship to Coalition*, Penguin, 2021

Fierce Allies, www.fierceallies.com

NAACP, https://naacp.org

Racial Equity Tools, www.racialequitytools.org/resources/plan/issues/reparations

Shakirah Bourne and Dana Alison Levy, *Allies*, DK, 2021

Showing Up For Racial Justice, https://surj.org

Indigenous rights

Center for World Indigenous Studies, www.cwis.org

Forest Peoples Programme, www.forestpeoples.org

International Work Group for Indigenous Affairs, www.iwgia.org/en/

Land Rights Now, www.landrightsnow.org/

Survival International, www.survivalinternational.org

LGBTQIA+

The Be You Project, https://thebeyouproject.co.uk/resources

Live Out Loud, www.liveoutloud.info

The Safezone Project, https://thesafezoneproject.com/resources

Stonewall, www.stonewall.org.uk

Trans Lifeline, www.translifeline.org/resources

The Trevor Project, www.thetrevorproject.org/explore

Disability

ADD International, https://add.org.uk

Americans with Disabilities Act (ADA), www.ada.gov

Belize Assembly for Persons with Diverse Abilities (BAPDA), https://disabilitybelize.org

EnAble India, www.enableindia.org

International Disability Alliance, www.internationaldisabilityalliance.org

Mencap, www.mencap.org.uk

Scope, the disability equality charity in England and Wales, www.scope.org.uk

Supportline, confidential emotional support, www.supportline.org.uk

Mental health

The Black, African and Asian Therapy Network (BAATN), www.baatn.org.uk

Black Minds Matter, www.blackmindsmatteruk.com

British Association for Counselling and Psychotherapy (BACP), www.bacp.co.uk

CALM, www.thecalmzone.net

CALM also provide a global list of mental health charities listed country-by-country, www.thecalmzone.net/2019/10/international-mental-health-charities

Gendered Intelligence, http://genderedintelligence.co.uk/professionals/therapists-and-counsellors.html

Mental Health America, https://mhanational.org

MIND, www.mind.org.uk

NHS, www.nhs.uk/mental-health

Psychology Today, www.psychologytoday.com

Samaritans, www.samaritans.org

Substance Abuse and Mental Health Services Administration (SAMHSA), www.samhsa.gov

Activism

Amnesty International, www.amnestyusa.org/take-action/resources-for-activists

Extinction Rebellion, extinctionrebellion.uk/act-now/resources

Friends of the Earth, https://campaigning.friendsoftheearth.uk

Global Justice Now, www.globaljustice.org.uk

Green and Black Cross, https://greenandblackcross.org

The United Nations, www.un.org/

Making nature accessible to all

A Growing Culture, www.agrowingculture.org

Avarna, https://theavarnagroup.com

Black Girls Hike UK, www.bghuk.com

BLM in the Stix (@blminthestix)

Disabled & Outdoors (@disablednoutdoors)

Disabled Hikers, https://disabledhikers.com

Diversify Outdoors, www.diversifyoutdoors.com

Dream Green, www.dreamgreen.earth

Flock Together, www.flocktogether.world

Groenemorgen: 1000 Geveltuinen (@1000Geveltuinen), www.groenemorgen.org/1000geveltuinen

Groundwork, www.groundwork.org.uk

Grow2Know, https://grow2know.org.uk

Incredible Edible, www.incredibleedible.org.uk

Land in Our Names (LION), https://landinournames.community

Le Permis de Végétaliser, www.paris.fr/pages/un-permis-pour-vegetaliser-paris-2689

National Park City, www.nationalparkcity.org

Nature is a Human Right, www.natureisahumanright.earth

Outside Voices Podcast, www.outsidevoicespodcast.com

Outdoor Afro, https://outdoorafro.com

Queer Nature, www.queernature.org

Right to Roam, https://righttoroam.org

The Ron Finley Project, https://ronfinley.com

The Rusty Anvil, www.the-rusty-anvil.land

Underground Plant Trade (@underground. planttrade)

Wild Diversity, www.wilddiversity.org

The Venture Out Project, www.ventureoutproject.com

We've done our best to make sure that the resources are as appropriate, accurate, and up-to-date as possible at the time of going to press. The publishers do not have any control over the content of the resources and cannot accept liability arising from use of any of them.

*

CREDITS

Publishing Director Katie Cowan
Art Director Maxine Pedliham
Managing Editor Ruth O'Rourke
Managing Art Editor Bess Daly
Senior Acquisitions Editor Stephanie Milner
Senior Editor Krissy Mallett
Editors Kiron Gill, Megan Lea, Jennette ElNaggar
DTP Designer Umesh Singh Rawat
Proofreader Katie Hewett
Indexer Lisa Footitt
Production Editor David Almond
Production Controller Kariss Ainsworth
Jacket Designer Bess Daly
Illustration by Nick Hayes
Author photography by Serena Brown

First American Edition, 2022
Published in the United States by DK Publishing
1450 Broadway, Suite 801, New York, NY 10018

A catalog record for this book
is available from the Library of Congress.
ISBN 978-0-7440-4805-6

DK books are available at special discounts when purchased
in bulk for sales promotions, premiums, fund-raising, or educational use.
For details, contact: DK Publishing Special Markets,
1450 Broadway, Suite 801, New York, NY 10018
SpecialSales@dk.com

Printed and bound in the United Kingdom

For the curious
www.dk.com